D0615426

GLOSSARY OF
LINGUISTIC TERMINOLOGY

GLOSSARY OF LINGUISTIC TERMINOLOGY

MARIO PEI

COLUMBIA UNIVERSITY PRESS
NEW YORK AND LONDON

Copyright © 1966 by Mario Pei
First published by Anchor Books,
Doubleday & Company, Inc., 1966

Columbia University Press edition, 1966

ISBN 231-03012-6
Library of Congress Catalog Card Number: 66-21013
Printed in the United States of America
10 9 8 7 6 5 4 3

FOREWORD

"Completeness" in a work of this kind is to be neither expected nor desired. To be "complete," a glossary of linguistic terminology would have to be a ten-volume encyclopedia, such is the number and proliferation of terms devised by the fertile minds of the linguists.

Neither can a work of this kind be expected to remain up-to-date for more than a very limited period. New linguistic works and new, ingenious terms are coming off the presses even as this book goes into print. There would be one way of keeping such a work fully up-to-date, and that would be to issue it not as a book, but as a card-index file, into which new cards could be inserted every year and revised cards substituted for existing ones. This idea is passed on, for what it may be worth, to others who may have similar glossaries in mind.

These considerations are offered not as an apology, but merely as a statement of fact. They may or may not ward off charges of "incompleteness."

The following items have been deliberately omitted: (a) old, traditional grammatical terms which laymen as well as linguists are supposed to be familiar with, and which can, at all events, be gleaned from ordinary grammars; this includes such items as *noun, adjective, verb, subjunctive mood, subordinate clause;* (b) figures of speech that bear on literary style rather than on language as such (*anacoluthon, chiasmus, hypallage, tmesis,* etc.); (c) names and descriptions of individual languages, save where they have a bearing on linguistic terminology or linguistic theory;[1] (d) new terminology that has not yet

[1] For an up-to-date treatment, see S. Muller, *The World's Living Languages,* Frederick Ungar Publishing Co., Inc., New York, 1964.

proved itself or gained general acceptance, though this may well find its place in future revised editions.

What I have tried to include is the general terminology used by linguists of a certain stature, historical, descriptive and geolinguistic, American and European, that has gained a measure of acceptance in the field. Failure to include a certain term may be a value judgment on my part, to the extent that I do not consider the term to be in wide enough use; it may also imply pardonable ignorance. No one is able to keep pace with all the writings in the field. Neither does inclusion of a term, or of a definition or interpretation of a term, imply that I approve or disapprove of such a term or acceptance. It is the function of a glossary, as of a dictionary, to record what goes on, not to pass judgment on it (the judgment may well be expressed elsewhere, however).

It is not the function of this book to trace the history of each term from its inception. Therefore, attribution of a term or definition to a given writer does not necessarily mean that the term or definition originated with him, but merely that he accepts and uses it. Often definitions and explanations have had to be cut down and condensed for glossary purposes. In such cases I have tried hard to avoid distorting in any way the writer's thought or concept. I may not have invariably succeeded, and in such instances I offer humble apologies. If aggrieved writers will get in touch with me and send in to me their own statements of how a given term should be defined in their concept, I promise that their own verbatim definition will appear in the earliest revision.

Different concepts and definitions of terms have been placed in juxtaposition and contrast, so that the reader may have as complete a picture as possible of what the terms mean to the linguists who use them. Often these definitions are contradictory, and for that there is no help. More often they are complementary, and illustrative of the way different minds run. The segmentation of reality in different ways is not merely a cultural and linguistic phenomenon. It may apply also to linguistic views. *Phonemic, distinctive, formant, marker,* even *fricative* and *spirant,* or *opposition* and *contrast,* may hold different connotations for different linguists, in the same fashion that *liberal, conservative, democracy* may hold different connotations for political writers. Terms that at first glance seem to be synonymous may hold delicate overtones of difference. Do Hockett's *morpheme,* Whatmough's *morphome,* and Martinet's *moneme* really mean exactly the same thing? Or is there only a general coincidence in the concepts? If a different cultural group from our own may be forgiven for labeling as "black" what we would label as "dark blue," surely linguists, dealing with concepts which too often are abstract, may be forgiven for not coinciding precisely in the way they use terms, or for preferring *oppositional* or *functional* to *relevant* or *significant.*

At the same time, the multiplication of equivalent or almost-equivalent terms seems, in some instances, to run beyond all reasonable bounds. When *phonemic* can have half a dozen synonyms; when the same type of sound change can be described by various writers as *combinatory, conditional, heteronomous, dependent, functional;* when one writer can use *prosodic* in the sense of *suprasegmental,* and another deny any identity between the two, it is not surprising that the student is confused. There are times when the field of linguistic terminology reminds one of what goes on in the field of constructed languages, where a new one is offered every week, it seems, despite the fact that over seven hundred such languages are already in existence, a good many of them fully functional and usable. There is perhaps need of an Academy of Linguistic Terminology, which will regiment and even repress ultra-creative flights.

At least equally confusing is the use of a single term in half a dozen different, sometimes contradictory acceptances. Beginning with *culture,* which means one thing to the "cultured" layman, quite a different thing to the anthropologist and the anthropological linguist, we can point to such terms as *derivation* (which has one historical and two descriptive meanings); *determinant,* with three acceptances (known to me; there may be more); side by side with *determinative,* one of whose acceptances is synonymous with one of those assigned to *determinant; source language* (four separate meanings); the above-mentioned *formant* and *marker,* concerning which there is no unanimity whatsoever. Then we have all sorts of confusing similarities: *syntagm* and *syntagma; second articulation* and *secondary articulation; associative etymology* and *folk etymology.* We can even go back to our older grammatical and historical terminology and discover that *voice* is used to denote at once an aspect of the verb and what is added to a sound when the vocal cords are vibrated; or try to establish what specific differences, if any, exist among such terms as *Ablaut, apophony, qualitative gradation* and *vowel mutation.*

One charge that cannot be leveled at linguistic terminology is that it fails to show the quality of imagination, or make use of metaphor. *Verbid, contoid, vocoid* sound like something out of science fiction. *Wrenched* and *switching, double cross juncture, coinage, clipped,* remind one of gangster films. Music is represented by such terms as *allegro, lento, vocalization;* the legitimate stage by *actor, prop* (*word*), *repertory;* medicine has *contamination, parasitic, infection, paraplasm, tainting, contagion, secretion, fixation;* from the physical sciences come *amalgam, atomic* (*language*), *centrifugal* and *centripetal, nucleus, molecule, radiation, characterology, feedback, environment, fissure, input* and *output, suction, unstable, redundancy.* Religion shows up with *cardinal* (*vowels*), *canonical* (*forms*), *relic, hierarchy, omnipotent* (*vowel*). *Onset* and *attrition* sound military; *transmutation, a priori* and *a posteriori* (*languages*) sound philosophical; *status, pedi-*

gree, family tree, proper and *improper* (*compounds*) sound social. *Acclimatization, alien, discrimination, equalization, integration, internalize, privilege* (*of occurrence*), *radical, reconstruction, solidarity, satellite,* (*allo*)*tax,* have sociological or historical overtones. *Corpus* is legal. There are straight Latin terms, like *figura* and *vox nihili;* picturesque or everyday terms, like *operator, lag, release, overlap, slot* and *slit, collation* and *collision, tap* and *bit, peak, kernel* and *core, fragment* and *frame.* There are humor-arousing terms, like *bow-wow, ta-ta, dingdong, pooh-pooh, sing-song* (all theories of how language began); *muddy transition* and *mucker pose, mock form* and *nesting, domesticated* and *intrusive, smear* and *slur, ghost* and *phantom* (*word*), *shifter, stretcher* and *stump* (*word*). There is no objection to all this, least of all from this writer, who is fond (perhaps overfond) of colorful language. These terms, however, are in somewhat strident contrast to mouth-filling words like *morphophonemic, paradigmatic, syntagmatic, metaphony, amelioration, cacuminal, suprasegmental, episememe.* But for this there seems to be no help. One wonders, on the other hand, precisely what advantage there may be in using *substitute* for the traditional *pronoun,* or *topic* for *subject,* or *exocentric construction* for *complete sentence.*

This book was originally aimed at the beginner in the field of linguistic studies. With the intervention of my editorial assistant, Mrs. Anita-Louise Cloutier de la Garza, a specialist in descriptive linguistics and phonetic-phonemic description, it was decided to include a fairly large number of more involved and technical terms and definitions, which will, it is hoped, make the work of value also to the more advanced student. It will be noted that her more technical explanations generally follow shorter and simpler ones, more readily accessible to the beginner.

There are only three previous specifically terminological works that are generally available to the American student of linguistics. One is Marouzeau's *Lexique de la terminologie linguistique,* revised and augmented in 1951; in addition to being outdated, this work, fairly satisfactory from the standpoint of historical linguistics, generally fails to take into account the work of American linguists, who have been in the forefront of terminological creativity. Hamp's *Glossary of American Technical Linguistic Usage to 1950* (published in 1958) is extremely brief and unsatisfactory by reason of unclear definitions (terms are presented only in their coiners' contexts). My *Dictionary of Linguistics,* done in collaboration with Frank Gaynor and with the editorial collaboration of Eugene Dorfman, appeared in 1954 and is badly out of date, in addition to dividing its efforts between purely linguistic terminology on the one hand, and traditional grammatical and stylistic terms, plus the description of individual languages, on the other. It is therefore hoped that the present offering may, at least for a time, serve a useful purpose.

In addition to Mrs. de la Garza, whose valid editorial collaboration has already been mentioned, I wish to express my indebtedness to Professor John Fisher, of Fairleigh Dickinson University, and to Professor Paul Gaeng, of Montclair State College, both of whom went carefully over the work in manuscript and offered valuable suggestions and corrections.

HOW TO USE THIS BOOK

Methodologically, I have endeavored to give, with each term defined, a list of synonyms, near-synonyms and opposites, so that the student may be able to tell at a glance whether the term he is looking up is substantially identical with or opposed to another term with which he may already be familiar.

Examples, in parentheses, have been given where feasible; they are drawn, where at all possible, from the more familiar languages. There are also, under each heading, abundant cross references to kindred topics. This means that the reader who is interested in exploring an entire corner of the field will be able to move from one related area to another, until that corner is covered.

Attention is called to two peculiarities of arrangement. Where a reference is followed by a numeral, as in *"See also* ALTERNATION 2" or *"Synonym:* PARASITIC 3," it means that the reference is to definition 2 or 3 under the heading, rather than to the heading as a whole. It has been found expedient, for reasons of space economy, to enclose in parentheses all words referring to the word that follows the closing of the parenthesis. Thus, *"See also* COMBINATORY (*also* CONDITIONAL, HETERONYMOUS, DEPENDENT, FUNCTIONAL) CHANGE" is used in place of *"See also* COMBINATORY CHANGE, CONDITIONAL CHANGE, HETERONYMOUS CHANGE, DEPENDENT CHANGE, FUNCTIONAL CHANGE."

SYMBOLS

Following is a list of symbols used in this work, with appropriate explanations. It has been found desirable to include also a certain number of symbols and diacritics which appear in linguistic works, even if not used here, along with the standard IPA chart of phonetic (broad transcription) symbols.

- Hyphen; often used to indicate the position of a letter or phoneme in a word; (*t-* for *t* in initial position; *-t-* for *t* in intervocalic position; *-t* for *t* in final position).

\> Historically, "became," "developed into," "to."

\< Historically, "developed from," "from."

* Asterisk; used in historical linguistics to indicate a non-attested, hypothetical, or reconstructed form.

[   ] Brackets; enclose PHONETIC TRANSCRIPTION (usually of the broad variety, based on IPA, *q.v.*).

/   / Bars; enclose PHONEMIC TRANSCRIPTION, based on phonemic pattern of specific language.

or ↑ Indicate rising intonation pattern.

or ↓ Indicate falling intonation pattern.

→ Indicates level intonation pattern.

↔ In TRANSFORMATIONAL GRAMMAR, indicates a change which may work in either direction.

{   } Braces; indicate CANONICAL FORM ({CVC} indicates a predominance of the syllabic structure consonant-vowel-consonant).

: :: : Indicates PROPORTIONAL ANALOGY, similar in nature to a mathematical proportion (x:y :: z:?).

~ "Alternates with," "is in alternation with."

+ Plus; /+/ in a phonemic transcription indicates PLUS or OPEN JUNCTURE.

− Minus; /−/ in a phonemic transcription indicates MINUS or CLOSED JUNCTURE (MUDDY TRANSITION).

/ "Varies between"; "either − or."

′ Acute accent; over a vowel of a word, normally indicates PRIMARY STRESS (*físher*); in a Chinese transcription, it indicates RISING TONE (*fú*); in some languages (Hungarian, Czech) it indicates VOWEL LENGTH; in others (French) it indicates a modification of the sound-quality; in others (Portuguese) it may indicate both primary accent and sound-quality. Note that in IPA phonetic transcription, primary stress is indicated by ′ before the stressed syllable: ['blæk-hɛd], *blackhead*. In some languages (Polish, Croatian) it is used over consonants to indicate a modified value of the consonant.

‵ Grave accent; over a vowel of a word, normally indicates SECONDARY or TERTIARY STRESS (*bláckbìrd, élevàtor*); in a Chinese transcription, it indicates a FALLING TONE (*lèi*); in the traditional orthography of some languages (Italian) it indicates final stress; in others (Portuguese) a modified sound-quality for the vowel.

˄ or ˆ Circumflex accent; used in some languages to indicate vowel length, or modification of sound, or position of stress, or a combination of two or all of these. In Esperanto, it is used over

certain consonants to indicate a palatalized value ($ĉ = [tʃ]$).

~ Til or tilde; over a vowel, usually indicates nasalization of the vowel ($[ɛ̃]$);
but while it is so used in Portuguese
conventional orthography ($ã$, $õ$), nasalization is otherwise indicated in
French, while in Spanish orthography
$ñ$ indicates palatalization of *n*.

‾ Macron; over a vowel, generally indicates
vowel length (Latin *mūrus*); in Chinese transcription, it indicates a level
tone (*fū*). Note that in IPA phonetic
transcription, vowel length is indicated
by: after the vowel (['fa:-rən], German *fahren*).

˘ Breve; over a vowel, generally indicates
shortness of vowel sound (Latin
portă); in Chinese transcription, it indicates a falling-rising tone (*hăo*); in
Rumanian, it indicates a modified
vowel value (*apă*). Over a consonant,
it is used in some orthographies to
indicate a modified value (Turkish
$ğ = [ɣ]$).

' Apostrophe; usually indicates elision; in
Russian transliteration, it is often used
to indicate palatalization of preceding
consonant (*govorit'*); in transliteration
of Arabic and Hebrew, it is used to
indicate glottal stop; in the Greek conventional alphabet, it represents a
smooth breathing (absence of *h*-sound
before initial vowel).

' Used in transliteration of Arabic and Hebrew to indicate pharyngeal sound
($[ʕ]$); in Greek conventional writing,

indicates rough breathing (*h*-sound prefixed to initial vowel).

˛ In historical linguistics, often used under *i* and *u* to indicate glide values ($e\underset{\smile}{i}$ = [ɛj]).

ᶋ Cedilla; used in conventional French and Portuguese orthographies to indicate [s] value for written *c;* in Rumanian, to indicate affricate value for *t* (t = [ts]) and palatal fricative value for *s* (s = [ʃ]); in Turkish, $ş$ = [ʃ], $ç$ = [tʃ].

ˇ Indicates modified, usually palatal, value for various consonants in many conventional orthographies (Czech, Croatian *č*). In phonetic transcription, some writers prefer [č] to [tʃ], and [ǧ] or [j] to [dʒ]; a few prefer [š] to [ʃ], [ž] to [ʒ]. Occasionally used over vowels in some orthographies (Czech *ě*) to indicate modified value.

° Over vowel; used in conventional orthographies of some languages (Swedish, Norwegian, Czech) to indicate modified value (*å*, *ů*).

· Used over or under consonants, occasionally vowels, in some conventional orthographies and transliterations to indicate modified values (Polish *ż*, Arabic *ẓ*).

″ or ¨ Umlaut; used in many conventional orthographies to indicate fronting of vowel sound (German, Swedish *ö*); while it is normally a matter of choice whether one uses a double dot or a double accent, in Hungarian orthography the double dot indicates a short middle rounded vowel, the double ac-

cent a long middle rounded vowel
(*ü* = [y], *ǘ* = [y:]). The same double
dot symbol may appear also as a diaeresis, to indicate that two adjacent
vowels are to be kept apart in pronunciation (French *Noël*), or that a *u*
that would normally be silent is to be
pronounced (Spanish *averigüe*).

₀ Under *l, r, m, n,* usually in transliterations, indicates vocalic value for liquids
and nasals (Sanskrit *ḷ, ṛ*).

ł Bar across *l* indicates in some conventional orthographies (Polish) back lateral value.

ø Symbol used in Danish and Norwegian
and adopted by IPA with same value
([ø]).

ͅ In historical linguistics, used under a
vowel to indicate open quality (*ę, ǫ* =
[ɛ], [ɔ]; used in traditional orthography of some languages (Polish) to indicate nasalization.

· Dot; used under vowels in historical linguistics to indicate closed value (*ẹ, ọ* =
[e], [o]).

GLOSSARY OF
LINGUISTIC TERMINOLOGY

THE INTERNATIONAL PHONETIC ALPHABET

CONSONANTS

	Bi-labial	Labio-dental	Dental and Alveolar	Retroflex	Palato-alveolar	Alveolo-palatal	Palatal	Velar	Uvular	Pharyngal	Glottal
Plosive	p b		t d	ʈ ɖ			c ɟ	k g	q ɢ		ʔ
Nasal	m	ɱ	n	ɳ			ɲ	ŋ	ɴ		
Lateral Fricative			ɬ ɮ								
Lateral Non-fricative			l	ɭ			ʎ				
Rolled			r						ʀ		
Flapped			ɾ	ɽ					ʀ		
Fricative	ɸ β	f v	θ ð s z	ʂ ʐ	ʃ ʒ	ɕ ʑ	ç j	x ɣ	χ ʁ	ħ ʕ	h ɦ
Frictionless Continuants and Semi-vowels	w ɥ	ʋ	ɹ				j (ɥ)	(w)	ʁ		

VOWELS

	Front	Central	Back
Close (y ʉ u)	i y	ɨ ʉ	ɯ u
Half-close (ø o)	e ø		ɤ o
Half-open (œ ɔ)	ɛ œ	ɜ ɞ	ʌ ɔ
Open (ɒ)	æ	a	ɑ ɒ

(Secondary articulations are shown by symbols in brackets.)

OTHER SOUNDS.—Palatalized consonants: ƫ, ȡ, etc. Velarized or pharyngalized consonants: ɫ, ɖ, ʮ, etc. Ejective consonants (plosives with simultaneous glottal stop): p', t', etc. Implosive voiced consonants: ɓ, ɗ, etc. ř fricative trill. ɕ, ʑ (labialized θ, ð, or s, z). ɕ, ʑ (labialized ʃ, ʒ). ʇ, ʗ, ʖ (clicks, Zulu c, q, x). ɺ (a sound between r and l). ʍ (voiceless w). ɪ, ʏ, ʊ (lowered varieties of i, y, u). ə (a vowel between ø and o).

Affricates are normally represented by groups of two consonants (ts, tʃ, dʒ, etc.), but, when necessary, ligatures are used (ʦ, ʧ, ʤ, etc.), or the marks ͡ or ͜ (t͡s or t͜ʃ, etc.). ɕ, ʑ may occasionally be used in place of tʃ, dʒ. Aspirated plosives: ph, th, etc.

LENGTH, STRESS, PITCH.—ː (full length). ˑ (half length). ˈ (stress, placed at beginning of the stressed syllable). ˌ (secondary stress). ˉ (high level pitch); ˍ (low level); ˊ (high rising); ˏ (low rising); ˋ (high falling); ˎ (low falling); ˆ (rise-fall); ˇ (fall-rise). See Écriture phonétique internationale, p. 9.

MODIFIERS.—˜ nasality. ̥ breath (ḷ = breathed l). ̬ voice (ṣ = z). ʰ slight aspiration following p, t, etc. ̣ specially close vowel (ẹ = a very close e). ̦ specially open vowel (ẹ = a rather open e). ̫ labialization (n̫ = labialized n). ̪ dental articulation (t̪ = dental t). ʲ palatalization (ż = ʒ). ˔ tongue slightly raised. ˕ tongue slightly lowered. ̹ lips more rounded. ̜ lips more spread. Central vowels ï (= ɨ), ü (= ʉ), ë (= ə˔), ö (= ɵ), ̩ (e.g. n̩) syllabic consonant. ̯ consonantal vowel. ʃ variety of ʃ resembling s, etc.

A

Abglitt   *See* OFF-GLIDE.

ablaut   1. Historically, the changes which occurred in a vowel sound according to the position of the pitch accent in the parent language, or of the stress accent at a later period; it reflects a mass shift of vocalic features in a language, and is an all-pervading, regular system of alternations, due to regular conditioning. (English *sing, sang, sung* represent ablaut variations reflecting conditions in the parent language where the accent was on the root, or on preceding or following syllables later lost; a descriptive example of such variation is the Spanish radical-changing verb *dormir,* where the *o* is retained wherever unstressed, but is replaced by *ue* when stressed, as in *duermo.*) The vowel alternation, gradation, or mutation regularly denotes a distinction in meaning (such as different tenses of a verb). Ablaut is subdivided into ABSTUFUNG and ABTÖNUNG (*q.v.*). *Synonyms:* ALTERNANCE VOCALIQUE, APOPHONY, QUALITATIVE GRADATION, (VOWEL) GRADATION, (VOWEL) MUTATION. *See also* CONDITIONED SOUND CHANGE, REGULAR SOUND CHANGE.

2. Descriptively, a REPLACIVE MORPHEME (*q.v.*) in INTERNAL MODIFICATION (*q.v.*).

abnormal vowel   A vowel representing an intermediate sound between a front and a back vowel (English *u* of *but*) (Dorfman). *Synonym:* CENTRAL VOWEL.

Absatz   *See* OFF-GLIDE.

absolute form   A word or morpheme in isolation, without a surrounding context. *Opposite:* SANDHI-FORM.

absolute pitch   *See* PITCH.

absorption   1. Phonetically, the suppression of a sound, or its incorporation into the sound(s) immediately preceding or following (in the current pronunciation of *often* as against its older spelling-pronunciation, the *t* is absorbed by the *f*).

2. Geolinguistically, as applied to the speakers of an immigrant language, the phenomenon occurring when the second generation goes over to the language of the receiving country, adopting it as an indigenous language and forgetting the language of their parents; as applied to native speakers of a language on their own soil, the process whereby they adopt as their own the language of colonization (Mexican Indian speakers of Spanish); as applied to an incoming conquering group, the process by which they adopt the language of the conquered population (people of French-speaking Norman stock who were absorbed into the body of English speakers in the centuries following the Norman Conquest).

Abstufung   The QUANTITATIVE GRADATION (*q.v.*) of vowels; a change as between normal grade and zero grade, caused by shifts in stress accent at a later date than the ABTÖNUNG changes (Greek *eptómēn,* with zero-grade vowel between *p* and *t,* as against *pétomai* and *pepótēmai,* both of which have normal *e* or *o* grade). *See also* ABLAUT.

Abtönung   The QUALITATIVE GRADATION (*q.v.*) of vowels; a change in the timbre or quality of a vowel (front or back, *e* or *o*), supposedly reflecting a difference in the pitch accent during the Indo-European period (Greek *pétomai,* with *e* grade; *pepótēmai,* with *o* grade; *eptómēn,* with zero grade; the root vowel, between *p* and *t,* shifts from *e* to *o* to zero; but for the last, *see* ABSTUFUNG). *See also* ABLAUT.

accent 1. Phonetically, an increase of stress (greater amplitude or loudness), or a change of pitch (higher or lower frequency), giving prominence to one syllable of a sequence over the adjacent syllables; syllabic prominence, depending on the degree of stress or the height of pitch. PITCH ACCENT may also be described as CHROMATIC or MUSICAL ACCENT; STRESS ACCENT may be described as EXPIRATORY or INTENSITY ACCENT. *See also* BOUND (*also* DYNAMIC, FIXED, FREE, PRIMARY, QUALITATIVE, QUANTITATIVE, RECESSIVE, RESTRICTED, SECONDARY, TONIC) ACCENT (or STRESS); FORESTRESS, MORPHOPHONEMIC STRESS, SENTENCE STRESS (or RHYTHM), WORD STRESS.
2. Graphemically, a diacritic mark indicating syllabic stress (Spanish *habló*); vowel quality (French *élève, fête*); or vowel quantity (Hungarian *jó* vs. *jobb*).
3. An individual's speech habits with respect to his own dialect or idiolect; or the phonetic traits of a learner's language carried over to his second language, resulting in a "foreign" accent.

accent of intensity *See* INTENSITY ACCENT.

accentual unit Martinet's term for a word or word group of which one syllable receives prominence by reason of stronger stress; it usually coincides with the word (Russian *nosoróg,* "rhinoceros," where *nos* loses its accent and vowel timbre and is subordinated to *rog*), or with the lexeme (German *Náshòrn,* where each element keeps its own stress).

accidence Variations in the form of a word to express distinctions of number, gender, case, tense, mood, etc. *Synonyms:* FLECTION, INFLECTION. *See also* CONJUGATION, DECLENSION, PARADIGM.

accidental gap A hypothetical sequence of phonemes not represented in the lexicon, but conforming to the distributional patterns of the language (*-sll-* in Spanish *desllevar*).

acclimatization Entwistle's term for the process by which foreign loan words are taken into the language. *See also* ALIEN WORD, BORROWING, DOMESTICATED WORD, LOAN WORD, NATURALIZED WORD.

accommodation   1. The partial assimilation of a phoneme, in which the assimilated phoneme takes over one, but not all, of the characteristics of the assimilatory phoneme (Latin **ag-tos* > *ac-tus,* with unvoicing of *g* to conform with *t;* but in the later progression of *actus* > Italian *atto,* the assimilation becomes complete, giving what Gray terms EQUALIZATION, *q.v.*).

2. The change effected in the form of a loan word to make it conform to the phonological and grammatical pattern of the borrowing language (English *show,* appropriated by Spanish speakers as *cho*).

acoustic allophone   An individual variation of a single phoneme, appearing on the spectrograph in successive recordings; these allophones are numerous, diverse, intersecting (resembling an allophone of another phoneme more than the other allophones of the same phoneme), and overlapping (not ending before the representation of the next phoneme begins) (Hockett).

acoustic change   A change due to defective imitation (a child's *frough* for *through*) (Sweet).

acoustic features   The sound features in an utterance, as they may be experimentally recorded (GROSS ACOUSTIC FEATURES). If they have a bearing on meaning and are thus essential to communication by speech, they are said to be DISTINCTIVE ACOUSTIC FEATURES; if they have no bearing on meaning and are not essential to the clarity of the message, they are called NON-DISTINCTIVE.

acoustic formants   Characteristic frequencies on a spectrogram that indicate sex, age, regional accent, and individual peculiarities of the speaker (Hughes).

acoustic phonetics   1. The study of significant speech sounds as they are perceived by the ear of the listener, and of the sound waves produced when they are ut-

tered; a branch of EXPERIMENTAL or LABORATORY PHO-
NETICS. *Synonym:* GENEMMIC PHONETICS.

2. One of the two developed branches of phonetics
which deal with the transmissional properties of speech;
it is treated under two aspects : (a) PHYSICAL PHONET-
ICS, which in turn includes PHONOGENETIC and VIBRA-
TORY PHONETICS; the phonogenetic aspect describes the
origin, in the body, or formation, in the vocal tract, of
sound waves; i.e., how air flow is converted into sounds;
the vibratory aspect deals with oscillations or sound
waves that are important for speech purposes and communication; direct interpretation of the very complex
air vibrations is done by means of oscillograms; resonants, fricatives and stops are described in terms of
their physical dimensions, as they are all different on
the oscillograms; acoustic terminology used in their description includes BURST, FORMANT, FRICTION, TRANSI-
TION; (b) PSYCHOLOGICAL PHONETICS, dealing with
hearing or sound perception, whereby stimulus-re-
sponse tests are given to determine how sounds and
words are recognized; the response investigates what is
of real import in the acoustic picture or stimulus; these
tests are usually called ARTICULATION TESTS, and described in terms of vocal tract articulation. *See also* AR-
TICULATORY PHONETICS, OSCILLOGRAM (de la Garza).

acrophony The use of the pictorial representation of an
object as the phonetic sign of the initial sound (or syllable) of the name of the object (the Semitic character
beth, originally representing a house, but later used to
indicate the sound of *b,* which was initial in the word).

actor The grammatical person-and-number reference of
an inflectional verb ending (the first singular connotation of Latin *amo;* the first plural connotation of French
chantons) (Hall). The term includes even the third
plural connotation of a passive form like Latin *amantur.* In this terminology, SUBJECT is restricted to a spe-

cific noun or pronoun form (Latin *ego* amo; *ei* amantur; French *nous* chantons).

actor-action-goal A sequence of forms in which the word order normally indicates the grammatical relationships ("The man bit the dog"; "The dog bit the man"; the action is the same, but the actor and goal are reversed) (Dorfman).

actualization The perceptible result of the articulation of one of the phonemic variants of a phoneme or archiphoneme (the phoneme, or ideal unit, *p* of American English can have objective existence only through the phones of *p* in *pit, spit, sip,* etc.; but these are allophones of the phoneme *p,* not the phoneme itself). *Synonym:* REALIZATION.

acute phoneme A phoneme showing concentration of energy in the higher frequencies of the spectrum (Jakobson). *Opposite:* GRAVE PHONEME.

adding A sporadic change whereby another allomorph with the same meaning, but different shape, is added to an already existing, older allomorph (in *children,* the original plural allomorph was [-r], and it was unique; then the allomorph [-en] was superimposed, thus yielding the unique allomorph [-ren] plural in English. *Synonym:* DOUBLING 2. *See also* UNIQUE MORPHEME (de la Garza).

addition A general term covering prefixation, suffixation and infixation (Hall). *Synonym:* AFFIXATION.

adjectival construction A construction which fulfills the functions of an adjective ("under-the-counter transactions"; "the now-you-see-it-now-you-don't method") (Hughes).

adjunct (word) A modifier; a word or word group that qualifies, amplifies, or completes the meaning of another word or word group, but is not itself one of the chief structural elements in the sentence (*all* and *well* in "All Americans eat well") (Webster III). *Synonym:* SECONDARY WORD. *See also* SUBSTANTIVAL ADJUNCT.

adstratum A term occasionally used for SUPERSTRATUM (*q.v.*), or to cover both SUPERSTRATUM and SUBSTRATUM (*q.v.*); a quasi-synonym occasionally used is LANGUAGES IN CONTACT (*q.v.*) (Weinreich); but the implication of the latter term is that the two languages coexist as separate entities, even while they influence each other; while ADSTRATUM, SUBSTRATUM and SUPERSTRATUM rather imply the disappearance of one language, even while it leaves its trace on the other. *See also* ARCHISTRATUM.

affective language The language of self-expression and emotion, as distinct from the grammatical language of communication; according to some, the AFFECTIVE LANGUAGE is the primary source of innovations leading to language change (Martinet).

affiliation The determination of the family or stock to which a language or dialect belongs, and of its relationship with other languages of the same group. *See also* LANGUAGE FAMILY.

affinity 1. Structural similarity or common origin.

2. A phoneme-by-phoneme correspondence between outgoing and incoming partners in REPLACEMENT 1 (*q.v.*); (*avunculus* and *oncle* have such correspondence, but *patruus* and *oncle* do not); AFFINITY may also be of the morphophonemic variety (*life* and *live*) (Hoenigswald).

affix A collective term used for PREFIXES, INFIXES and SUFFIXES (*q.v.*); a bound form attached to the beginning or end of a word, base or phrase, or inserted within a word, to produce DERIVATIVES (*un-do, iodide, morning-after-ish*), INFLECTIONAL FORMS (*cat-s, talk-s*), or the basis of part or all of a paradigm (*vi-n-cit* as opposed to *vi-cit*). *See also* BOUND MORPHEME, DERIVATIONAL AFFIX, FORMANT 4, FORMATIVE, PRESENTATIONAL AFFIX.

affixation A morphological process consisting of adding affixes to a root or stem. *Synonym:* ADDITION.

affix clipping Webster III's term for METANALYSIS
   (*q.v.*).

affricate 1. A sound articulated as a stop, immediately
   followed by a sharp release through the articulatory
   position for a homorganic fricative; a combination
   sound in which the mode rather than the point of articulation is shifted (if the occlusion and release involved in the production of *t* are immediately followed
   by the continuant, fricative sound of *sh,* the over-all
   result will be the *ch* of *why choose,* differentiated only
   by juncture from the *t* + *sh* of *white shoes;* similarly,
   we may produce the combination sounds *ts* and *dz,*
   which the orthography of some languages represents
   with the single letter *z*). Some phoneticians prefer to
   represent the affricates of *chair* and *jaw* by means of a
   double symbol [tʃ], [dʒ], others treat them as the
   plosive counterparts of the palatal fricatives [ʃ], [ʒ],
   and represent them with a single symbol: [č], [j].
   Synonym: SEMI-PLOSIVE. *See also* ASSIBILANT.
   2. A stoppage followed by frictional release of en-
   trapped air; thus, HOMOTOPICAL SOUNDS in CLOSED
   JUNCTURE; a stop in which the opening or release is
   relatively slow; a stop plus movement into the fricative
   position. Phonetic factors prove that these sounds can
   be considered as single units; IPA does not group them
   as a distinct class, though linguists are divided in their
   opinions on the subject; how these sounds are classified
   depends upon the phonemic structure of the particular
   language; in some languages, fricatives and affricates
   are in contrast, and must be considered as two sets of
   sounds (Polish [czy] ~ [trzy]) (de la Garza).

age-area theory A theory of diffusion of cultural traits,
   first advanced by Bartoli, to the effect that a trait spread
   over a wider area is older than one spread over a
   smaller territory, and that traits lying close to the center
   of distribution are relatively new, and those lying far-
   thest from it relatively older. *See also* LATERAL AREAS.

agglomeration The amalgamation of units which are for the most part semantically self-sufficient, occurring particularly in Papuan and Australian languages (Entwistle).

agglutination 1. The process of addition of suffixes to a word-root.

2. The process whereby two or more units are blended into one (French *encore* from Latin *hanc horam*) (Saussure).

3. The formation of derivative or compound words by putting together constituent elements each of which expresses a separate, definite meaning (Hungarian *házakban,* "in houses" : *ház,* "house"; *-ak-,* sign of plural; *-ban,* "in," as contrasted with Latin *am-ō,* where the inflected morpheme *-ō* is a CUMUL (*q.v.*) which expresses person, number, tense, voice and mood).

agglutinative (or **agglutinating**) **language** A language combining into a single word various linguistic elements, each having a distinct, fixed connotation and separate existence (*see above*).

agreement Correspondence of one word with another as to gender, number, case, person, etc. (Spanish *las buenas muchachas,* where *las* and *buenas* are both feminine and plural to agree with *muchachas*). *Partial synonyms:* BONDING, CONCORD, CONCORDANCE, CONGRUENCE.

akousma The hearing idea about speech sounds; as opposed to GRAPHEMA, KINEMA, LEGEMA, ORAMA, (*q.v.*).

Alarodian *See* JAPHETIC, NOSTRATIC.

alien word A borrowed word that still retains part of the phonemic pattern, stress, written form, etc., of the language of origin (*chic, garage, naïveté, episcopal*). *See also* ACCLIMATIZATION, DOMESTICATED WORD, NATIVE WORD, NATURALIZED WORD.

allegro forms Forms cut down in pronunciation by rapid use (*cute* from *acute;* the current pronunciation of *Mrs.* as against the original *Mistress,* which also survives)

(Gray). *Synonym:* WEAK FORMS. *Opposites:* LENTO FORMS, STRONG FORMS. *See also* CLIPPED WORD, REDUCTION, SHORTENING, STUMP WORD.

alliteration The recurrence of the same sound or sound group, usually initial, in successive words ("*w*ild and *w*oolly," "*pr*incess of *pr*omise *pr*imeval").

allo- Combining form indicating one of a group whose members constitute a linguistic unit. *See below.*

allograph A positional or other variant of a written symbol or GRAPHEME (*q.v.*) : (the Greek letter *sigma,* written *σ* save in final position, where it appears as ς; English *p* in *hop,* which is doubled in *hopped;* the Italian unvoiced palatal affricate [č], written as *c* before *e* or *i,* as *ci* before *a, o* or *u*).

allokine A member of a KINEME (*q.v.*), analogous to an allophone (Birdwhistell).

allokinemorph A member of a KINEMORPHEME (*q.v.*), analogous to an allomorph (Birdwhistell).

allomorph A positional variant of a morpheme, occurring in a specific environment (*am, art, is* are allomorphs of *be,* occurring respectively in the environments of *I, thou, he* or *she* or *it;* the prefixal morpheme *in-,* meaning *not,* appears under the allomorphic guise of *il-* in *illiterate, im-* in *improper, ir-* in *irrespective,* depending on the environment supplied by the following consonant). *See also* ALTERNANT, COMBINATORY VARIANT, CONDITIONAL VARIANT, MORPHEMIC ALTERNANT, PREFIXAL MORPHEME, SHAPE, ZERO ALLOMORPH.

allophone 1. A positional variant of a phoneme, which occurs in a specific environment and does not differentiate meaning (the *p*-sounds appearing in *pin, spin, sip,* though phonetically different, are accepted by American English speakers as "the same sound," because the phonetic differences between them do not lend themselves to confusion of meaning, even if one is accidentally substituted for another). *Synonyms:* COMBINA-

TORY (or CONDITIONAL, or CONTEXTUAL, or POSITIONAL)
ALTERNANT (or VARIANT).

2. Sound types which are members of a phoneme class;
the individual sounds which compose a phoneme (such
variation is subphonemic); a class of phones such that
all are members of the same phoneme; they may occur
in the same phonetic environment (FREE VARIATION),
or in different positions, with non-distinctive differences
among them (COMPLEMENTARY DISTRIBUTION). *Synonym*: SUBPHONEMIC VARIANT. *See also* FREE VARIANT
(de la Garza).

allophonic Not involving a phonemic distinction; subphonemic. *See above.*

allophonic analogy The tendency of an allophone to become a separate phoneme by developing a contrast in
the same environment (Caribbean Spanish turns final
-*s* into [h] before consonants; later this change is extended analogically to a position before vowels, so that
ultimately a contrast develops between the intervocalic
s of *asar* and the intervocalic [h] of *loh americanoh*
for *los americanos*) (Hockett). A phenomenon occurring when one allophone of a phoneme comes to occur
in positions previously open only to some other allophone of the same phoneme, thus creating a new phonemic contrast and bringing about phonemic change in
a language (*las animas* > *las animah, las casas* > *lah
casah;* no phoneme /-h/ existed previously; therefore
the phoneme /s/ bifurcates into [s] and [h]; by conditioned variation, [h] occurs finally and before consonants, [s] before vowels. Now the phoneme /s/ has
two allophones, [s ~ h], and a word like *las* will
appear as [las ~ lah]; but by morphological analogy,
there is a tendency for the whole system to become
simplified, with the result that [lah] gets to be used
even before a vowel ([lah animah]); the original intervocalic [s] of *casas,* however, is not affected, so that
in word-final position we have [h] before either vowels

or consonants, but in intervocalic position within the word we have [s]. The phonemic structure is now changed, and we have both /s/ and /h/) (de la Garza).

allophonic change 1. *See* ALLOPHONIC ANALOGY.
2. A change in form (or features) on the part of an allophone (de la Garza).

allophonic confusion The gradual change of an allophone in some speech variants, such as the voicing of intervocalic *t* in some American English varieties, to the point where the change is ultimately reflected in semi-literate spelling (*bleeding* for *bleating, should of* for *should have*) (Dykema).

allophonic extension *See* ALLOPHONIC ANALOGY.

alloseme A meaning which functions as a member of a sememe (Hall). (Connotation of *profits* to a corporation executive and to a labor leader.)

allotax A positional variant of a taxeme (the position of the object pronoun in French *regardez-moi,* as opposed to its normal position in *vous me regardez*) (Hall).

allotone A tone which functions as a member of a toneme (Hall). (French *l'homme própose, Dieu díspose.*)

alphabet The written characters of a language, originally based on a sound-for-symbol correspondence, arranged in a conventional order (*a, b, c, d,* etc.), exclusive of logograms (such as the symbols $, &) and punctuation signs.

alternance vocalique *See* ABLAUT.

alternant One of the non-significant variants (allophones, allomorphs) of a phoneme or morpheme (the different articulation of the plural ending or marker in *cat-s, cad-s, glass-es,* where the alternants are phonetic, regular and automatic; in *mice, children, oxen,* where the alternants are irregular; in *sheep, deer,* where they are zero alternants; and in languages like

Greek or Latin, where they are not phonetic, but morphological. *Synonyms:* ALLOMORPH (for morphological alternant), ALLOPHONE (for phonemic alternant).

alternation 1. A correspondence existing between two definite sounds or groups of sounds, and shifting regularly between two series of coexisting forms (Saussure). *See also* AUTOMATIC ALTERNATION, COMPLEMENTARY DISTRIBUTION, COMPLEMENTATION, SPORADIC ALTERNATION.
2. For Hjelmslev's use of the term, *see* COMMUTATION, PROCESS, SYSTEM.

alternation change A phenomenon occurring when all the forms of an already existing alternation are borrowed from another language, thus supplying additional patterns of alternation to the borrowing language; competition often results between borrowed and native patterns, and the existence of DOUBLETS in the borrowing language is common; the borrowed form also often has a more learned connotation than the native (the borrowing by English from Latin of forms like *datum: data,* or *matrix: matrices;* note *index,* with its double plural *indices* (borrowed) and *indexes* (native). *See also* DOUBLET, CONNOTATION, LOAN WORD (de la Garza).

alveolar A consonant produced by placing the tip or blade of the tongue in contact with the alveoli, or gingival ridge of the upper gums (English /t/, /d/, /n/, /s/). *Synonyms:* GINGIVAL, POST-DENTAL 1.

amalgam The blending of two or more meanings (SIGNIFICATA, SIGNIFIEDS) into one signifier (SIGNIFICANS) (French *au,* blending *à* and *le;* Latin *-ōrum,* blending genitive and plural, though itself indivisible, are FORMAL AMALGAMS; English *bull's-eye* is a SEMANTIC AMALGAM) (Martinet). *Synonyms:* CUMUL, PORTMANTEAU FORM.

amalgamating language A flectional language in which the affixes are intimately fused with the roots of the words, and do not possess or retain independent entity. *Approximate synonym:* FLECTIONAL LANGUAGE. *See also* AGGLOMERATION.

ambisyllabic Term applied to a single contoid between two vocoids; its onset comes before the end of the first syllable, the syllable boundary falls during the hold, and the release comes after the beginning of the next syllable (Hall).

amelioration Betterment or enhancement in the meaning of a word (Germanic *marah skalk,* "horse groom," eventually turns into *marshal,* even in the sense of "a marshal of France"). *Synonyms:* ELEVATION, ENHANCEMENT, MELIORATION. *Opposites:* DEGENERATION, PEJORATION.

amorphous change Cases of disappearance or emergence of words for which there is no replacement (the disappearance of *igitur* in Romance development, or the emergence of *boy* in Middle English). Such changes affect the phonemic structure of the language only by accident (Hoenigswald). *Partial synonyms:* COINAGE, LOSS OF WORDS.

amorphous language A term applied by Russian linguists to languages which have no flectional endings, such as Chinese (Entwistle).

amplificative *See* AUGMENTATIVE.

analogical extension A modification of form (MORPHOLOGICAL EXTENSION) or of meaning (SEMANTIC EXTENSION) of a word in imitation of an existing or widely used pattern (*five-thirtyish,* formed on the analogy of *yellowish, Spanish,* etc.). *See also* ANALOGY.

analogue A word in one language corresponding to a word in another (*house, maison, casa*); all the connotations of analogues do not have to be identical.

analogy (analogical change) The occasional and unpredictable tendency of a word or form to be pulled out of its natural orbit of development by the attraction of another word or form with which it has a real or fancied resemblance; the process of modifying words on the model of existing patterns, or of creating new words on the basis of such patterns (a child's use of *deers* as the plural of *deer* because *beans* is the plural of *bean;* the creation of *helped* as the past tense of *help,* replacing an earlier *holp,* because most verbs form the past tense by the addition of -*d* or -*ed*). *Synonyms:* EXTENSION (ALLOPHONIC, ANALOGICAL, MORPHOLOGICAL, PROPORTIONAL, SEMANTIC). *See also* PHONOSYMBOLISM, PRIMARY ANALOGY, PROPORTIONAL ANALOGY.

analysis 1. In descriptive linguistics, the study of words and forms which have been gathered and collated, for the purpose of isolating and listing the various phonemes of a language with all their allophones (PHONEMIC ANALYSIS), the morphemes and allomorphs (MORPHEMIC ANALYSIS), the syntactical system of the language (SYNTACTICAL ANALYSIS), and the word-stock of the language (LEXICAL ANALYSIS); the end product of linguistic analysis is a complete descriptive grammar of the language under consideration. *Synonym:* LINGUISTIC ANALYSIS. *See also* DISCOURSE ANALYSIS. 2. In historical linguistics, the use of separate words to convey the concept previously expressed by a single, usually longer word (Latin *amabo,* "I shall love," replaced by Vulgar Latin *amare habeo,* which eventually contracts into *amerai, amaré, amerò,* and other Romance forms). *Opposite:* SYNTHESIS.

analytical language A language in which AUXILIARY WORDS (*q.v.*) are the chief means of indicating grammatical relationships, to the total or partial exclusion of inflections, and where the separate meanings are expressed by words that can be used in isolation (FREE MORPHEMES). (English *I shall wait,* where *I* expresses the notion of first person singular, *shall* expresses futurity, and *wait* conveys the basic idea of the action, as contrasted with Latin *amabō,* where *ama-* conveys the basic idea, -*b*- expresses futurity, -*ō* expresses first person singular.) *Synonyms:* AMORPHOUS (*also* ATOMIC, FORMLESS, ISOLATING, RADICAL) LANGUAGE. *Opposite:* SYNTHETIC LANGUAGE. *See also* AGGLUTINATIVE, FLECTIONAL, POLYSYNTHETIC LANGUAGE.

anaphora   Reference to something already mentioned (the thing referred to is called the ANTECEDENT, even if it follows). An ANAPHORIC WORD refers to another word already spoken or written ("You have a black suit, I have a gray *one*"). ZERO ANAPHORA occurs where the anaphoric word or its antecedent is omitted or understood ("I wanted to go, but I couldn't"; here *go* would be the antecedent, *do so,* or some similar expression, the anaphoric word). *Synonym* for ANAPHORIC WORD : PROP WORD.

anaptyctic vowel   A vowel arising by ANAPTYXIS (*q.v.*). *Synonyms:* EPENTHETIC (*also* EXCRESCENT, INTRUSIVE, PARASITIC) VOWEL.

anaptyxis   The insertion of a vowel or vowels to break up a troublesome consonant cluster (Italian *lanzichenecco,* "foreign mercenary," from German *Landsknecht;* French borrows Scandinavian *knīf,* but finds it expedient to insert an anaptyctic vowel between *k* and *n,* and the result is *canif*). Bloomfield defines the phenomenon as the rise of a vowel beside a sonant, originally syllabic, which then becomes non-syllabic (Gothic *fugls,* where the *l* is syllabic, as against Anglo-Saxon *fugol,* in which an anaptyctic vowel *o* has arisen). *Synonyms:* EXCRESCENCE, VOWEL EPENTHESIS.

Anlaut   1. The ONSET (*q.v.*) of the vocal stream.

2. The initial position in a word or utterance.

antecedent   *See* ANAPHORA.

anticipation   Regular or sporadic sound change; the effect of a phoneme on a preceding phoneme as the vocal organs prepare for the second while still uttering the first. *Synonyms:* in a broader sense, RETROGRESSIVE

ASSIMILATION; as applied to vocalic phenomena only, FRONTING, METAPHONY, UMLAUT.

anticipatory expansion The addition of new elements before what was already present in a construction ("the man" by ANTICIPATORY EXPANSION becomes "the good old man") (Hall). *See also* EXPANSION.

antonym A word meaning the opposite of another (*big* is the antonym of *small*). *Synonym:* OPPOSITE. *Opposite:* SYNONYM.

aorist A verb-tense, expressing an action, usually past, where the time is indefinite or unimportant (Greek *epempsa,* "I sent," vs. *pepompha,* "I have sent").

aphasia The loss of the speech function owing to injury to the brain or nervous system.

apheresis The disappearance of an initial vowel, often by reason of absorption by the final vowel of the preceding word (Vulgar Latin *illa abbatia* > Italian *la badia;* English *cute* from *acute, mid* from *amid*). *Opposite:* PROTHESIS.

aphesis Omission of the initial part of an utterance ("Morning!" for "Good morning!"; "That do?" for "Will that do?") (Jespersen). *Synonym:* PROSIOPESIS.

aphoristic clause A clause or sentence used chiefly in proverbs and aphorisms ("First come, first served!") (Hall).

apical (combining form : APICO-) A sound produced with the tip or apex of the tongue as the articulator (Castilian apical *s*).

apico-alveolar A sound produced with the apex or tip of the tongue touching the alveoli, or upper gum ridges (English /t/, Castilian /s/) (Martinet). *See also* APICO-DENTAL.

apico-alveolar lateral *See* APICO-DENTAL LATERAL.

apico-dental A sound produced with the tip of the tongue touching the back of the upper teeth (French /t/) (Martinet). *See also* APICO-ALVEOLAR.

apico-dental lateral 1. A LATERAL (*q.v.*) produced with the closure of the tip of the tongue touching the back of the upper teeth (French *l* in *loup*); in English, the lateral is pronounced with the tip of the tongue touching the alveoli, and may thus be described as an APICO-ALVEOLAR LATERAL (Martinet).

2. A sound produced with the apex of the tongue making a medial occlusion in the dental (or alveolar) region, and the sides relaxed so that the breath stream flows between the teeth near the first premolars; this sound, which results from the position of the convex upper surface of the blade of the tongue near the palatal or prepalatal region, is called LIGHT or CLEAR [l] (as in French); sometimes the lateral sound is articulated with the back of the dorsum of the tongue elevated in the prevelar or mediopalatal region; this back elevation produces a concave upper surface of the tongue behind the alveolar occlusion, and the sound that results is slightly velarized; this is referred to as DARK [l] (as in English) (de la Garza).

apocope (or **apocopation**) The loss of a final vowel (Middle English *helpe* > Modern English *help*). *Opposite:* PARAGOGE.

apophony *See* ABLAUT.

aposiopesis Omission of the final part of an utterance ("I'm going to St. Paul's," with "Church" understood) (Jespersen). *Opposites:* APHESIS, PROSIOPESIS.

a posteriori language An artificial language constructed with reference to and on the basis of existing languages, and blending different living language elements (Volapük, Esperanto, Ido, Interlingua, etc.). *Opposite:* A PRIORI LANGUAGE. *See also* ARTIFICIAL (*also* AUXILIARY, CONSTRUCTED, INTERNATIONAL, UNIVERSAL) LANGUAGE, INTERLANGUAGE.

appellative That aspect of language which characterizes the hearer, as against EXPRESSIVE (characterizing the speaker) and REPRESENTATIONAL (characterizing the

subject of discourse) (Trubetskoi). *See also* FUNCTIONS
OF PITCH.

applied linguistics *See* LINGUISTICS.

a priori language An artificial language constructed
without reference to or similarity with existing lan-
guages (Solresol, Suma, Ro, etc.). *Opposite:* A POS-
TERIORI LANGUAGE. *See also* ARTIFICIAL (*also* AUXIL-
IARY, CONSTRUCTED, INTERNATIONAL, UNIVERSAL)
LANGUAGE, INTERLANGUAGE.

archaic No longer in use; old-fashioned; obsolete (Middle English *yclept, hight*).

archaism A form no longer in current use. *See also* OB-
SOLETE, OBSOLESCENT.

archiphoneme The phonemic unit consisting of two or
more phonemes subject to NEUTRALIZATION (*q.v.*),
plus all their allophones; the sum total of the relevant
features common to two mutually neutralizable phonemes (Dorfman); the single phoneme replacing two
phonemes normally distinct when they are neutralized
in certain environments (/t/, /d/ in intervocalic position in some modern German dialects) (Hughes); a
neutralized or environmentally determined variant (in
Spanish, /r/ occurs finally, but not initially; /rr/ occurs initially, but not finally; both occur between
vowels; a single archiphoneme covering both phonemes, /r/ and /rr/, may be postulated, with the understanding that a phonemic difference between the two
variants occurs only in a determined position or environment, as in *pero* vs. *perro*) (Trubetskoi). *See also*
NEUTRALIZATION, PARTIAL COMPLEMENTATION.

archistratum The cultural over-layer of a language, generally common to all the languages of Western civiliza-
tion, and made up largely of Greek and Latin roots
(Migliorini). *See also* ADSTRATUM.

area and language studies Geolinguistically, the study
of a political or geographical area with reference to its
history, geography, economic and political status, cul-

tural features, combined with the study of that area's language or languages.

area language   Geolinguistically, a language that is predominant in a region but not native to or predominant in all of that region (Russian in the Soviet Union and some of its European satellites). *See also* COLONIAL LANGUAGE, REGIONAL LANGUAGE, SECONDARY LANGUAGE 3, SPHERE OF INFLUENCE, SUPERIMPOSED LANGUAGE.

area (or **areal**) **linguistics**   The pursuit of a school of historical and comparative linguistics denying the exceptionless working of SOUND LAWS (*q.v.*), and emphasizing the study of dialects. *See also* DIALECT LINGUISTICS, DIALECTOLOGY, LINGUISTIC GEOGRAPHY, NEOLINGUISTS.

argot   A class jargon, or special vocabulary, not intelligible to the uninitiated listener. *See also* CANT, JARGON, JOBELYN.

articulation   The formation of a speech sound by the vocal organs; the totality of the movements of the speech organs required to produce a distinct speech sound. Articulations are described as DOUBLE or SECONDARY when accompanied by LABIALIZATIONS, PALATALIZATIONS, etc. (Gleason). *See also* EMPHATIC ARTICULATION, FIRST ARTICULATION, POINT OF ARTICULATION, SECOND ARTICULATION.

articulation test   *See* ACOUSTIC PHONETICS.

articulator   An organ of speech, such as the tongue, lips or uvula, that can be moved more or less freely to open or close the mouth, or to form a narrow passage for the breath stream. *Synonym:* MOVABLE SPEECH ORGAN. *Opposite:* IMMOVABLE SPEECH ORGAN.

articulatory phonetics   1. The study of the mechanism of production of speech sounds, basing itself upon the point of articulation and the mode of production of the sounds, giving an objective description of the sounds and how they are produced, and establishing a broader or narrower classification among them, as reflected in the INTERNATIONAL PHONETIC ALPHABET (*q.v.*). *Synonyms:* GENETIC PHONETICS, PHYSIOLOGICAL PHONETICS. *See also* ACOUSTIC (GENEMMIC) PHONETICS.

2. One of the two branches of phonetics which have been developed to deal with the transmissional properties of speech. Articulatory phonetics is treated under two aspects : (a) the MOTOR (or ACTIVE) aspect, which deals with how sounds are produced in terms of muscular activity, i.e., how, during speech, the normally slow-moving air flow of the vocal tract is set in motion by the muscles of the pulmonary and articulatory regions; (b) the VOCAL TRACT (PASSIVE) aspect, which treats of how the vocal tract is shaped and how it moves during articulation; this second phase of articulatory phonetics is concerned with air flow, and is better developed than motor phonetics; it is usually described by linguists in terms of POSITION OF ARTICULATION and the SECONDARY (or PROSODIC) features involved (de la Garza).

artificial language A language constructed or created, by an individual or a group of individuals, for purposes of international communications or for use by a special group (Esperanto, Interlingua, etc.). *Synonym:* CONSTRUCTED LANGUAGE. *See also* A PRIORI (*also* A POSTERIORI, AUXILIARY, INTERNATIONAL, UNIVERSAL) LANGUAGE, INTERLANGUAGE.

aspect A verbal category indicating whether an action or state is viewed as completed or in progress, instantaneous or enduring, momentary or habitual, etc. *See also* IMPERFECTIVE, PERFECTIVE.

aspects of sound (a) FEEDBACK, which includes the auditory, vibratory, kinesthetic and tactile sensations, and intention types (*q.v.*); (b) TRANSMISSION, which includes intention and the nervous system (de la Garza).

aspirate 1. The sound [h] and its variants.

2. A stop consonant characterized by the addition of a puff of breath, or ASPIRATION (*q.v.*); a sound whose pronunciation involves intensity in the expulsion of air from the oral cavity (English word-initial *p, t, k;* the Greek sounds indicated by the letters *phi, chi, theta* in the earlier stages of the language; Sanskrit and Hindi sounds indicated in transcription by such combinations as *bh, dh, jh*).

aspiration The addition to a stop consonant of a perceptible puff of breath (or an *h*-sound unmarked in English writing; in English, /p/, /t/, /k/ are usually aspirated in the initial position, but unaspirated after *s*-). *See also* SECONDARY FEATURES.

assibilant (or **assibilate**) A special variety of AFFRICATE (*q.v.*) consisting of a stop contoid plus a sibilant release ([ts], [dz]), articulated at a dental point of articulation.

assibilation The process of ASSIMILATION (*q.v.*) whereby a non-sibilant becomes an assibilant (Latin *vitium* > Italian *vezzo*).

assimilation A phonetic process whereby two phonemes acquire common characteristics or become identical. The assimilation may be PARTIAL (Latin *in-possibilis* to *impossibilis,* where the *n* acquires the labial feature of the *p,* but not its unvoiced stop character; *synonym:* ACCOMMODATION); or TOTAL (Latin *ad-porto* to *apporto,* where the voiced dental *d* turns into the unvoiced labial *p,* to assimilate fully to the ASSIMILATORY PHONEME *p; synonym:* EQUALIZATION). When both phonemes affect each other, the assimilation is RECIPROCAL (Latin *rapidum* to *rap'du* to Italian *ratto,* with unvoicing of *d* to conform to *p,* and dentalizing of *p* to conform to *d*). If the two phonemes are adjacent, as in the above examples (or in English *haf to* for *have to*), we have CONTIGUOUS ASSIMILATION; if they are not adjacent (Latin *denarium* to Italian *danaro,* where the *e* of the initial syllable is assimilated to the *a* of the stressed syllable), we have NON-CONTIGUOUS or IN-CONTIGUOUS ASSIMILATION. (*Synonyms:* DILATION, DISTANT ASSIMILATION; UMLAUT and VOWEL HARMONY (*q.v.*) are forms of DISTANT ASSIMILATION.) When the phoneme which produces this phenomenon (ASSIMILATORY PHONEME) precedes the ASSIMILATED PHONEME, the assimilation is PROGRESSIVE (Latin *hominem* to *hom'ne* to French *homme,* or *femina* to *fem'na* to *femme;* Cockney *Lunnon* for *London,* vulgar American *wunnerful* for *wonderful*). When the ASSIMILATORY PHONEME follows the ASSIMILATED PHONEME, the assimilation is REGRESSIVE or RETROGRESSIVE (Latin *domina* to *dom'na* to Italian *donna;* English *give me* to *gimme*). *Opposite:* DISSIMILATION. *See also* COMBINATIVE CHANGE, INFECTION, METAPHONY, MORPHOLOGICAL ASSIMILATION.

assimilatory phoneme *See* ASSIMILATION. *Synonyms:* ASSIMILATING (INDUCING) PHONEME, INDUCER.

associative etymology Orr's synonym for FOLK ETYMOLOGY (*q.v.*).

associative field The network of associations connecting every word with other terms related to it in form, meaning, or both (Bally).

assonance The repetition in verse of stressed vowel sounds, but not of the accompanying consonants (Old French *magnes, Espaigne, fraindre, aimet, ataignet,* all occurring at the end of verses in a single *laisse* of the *Chanson de Roland,* have in common the stressed vowel *a,* followed or not by a *y*-glide). *See also* CONSONANCE, RHYME.

asterisk *See* STARRED FORM.

asyllabic Said of a phoneme incapable of forming a syllable by itself, or of serving as a syllable nucleus (*d, t, k*). *Synonym:* NON-SYLLABIC. *Opposite:* SYLLABIC.

asyntactic compound *See* COMPOSITION.

athematic Not related to or constituting a stem; applied to a flectional form where a prefix or suffix is added to

the root without a thematic morpheme. *Opposite:* THE-
MATIC.

atlas   *See* DIALECT ATLAS, LINGUISTIC ATLAS.

atomic language   Marouzeau's term for ISOLATING LAN-
GUAGE (*q.v.*).

atomistic approach   The view of language which considers every phoneme as an individual, isolated unit, in
contrast to the STRUCTURAL LINGUISTICS (*q.v.*) approach.

atonic   Without stress or pitch accent (in *furthering, -er-*
and *-ing* are atonic syllables, and *-e-* and *-i-* atonic
vowels). *Synonyms:* UNACCENTED, UNSTRESSED. *Opposites:* ACCENTED, STRESSED, TONIC.

attested form   A form recorded as actually in use at some
time or other. *Opposites:* STARRED FORM, UNATTESTED
FORM.

attraction   1. Phonemically, an attempted completion of
the regularity of the phonemic pattern, usually manifested by filling the HOLES IN THE PATTERN (*q.v.*).
2. Morphologically, the tendency toward a morphological change in a word under the influence of adjacent
words; the change may be of number, gender, case,
mood, tense, etc. ("Neither of these books *were* sold";
"*These* kind of books"). *Synonym:* MORPHOLOGICAL
ASSIMILATION. *See also* SYNONYMIC ATTRACTION.

attribute   The word or group of words denoting qualities
of the HEAD, HEAD WORD or CENTER of the CONSTRUC-
TION (in "The new houses now being built," *houses* is
the HEAD, *the, new* and *now being built* are ATTRI-
BUTES) (Hockett).

attributive construction   Bloch and Trager's term for
SUBORDINATIVE CONSTRUCTION (*q.v.*).

attrition   The phonological process whereby a word is
worn down to the point where it has to be replaced
(Old French *ef* from Latin *apem,* ultimately replaced
by *abeille* from the Latin diminutive *apicula*) (Entwistle).

audio-lingual The combination of listening and speaking, the two basic language skills, and teaching designed to produce them (Brooks). *Synonym:* AURAL-ORAL.

auditory discrimination The ability to distinguish between sounds in one language, or between similar sounds in two or more languages (Walsh). *Synonym:* AURAL (or LISTENING) DISCRIMINATION.

auditory feedback Hearing ourselves talk. *See also* KINESTHETIC FEEDBACK.

Aufhebung *See* NEUTRALIZATION.

augment A prefixed element (vowel, diphthong, or vowel-lengthening) used in Classical Greek (imperfect *epempon* from *pempō; ērchon* from *archō*).

augmentative A word formed from another, usually by the addition of a suffix, to indicate the accessory notion of bigness (Spanish *hombrote,* "big man," from *hombre,* "man"; Italian *casone,* "big house," from *casa*). *Synonym:* AMPLIFICATIVE. *Opposite:* DIMINUTIVE.

aural discrimination *See* AUDITORY DISCRIMINATION.

aural-oral *See* AUDIO-LINGUAL.

Auslaut 1. The end of the vocal stream. *See also* OFF-GLIDE.

2. FINAL POSITION (*q.v.*) in a word or utterance.

automatic alternation An alternation that must take place under penalty of violating the phonemic structure of the language (Italian, until recent times, would not tolerate an *s*-impure cluster after ᴀ consonant; therefore, the shift from *strada,* as in *la strada,* to *istrada,* as *per istrada,* was automatic; *strada* was the base form, and *istrada* replaced it only under specific conditions) (Hockett). A predictable, formal alternation which is determined by the phonemes of the accompanying form, which can be described in terms of phonetic modification, and which applies to all morphemes in general when they occur in that particular conditioned environment (the alternation of English [-s $\sim$ -z $\sim$ -iz] in the regular plural suffix of nouns, which is determined by the final phoneme of the noun stem; this differs from phonetic alternation, since not every [s] in English is subject to this alternation, but only the allomorphs of this particular morpheme). Most automatic alternations are regular. Automatic alternation is always phonemic, but phonemic alternations are not always automatic (de la Garza). *Opposite:* NON-AUTOMATIC ALTERNATION. *See also* ALTERNATION, COMPLEMENTARY DISTRIBUTION, COMPLEMENTATION, PHONEMICALLY CONDITIONED ALTERNATION, REGULAR ALTERNATION.

autonomous moneme   *See* MONEME.

autonomous sound-change   *See* SPONTANEOUS SOUND-CHANGE.

autonomous syntagm   *See* SYNTAGM.

auxiliary   A word having no complete meaning in itself, and used in combination with or reference to another word which has a meaning of its own (prepositions, conjunctions, auxiliary verbs such as *may, shall*).

auxiliary language   1. Geolinguistically, a language that may be used to a varying degree in substitution for another language which is native to the area (French in Tunisia, English in India, German in Czechoslovakia). *Partial synonyms:* CULTURAL, SECONDARY, SUBSTITUTE, TERTIARY LANGUAGE.

2. An INTERNATIONAL LANGUAGE or INTERLANGUAGE, such as Esperanto, designed to serve for international communications among people speaking different languages. *Additional synonym:* UNIVERSAL LANGUAGE.

auxiliary numeral   One of a set of CLASSIFIERS (*q.v.*) used in some languages, like Japanese, in addition to the cardinal numbers, to indicate the class to which the noun modified by the numeral belongs. *Synonyms:* CLASSIFIER 1, ENUMERATIVE, NUMERAL (or NUMERATIVE) CLASSIFIER.

avulsive   Marouzeau's term for CLICK or CLOSING SOUND (*q.v.*).

axis In an exocentric, directive construction, the portion which complements the director (in "on the table," *on* is the director, *the table* is the axis) (Hockett); the direction along which the relation between the indicator and its complement lies; usually the object of the preposition or postposition (Hall).

B

back formation The derivation of new words from existing ones assumed to be derivatives (*sculpt* from *sculptor, buttle* from *butler,* on the analogy of *act* from *actor*); forming one word from another by cutting off a real or supposed suffix (French *cri* from *crier,* English *peddle* from *peddler*); this process normally involves the transformation of one part of speech into another. *Synonyms:* INVERSE DERIVATION, RE(TRO)GRESSIVE FORMATION, RÜCKBILDUNG. *See also* FUNCTIONAL CHANGE, RECUTTING, RESHAPING, STUMP WORD.

back sound *See* BUCCAL SOUND.

back vowel A vowel whose point of articulation is in the rear of the oral cavity, and which is pronounced with the back part of the tongue arched toward the soft palate ([o], [u]). *Synonyms:* BROAD (*also* DARK, DEEP, VELAR) VOWEL. *Opposites:* BRIGHT (*also* FRONT, PALATAL, SLENDER) VOWEL.

base 1. The simple form of a word, to which inflectional endings are appended; it may be the primary root of the word, or the root with a THEMATIC SUFFIX (*q.v.*) (in Latin *agimus, ag-* could be regarded as the root, *agi-* as the stem, with addition of the thematic morpheme *-i-;* either *ag-* or *agi-,* which represent simply different GRADES (*q.v.*), could be regarded as the base) (Gray). *Partial synonyms:* KERNEL, NUCLEUS, RADICAL 1, ROOT, STEM, THEME.

2. In historical linguistics, the reconstruction of the relationship among words in several languages (Indo-European base **bher-,* reconstructed from Greek *phero,* Latin *fero,* Anglo-Saxon *beran,* etc.).

3. *See* HEAVY BASE, LIGHT BASE.

4. In descriptive linguistics, a word or morpheme which may be a bound form but not an affix, chosen as the convenient point of departure for the analysis of complex words or derivatives (*play* as the base from which *played, playing, player,* etc., are derived) (Webster III). *Synonym:* KERNEL.

base compound A compound formed of two bases with no connecting element (*telephone*) (Hall). *Synonyms:* BASE FORM, PRIMARY COMPOUND. *See also* SOCIATIVE MORPHEME.

base form The allomorph of a given morpheme having the greatest frequency of occurrence, with the others regarded as REPLACIVES or VARIANTS (for the past-indicating morpheme in English verbs, /d/ might be considered the base form, with /t/, /ed/, internal vowel change [as in *sing, sang, sung*], zero change [as in *put,* past *put*], considered as replacives) (Gleason).

base of comparison In phonemics, the relevant features which two or more phonemes have in common (voiced or unvoiced, dental or labial, etc.); in bilateral oppositions, this is the ARCHIPHONEME (*q.v.*); in all oppositions, this is what permits the setting up of ORDERS and SERIES (*q.v.*).

base of inflection The simple or basic form of a word, to which inflectional endings are appended; it may be the primary root of the word (ROOT BASE), or the root with a thematic suffix (STEM BASE). *Synonyms:* BASE 1, ROOT BASE, STEM BASE.

basic alternant An alternant which has wider range than the others (*keep, run,* as against *kep-, ran*) (Bloch and Trager). *Partial synonyms:* BASE 4, BASE FORM.

basic language A language functioning with a small number of words, out of which are built, by a process of paraphrase, the equivalents of other words (Basic English "without thought of others" for *selfish,* "small tree" for *shrub*).

basis of articulation The over-all neutral position of the speech organs and their various parts when not speaking which is characteristic of a speech community or of the native speakers of a language (Dorfman).

bidirectional In TRANSFORM (or TRANSFORMATIONAL) GRAMMAR, a transformation that can proceed in either direction ("Dog bites man" ↔ "Man bites dog") (Hall).

bilabial A sound produced with both lips (*p, b, m*).

bilateral opposition This occurs when two phonemes, often having the same ARCHIPHONEME (*q.v.*), share most features, but differ in only one relevant feature (German /k/ and /χ/ are both oral, velar, and voiceless; but the first is a plosive, the second a fricative (Trubetskoi, Jakobson). A minimal contrast or differentiation between only two phonemes (de la Garza).

bilingualism The state of being able to speak two languages with approximately equal ease and a native-speaker accent.

bilingual text A text appearing in two languages.

binary principle The theory that every phonemic opposition presents a common denominator, both on the acoustic and the articulatory level, in a dichotomy imposed by the nature of the language (the relation strong/weak is measurable physically and physiologically) (Jakobson). *See also* CORRELATION, OPPOSITION.

binit The unit of information to communications and information engineers. *Synonym:* BIT.

biolinguistics The study of language as a biologically determined activity of the organism, with emphasis on neurophysical, embryological and genetic features (Meader and Muyskens).

bipartite system A morphological system in which there are only two major parts of speech (e.g., inflected, with the same type of inflection applying to words used as nouns and to words used as verbs; and uninflected) (Hockett). *See also* MULTIPARTITE, TRIPARTITE.

bit *See* BINIT.

blade of the tongue The part of the tongue which is just past the tip or apex, and up to the front, often coinciding with the hard palate. *See also* ARTICULATOR.

blending The combination into a single word of two words from different sources, or even from different languages; a process of division followed by addition (*motor* + *hotel* > *motel; smoke* + *fog* > *smog;* Germanic *hoch* + Latin *altum* > Old French *halt,* Modern French *haut*). *Synonyms:* CONTAMINATION, (WORD) CROSSING. *See also* PORTMANTEAU WORD, TELESCOPED WORD. A sporadic change which consists of combining part of one word with part of another to form a single new word (de la Garza).

blocked syllable *See* CHECKED SYLLABLE, CLOSED SYLLABLE.

blocked vowel *See* CHECKED VOWEL, CLOSED VOWEL 2.

bonding That feature of AGREEMENT or CONCORD (*q.v.*) whereby a feature of gender, number, case, etc., in the noun is reflected in the accompanying article or adjective, and that of the subject in the verb (Spanish *las malas muchachas han sido castigadas*) (Hughes). *See also* CONGRUENCE, GOVERNMENT.

book word *See* LEARNED WORD.

border *See* TROUGH.

borrowed word *See* LOAN WORD.

borrowing 1. A borrowed word or LOAN WORD (*q.v.*).
2. The process whereby one language absorbs words and expressions, possibly also sounds and grammatical

forms, from another, and adapts them to its own use, with or without phonetic and semantic adaptation (Old French *verai* [Modern French *vrai*] borrowed by English and adapted as *very*). *See also* ACCLIMATIZATION, ALIEN (*also* DOMESTICATED, NATURALIZED) WORD, LOAN BLEND, LOAN SHIFT, LOAN TRANSLATION.

bound accent *See* BOUND STRESS, FIXED STRESS.

boundary *See* LANGUAGE BOUNDARY.

bounded noun A noun that in the singular requires a determiner, such as *the* or *a;* the class meaning is "species of object occurring in more than one specimen, such that the specimens cannot be subdivided or merged" (*the house, a house*) (Bloomfield). *Synonym:* COUNT NOUN. *Opposites:* MASS NOUN, UNBOUNDED NOUN. *See also* DETERMINER, MARKER.

bound form A morpheme which has distinct meaning only when it is attached (prefixed or suffixed) to a word (*-s* in *dogs*). On the level of inflection, such a form is said to be INFLECTIONALLY BOUND (*walls*); if it replaces a phrase, it is PHRASALLY BOUND (*wall's*); if it requires a clause, it is CLAUSALLY BOUND (*considering that*); if it appears in the predicate, it is PREDICATIVELY BOUND (French *il* in *mon frère, est-il venu?*) (Hall). *Synonyms:* BOUND MORPHEME, MORPHEME (as opposed to FORMANT). *Opposites:* FORMANT, FREE FORM, FREE MORPHEME. *See also* DEGREE OF BOUNDNESS, DERIVATIONAL AFFIX, FORMATIVE.

bound morpheme *See* BOUND FORM.

bound stress Stress which must always fall on a given syllable of the word (initial stress of Czech, penultimate stress of Polish). *Synonyms:* BOUND ACCENT, FIXED STRESS. *Opposite:* FREE STRESS.

boustrophedon "As the ox plows"; used to describe a system of writing in which one line runs left to right, the next right to left, the next left to right again, etc., as in Archaic Greek.

bow-wow theory The belief that language rose in imita-

tion of sounds heard in nature. *Synonym:* ONOMATO-
POETIC THEORY.

branlant　Saussure's term for VIBRANT (*q.v.*).

breaking　The change of a simple vowel into a diphthong
(Anglo-Saxon *werc* to *weorc;* Latin *novum* to Italian
nuovo). *Synonyms:* BRECHUNG, DIPHTHONGIZATION,
VOWEL FRACTURE. *Opposites:* DEDIPHTHONGIZATION,
MONOPHTHONGIZATION.

breath group　A chain of sounds produced in one breath
(Gleason); the stretch of utterance between two pauses
sufficient for an intake of breath at each pause (Webster III).

breathing　A mark appearing in Greek over initial vowels
and *r* to indicate the presence of aspiration (ROUGH
BREATHING, SPIRITUS ASPER) or its absence (SMOOTH
BREATHING, SPIRITUS LENIS); the rough breathing is
usually transcribed by *h,* the smooth breathing is left
untranscribed.

breathy voice　*See* MURMURED VOWEL.

Brechung　*See* BREAKING.

breve　1. As a diacritic (*q.v.*), a mark placed over a
vowel to indicate a special sound (Rumanian *casă*).
2. As a quantity mark, an indication that the vowel is
short (Latin *portă*). *Opposite:* MACRON.

bright vowel　Gray's term for FRONT VOWEL (*q.v.*). *Synonyms:* PALATAL (*also* SLENDER) VOWEL.

broad consonant　In Irish phonetics, a consonant immediately preceding or following a broad vowel (*q.v.*) in
the same word. *Opposite:* SLENDER CONSONANT.

broad transcription　1. Technically, a simplified form of
phonemic transcription, in use since the phonemic principle has been clearly recognized, whereby one symbol
represents each phoneme in a language (de la Garza).
Opposite: NARROW TRANSCRIPTION.
2. A form of transcription used by some linguists and
writers of grammars to represent only the gross phonetic

features of utterance, and approaching a phonemic transcription.

broad vowel *See* BACK VOWEL.

broken plural Those plural forms of the Semitic languages (originally feminine singular collectives) which are formed by the change of internal vowels (Arabic *kalb,* "dog," plural *kilāb; kitāb,* "book," plural *kutub*).

buccal cavity The mouth, acting as a filtering cavity.

buccal sound 1. A sound produced with the uvula pressed back against the wall of the mouth so as to prevent an escape of air by way of the nose. *Synonym:* BACK SOUND.

2. A non-nasal (Entwistle). *Synonym:* ORAL SOUND.

burst The acoustic cue, on the spectrogram, for the articulation of a stop or consonant constriction (fricative); the burst of constriction sounds is produced during, or just following, the point of greatest closure in consonant articulation; it reflects little if any of the consonant's movement (point of articulation); frequently the position of the bursts enables the listener to distinguish among the voiceless stops [p, t, k]; the presence of a constriction (burst) is important as it marks the *manner* of articulation of a sound (de la Garza). *See* ACOUSTIC PHONETICS.

C

cacophony A harsh, discordant sound effect, unpleasant to the ear. *Opposite:* EUPHONY.

cacuminal A sound produced by placing the tip of the tongue against the hard palate behind the alveolar ridge.

Synonyms: CEREBRAL, DOMAL, INVERTED, RETROFLEX.

cadence 1. The modulation of the voice, leading to the flow of language; the rise and fall produced by the alternation of louder and softer syllables in accentual tongues.

2. The fall of the voice at the end of a sentence or at a pause.

calque A translation loan word; the translated imitation of a special meaning (English *foot* as a unit of measure is a calque, or loan translation, of Latin *pes* used in that sense). *Synonyms:* HETERONYM 2, LOAN-SHIFT, LOAN TRANSLATION, TRANSLATION LOAN WORD.

canonical form 1. The normal form of a language's lexemes (Martinet); a generalized, typical phonemic shape of morphs or syllables (Hockett) (the Chinese canonical form is typically monosyllabic; the Semitic consists of three consonants ({CCC}); the English often assumes the shape consonant-vowel-consonant ({CVC}), as in *far* or *met,* or consonant-vowel-consonant-vowel-consonant ({CVCVC}), as in *leather* or *bottom*). *See also* SYLLABIC PATTERN.

2. A generalized phonemic shape among words of the same positional class (French adjectives of a single syllable such as {bõ} and {rõ} have the canonical form {CV}) (de la Garza).

cant The special vocabulary of a particular group, especially criminals. *See also* ARGOT, JARGON.

cardinal vowels A system of eight vowels, four front, four back, devised by Daniel Jones ([i], [e], [ɛ], [æ], [a], [o], [ɔ], [ɑ]) and arranged in a vowel trapezoid or triangle; these vowels are said to have approximately equal acoustic intervals between them, with characteristic tongue and lip positions and well-defined acoustic qualities; modifications of the system increase the number of vowels up to sixteen. *See also* PRIMARY VOWEL, SECONDARY VOWEL.

cases vides *See* HOLES IN THE PATTERN (Martinet).

caste A group of nouns denoting a class of beings (rational, irrational, animate, inanimate, etc.). *See also* GENDER.

catacresis A form of metonymy in which there is an inherent contradiction of terms ("a mule shod with silver shoes") (Migliorini).

catch *See* GLOTTAL STOP. *Synonyms:* GLOTTAL CATCH, IMPULSION, STØD.

categories (grammatical) *See* GRAMMATICAL CATEGORIES. *See also* OBLIGATORY CATEGORIES, SYNTACTIC CATEGORY.

catenative verb A verb that links the subject and predicate (Walsh).

cavities of speech organs The pulmonary, gastric, esophagal, pharyngeal, laryngeal, velic, oral and nasal cavities.

cedilla A diacritic mark placed under certain letters to indicate the proper sound; originally a small letter z, indicating palatalization of the c under which it was written (ç).

ceneme 1. Linguistically, a phoneme, or anything pertaining to phonology (Hockett).
2. The smallest unit of expression without corresponding content, differing from a phoneme in that it does not necessarily consist of sound, but may include letters and other semantic indicators (Hjelmslev). *Opposite:* PLEREME. *See also* CENETICS, FIGURA, TAXEME OF EXPRESSION.

cenetics The aspect of language which is concerned not with grammar, but with the levels of expression; i.e., phonetics (substance) and phonemics (form) (Hjelmslev).

census An enumeration of the inhabitants of a given area, with pertinent information about them; a linguistic census lists languages and their speakers, or individuals with the languages they speak, for geolinguistic purposes.

center (of an INTONATION or MACROSEGMENT) The most prominent syllable of an intonation (Hockett); a sound articulated with a peak of sonority (Hall). *Synonym:* NUCLEUS.

centering A weakening of vowel articulation (Latin final *-a* to French *-e* mute) (Hall).

center of Broca The area in the front of the brain where KINEMATA (*q.v.*) are stored.

central vowel 1. A vowel midway in point of articulation between a front and a back vowel, according to a vowel triangle (the *a* of *father,* midway between *e, i* on the one side, *o, u* on the other) (Gray). *Synonyms:* ABNORMAL VOWEL, MIDDLE VOWEL.
2. A vowel articulated in the absolute center of the mouth ([ə]).

centrifugal Linguistically, the inherent, natural force which impels a language to branch out into different regional dialects; the inherent tendency of language to change in time and diverge in space. *Opposite:* CENTRIPETAL.

centripetal Linguistically, the man-made tendency of language to unify and standardize under the influence of strong centralizing factors, such as a firmly established central government, good communications, a national spirit, a literary tradition, etc.; natural geographic barriers and political barriers may also have a centripetal effect. *Opposite:* CENTRIFUGAL.

centum languages Those Indo-European languages in which the velar stops ([k], [g], etc.) did not palatalize or turn into alveolars (Celtic, Germanic, Greek, Italic, Hittite, Tokharian). *Opposite:* SATEM LANGUAGES.

cerebral *See* CACUMINAL.

characterology of speech The STYLISTICS (*q.v.*) of a language or of an individual; the notion of choice between various ways of obtaining a given logical effect (Entwistle). *See also* DIALECT, EMPHATICS, EXPRESSIVE FEATURES (Jakobson), IDIOLECT, INTELLECTUAL VARI-

ATIONS (Trubetskoi), NON-DISTINCTIVE, RANDOM VARI-
ATIONS.

checked position Descriptive of a vowel followed by a consonant in the same syllable (Latin *par-tem*). *Opposite:* FREE POSITION.

checked syllable A syllable that ends in a consonant phoneme (in Latin *partem,* the stressed syllable *par-* is checked). *Synonyms:* BLOCKED (or CLOSED) SYLLABLE. *Opposites:* FREE (or OPEN) SYLLABLE.

checked vowel A vowel followed by a consonant in the same syllable (in Latin *partem,* the stressed *a* is checked). *Synonym:* BLOCKED VOWEL. *Opposite:* FREE VOWEL.

chest pulse A sudden expiratory movement of the chest muscles; the outward impulse of breath so produced.

chromatic accent Marouzeau's term for PITCH ACCENT (*q.v.*).

chroneme Daniel Jones' term for a unit of DURATION (*q.v.*).

chronological theory The belief that the differences among the Romance languages have their root in the changing Latin of the different periods of Roman conquest and colonization.

class The totality of linguistically (phonetically, morphologically, etc.) comparable or equivalent elements; a group whose members share some common peculiarity or function. *Synonyms:* CONSTITUENT CLASS, FORM CLASS.

class cleavage 1. Descriptively, the occurrence of a linguistic form in more than one FORM CLASS (*q.v.*); i.e., in entirely different functions (the word *one* in "one book," "one cannot do that," "this one or the other one") (Webster III).
2. Geolinguistically, the subdivision of a unified language into variant forms used by the various social classes. *See also* CLASS LANGUAGE, JARGON, SOCIAL STRATIFICATION, SUBSET.

classical A stage of a language, often archaic, appearing in literary texts of high standing, and used as the basis for teaching that language (Classical Latin, Classical Arabic).

classification of languages The arrangement of languages into classes or families, on the basis of GENETIC (*q.v.*) relationship, similarity of structural factors (*see* TYPOLOGY), geographical location (*see* AREAL LINGUISTICS), etc. ("Romance languages" is a genetic, "isolating languages" a typological, "African languages" a geographical classification).

classificatory language A language where prefixes are used to indicate the class to which any given word belongs; the modifiers then carry the same prefix (Swahili *mtu mrefu,* "tall man," where the prefix *m-* is used for human beings in the singular, and is prefixed to each word associated with *tu,* "man").

classifier 1. A word or prefix used to indicate the semantic or grammatical classification of words (English *head* in "five head of cattle" classifies *cattle;* Bantu *mu-* in *muntu,* "man," indicating singular human being, vs. *ki-* in *kintu,* "thing," indicating singular object). *See also* AUXILIARY NUMERAL, ENUMERATIVE, NUMERATIVE.

2. In logographic writing, an additional symbol added to the PHONETIC (*q.v.*) to form a compound ideographic character. *See also* DETERMINATIVE, KEY, RADICAL 2, SEMANTIC COMPLEMENT, SEMANTIC INDICATOR.

class language A type of language peculiar to one social or educational group, and not to others in the same speech community (British "U" and "non-U"). *Synonym:* SUBSET. *See also* CLASS CLEAVAGE 2, JARGON, SOCIAL STRATIFICATION.

class meaning The functional meanings in which the forms of a form-class appear; a common feature of meaning present in every lexical form within a given FORM CLASS (*cars, names, ideas,* as members of the form class of plurals, all have the class meaning of "more than one").

class sign   A characteristic mark identifying a linguistic form as a member of a particular linguistic class or part of speech (Spanish *-mente* is the identifying mark of the class of adverbs).

class word   A word that can be fitted into a class on the basis of the way it functions in specific frames (all words that may be inserted into the frame "The — is good" may be considered members of the same class) (Fries).

clause terminal   What is popularly known as a pause, at the end of a sentence or clause, and indicated in writing by appropriate punctuation. Phonetically, the terminal may be fading (characterized by a marked decrease in pitch and volume), rising (with a sudden, rapid, short rise in pitch, and volume suddenly shut off), or sustained (with pitch held, the last syllable prolonged, and some diminution of volume) (Gleason).

clear lateral   A lateral (*q.v.*) pronounced with the back of the tongue held up (Hockett). *See also* APICO-DENTAL LATERAL.

cleavage   *See* CLASS CLEAVAGE.

click   A velaric suction stop, made by drawing back the dorsum while maintaining both the inner and the outer closure (Bloch and Trager); an oral sound, made by drawing back the dorsum against the velum while maintaining a closure further forward in the mouth; the air in the small chamber thus established is either compressed or rarefied, and the frontmost closure is released first ([tsk-tsk]) (de la Garza); clicks occur as regular speech sounds in some South African languages, such as Zulu and Xhosa, but in Western languages they do not occur as speech sounds (the smack of a kiss is a bilabial click; the cluck given to a horse is a lateral click); clicks may be voiced or voiceless, and oral or nasal. Clicks are not to be confused with COARTICU-

LATED STOPS (*q.v.*). *Synonyms:* AVULSIVE, CLOSING
SOUND.

clipped   As applied to pronunciation, characterized by a
more fortis articulation, more frequent syncopation,
more rapid tempo (exemplified in part by southern
British *city,* with *t* pronounced as an alveolar stop instead of the American flap, or by British vigorously
flapped consonant *r* of *very,* as opposed to the more
lax vocalic American *r*) (Webster III).

clipped word   A word that has been turned into a new
morpheme by clipping the initial or final part, or both,
of a preexisting morpheme (*cab* from *cabriolet, flu*
from *influenza, skeet* from *mosquito, anthro* from *an-
thropology*). *Synonyms:* CREATIVITY BY SHORTENING,
STUMP WORD. *See also* ALLEGRO FORM, REDUCTION 1,
SHORTENING 2.

clipping   *See* AFFIX CLIPPING.

clock   A style matrix for American English, with five
categories: intimate, casual, consultative, formal, fro-
zen (the last is only written, not spoken) (Joos).

closed-class words   Crystal's term for FUNCTION WORDS.

closed construction   A construction not susceptible of
further development (*Ouch!, Hey!*) (Hall).

closed list   *See* LIST.

closed repertory   *See* OPEN REPERTORY.

closed syllabification   A type of syllable structure where
the majority of syllables end in consonants (English,
German) (Hall). *Opposite:* OPEN SYLLABIFICATION.

closed syllable   A syllable ending in a consonant sound.
Synonyms: BLOCKED (or CHECKED) SYLLABLE. *Opposites:* FREE (or OPEN) SYLLABLE.

close(d) juncture   The transition found in a simplex
word (*q.v.*) from one sound to another, not marked by
a pause (Bloch and Trager); a term usually applied to
juncture phenomena occurring between phonemes in
the same word (in *spit,* closed juncture appears between
s and *p,* between *p* and *i,* between *i* and *t*) (Hockett).

Synonym: MUDDY TRANSITION (or JUNCTURE). *Opposites:* OPEN JUNCTURE (or TRANSITION).

close(d) vowel 1. A vowel pronounced with the mouth less open and the tongue raised toward the palate (*i* is more closed than *a*). *Synonym:* HIGH VOWEL.

2. Sometimes used for BLOCKED or CHECKED VOWEL (*q.v.*).

3. *See* NARROW VOWEL, TENSE VOWEL.

closing sound A sound attended by an implosion, or sucking in of the breath (Saussure). *Synonyms:* AVULSIVE, CLICK.

closure *See* INNER CLOSURE.

cluster 1. Phonetically, two or more consecutive consonants or vowels in a speech segment (w*inch* sp*r*ocket) (Webster III); a group of phonemes, not necessarily constituting a syllable (Walsh). *Synonym:* COMPLEX (Marouzeau). *See also* NUCLEUS 3, 4, 5; VOWEL CLUSTER.

2. Generally, a group of elements (consonants, vowels, nouns, adjectives, etc.) in sequence. *See also* NOUN CLUSTER, VERB CLUSTER.

coalescence The coming together of certain phonemes in certain positions, but not in others (in Southern pronunciation, *fine* and *fin'* [for *find*] are merged, but this does not mean that *d* has disappeared as a separate phoneme in that dialect; it still appears in other environments) (Hockett). *See also* ARCHIPHONEME, NEUTRALIZATION.

coarticulated stop A sound in the production of which two oral closures are made simultaneously, one of them apparently always dorso-velar; both closures are released at once, but with no compression or rarefaction of the air between the closures; such sounds are functional or distinctive in languages of West Africa and New Guinea; do not confuse COARTICULATED STOP with COARTICULATION, or with CLICK SOUNDS (de la Garza).

coarticulation 1. A secondary feature added to the utterance of a primary phoneme (the palatalization added by Russian to /l/ in certain positions); any part of the oral cavity not actively involved in a position of articulation is free to do something which may modify the coloring of the resulting sound (Hockett); the action of an articulator (*q.v.*) which is not directly participating in the articulation. *Synonyms:* SECONDARY ARTICULATION, SECONDARY FEATURES.
2. Phenomena of FUSION (*q.v.*) and OVERLAPPING (*q.v.*) occurring when articulatory movements belonging to new speech sounds are accomplished while neighboring sounds are still being articulated; do not confuse COARTICULATION with COARTICULATED STOP (de la Garza).

coda (of syllable) Any consonant or sequence of consonants at the end of a microsegment or in word-final position (/rts/ in *quartz*) (Hockett); that part of a syllable which comes after the peak and before the onset of the next syllable (Hall).

code switching The interpretation of phonemes as produced by different persons under different conditions (the interpretation of a child's *putty* as *pussy*) (Gleason).

coexistence *See* COMMUTATION, PROCESS, SYSTEM (Hjelmslev).

cognates Words in two languages from the same original source (English *man,* German *Mann*). DECEPTIVE COGNATES result from a shift of meaning in one of the languages (English *rent,* French *rente;* English *knight,* German *Knecht*). FALSE COGNATES may result from accidental resemblance of form (*grosseria,* which means "vulgarity" in Portuguese, used in the sense of English *grocery* by Portuguese immigrants to the United States; this is a LOAN-SHIFT).

coinage 1. The creation, usually deliberate, occasionally accidental, of a new, artificial word which had no previous membership in the language (Burgess' *blurb,* Lewis Carroll's *chortle*). *See also* NEOLOGISM, NONCE WORD, PORTMANTEAU WORD.

2. A relatively rare phenomenon of linguistic creation, which may result from ONOMATOPOEIA, SLANG, the need of a new practical or technical name for an object, SEMANTIC CHANGE due to expansion and obsolescence of meaning, new COMPOUNDS or DERIVATIONS, and BORROWINGS (*q.v.*) (de la Garza).

collation The gathering of language samples, obtained from informants, for phonemic or morphemic analysis, and the study of such samples. *See also* GATHERING, LINGUISTIC ANALYSIS.

collision The coming together into homonyms, in the course of historical development, of two words originally separate and distinct (Latin *statum* and *aetatem* both become *été* in French) (Marouzeau).

collocation The likelihood that any particular lexical item will occur in the immediate environment of any other ("through thick and thin") (Crystal).

colloquial Informal spoken language widely used in daily intercourse by all classes, but not used in formal speech or in writing ("I've got three books").

colloquialism A colloquial form. *See also* SLANG, SUB-STANDARD, VULGARISM.

colonial lag Post-colonial survivals of earlier phases of mother-country culture, including speech features; retention of earlier speech features (colloquial Canadian French /mwe/ for standard French *moi*) (Marckwardt).

colonial (or **colonizing**) **language** The language of colonizers, superimposed on the native language of a conquered country (English in India), and occasionally turning into the indigenous language of the majority of the population (English in the United States, Australia, New Zealand; Latin in Gaul and Iberia). *Synonyms:* LANGUAGE OF COLONIZATION, SUPERIMPOSED

LANGUAGE. *See also* AREA LANGUAGE, SECONDARY LANGUAGE 3.

combinative change   A change due to some sort of assimilative influence and dependent on phonetic environment (Primitive Germanic *mūsi to Anglo-Saxon *mȳs,* Modern English *mice,* where the root vowel anticipates the mouth-position of the final vowel) (Sweet). *Partial synonyms:* ANTICIPATION, DISTANT RETROGRESSIVE (or PROGRESSIVE) ASSIMILATION, FRONTING, LAG, METAPHONY, UMLAUT, VOWEL MUTATION.

combinatory change   *See* CONDITIONED (*also* DEPENDENT, HETERONOMOUS) SOUND CHANGE. *Opposites:* SPONTANEOUS (or UNCONDITIONED) CHANGE.

combinatory phonology   Phonemics, particularly in relation to the interdependence (conditioning) and environment of the phonemes (Saussure). *Opposite:* SPONTANEOUS PHONOLOGY.

combinatory variant   *See* ALLOMORPH, ALLOPHONE.

comment   Roughly, for most languages, what traditional grammar defines as the predicate (Hockett). *See also* PREDICATIVE CONSTRUCTION, TOPIC.

common case   The uninflected form of the word, used in uninflected languages, with or without prepositions, in all instances where inflected languages would use different case forms (Italian *muro* vs. Latin *mūrus, mūrī, mūrō, mūrum*).

common core   *See* CORE.

common gender   In languages which distinguish grammatical genders, applied to adjectives, pronouns, and occasionally nouns having only one form for all genders (English *they, child*); in languages which do not distinguish grammatical genders, applied to nouns, pronouns, etc., which denote men, women, or men and women alike (Hungarian *ő*).

communication   The process by which meanings are exchanged between individuals through a common system of symbols (language, signs, gestures, etc.) (Webster III).

commutation The process by which one word is transformed into another by replacing each phoneme with another (*set* to *bid*) (Hjelmslev); the process of substituting one phoneme for another, with consequent change of meaning (replacing the *f* of *fit* with *p* (Martinet). *See also* PROCESS, SYSTEM.

commutation test Hjelmslev, in "Glossematics," tries to replace any part of an utterance with other linguistic material, in order to determine whether the utterance is divisible, and how best to divide it; this is basic to Hjelmslev's entire theory, and he applies this technique to all kinds of material, on every level of the language, from the complete utterance down to the phone; Harris calls the same process or technique SUBSTITUTION (de la Garza).

compact phoneme A phoneme showing concentration of energy in a relatively narrow central region of the spectrum (Jakobson). *Opposite:* DIFFUSE PHONEME.

comparative linguistics A study of the similarities and differences between two or more languages at one point in time, or of the same language at different points in time; it can thus be conducted either on a synchronic or on a diachronic plane; the purpose of comparing different languages is often to determine or reconstruct their common ancestry.

comparative method A method consisting in laying side by side forms from various languages to determine their similarities and differences, their phonological and morphological correspondences, their common and divergent lexical features, and ultimately the relationship among the languages in question, and the probable structure of the common parent tongue, if any.

comparison of languages *See* COMPARATIVE METHOD.

compensatory lengthening The lengthening of a vowel phoneme when the following consonant phoneme is dropped (English *night,* originally pronounced [niχt], becomes [najt], with lengthening of [i] to [i:], which later opens into the falling diphthong [aj]; Latin *isdem* to *īdem*). *Opposite:* COMPENSATORY SHORTENING.

compensatory shortening The shortening of a vowel when the following consonant is doubled (Latin *lītera* to *littera*). *Opposite:* COMPENSATORY LENGTHENING.

complementary distribution The distribution of groups of related speech sounds or linguistic forms in such a way that one is found only in environments in which the others do not appear (the aspirated *t* of *tone,* appearing initially, vs. the unaspirated *t* of *stone,* appearing after *s; your,* used in an adjective function, vs. *yours,* used as a pronoun); complementary distribution forms the basic prerequisite for the classification of non-identical sounds as allophones of a single phoneme, or of non-identical grammatical forms as allomorphs of a single morpheme (Webster III); the arrangement of two or more common elements in such a way that one occurs in one environment in which the others never appear (save by accident or deliberate distortion), and there is no environment in which they all occur (Walsh); characterized by the feature of non-interchangeability; the allophones together cover all possible positional occurrences, but one may not trespass on the territory of another, one allophone differing from another phonetically, but not phonemically (Fowkes). *Synonyms:* ALTERNATION, COMPLEMENTATION, NON-CONTRASTIVE DISTRIBUTION. *See also* PARTIAL COMPLEMENTATION.

complementation *See* COMPLEMENTARY DISTRIBUTION.

complete assimilation *See* ASSIMILATION.

completive (sentence) A minor clause which supplements a situation, such as earlier speech, an earlier gesture, or the presence of an object, and which refers back to a known context ("This one" in reply to

"Which book do you want?"; "Tomorrow morning" in reply to "When do we start?") (Bloomfield).

complex Marouzeau's term for CLUSTER (*q.v.*).

complex (vowel) nucleus A combination of any simple vowel with a following glide or semi-vowel; a diphthong (Bloch and Trager). *Partial synonyms:* COMPOUND PHONEME, DIPHTHONG.

complex peak A PEAK (*q.v.*) consisting of a diphthong or triphthong.

complex vowel nucleus *See* COMPLEX NUCLEUS.

complex word A word having a bound form (*q.v.*) as one or both of its immediate constituents (*un-man-ly*) (Webster III). *See also* COMPOUND (SIMPLEX) WORD.

component One of the elements out of which a construction (*q.v.*) is formed (Hockett). *Synonym:* ELEMENT. *See also* CONSTITUENT.

composition The putting together of two roots (or free morphemes) to form a word that differs in meaning from both of its components (*railroad*); the monemes that go into the compound must have separate existence elsewhere than in the compound itself (Martinet). The compound is described as SYNTACTIC if it corresponds to a phrase (*blackbird*); ASYNTACTIC if it does not correspond to a phrase (*doorknob*); SEMISYNTACTIC if it consists of two adjectives, the second of which comes from a noun (*blue-eyed*) (Hall). *See also* COORDINATION, DERIVATION, FORESTRESS.

compound *See* COMPOUND WORD.

compound grapheme A group of two or more letters representing a single sound (English *th* in *this* or *think*, *ph* in *telephone*) (Hall). *See also* DIGRAPH, TRIGRAPH.

compound phoneme 1. The combination of two or more primary phonemes, such as a diphthong or triphthong (English /ow/ in *own*, Italian *buoi* /bwɔj/, "oxen").

2. A combination of simple phonemes which act as a unit so far as meaning or word structure is concerned;

they resemble a succession of two or more phonemes of the same language, but they are somehow distinguished from such a succession, and function as a separate phoneme; note that phonemic theory does not admit of a "compound phoneme" (de la Garza).

compound word 1. A word whose components are two or more words having full separate existence elsewhere than in the compound (Martinet).

2. A word containing more than one free form (*redcap, doorknob*) (Bloomfield).

3. A word and a combining form (*centimeter*); a word and a non-inflectional affix (*builder*); a word consisting of two or more combining forms (*biology*); a word consisting of a combining form and a non-inflectional affix (*chloride*) (Webster III). *See also* BASE COMPOUND, COMPLEX WORD, COMPOSITION (Hall), DERIVED SECONDARY WORD, FUSED COMPOUND, IMPROPER COMPOUND, PRIMARY COMPOUND, PRIMARY WORD, PROPER COMPOUND, REPETITIVE COMPOUND, SECONDARY COMPOUND, SEMI-SYNTACTIC COMPOUND, SIMPLEX WORD, SOLID COMPOUND, STEM COMPOUND, SYNTACTIC COMPOUND, SYNTHETIC COMPOUND.

compromise language *See* KOINE.

conative A verbal formation expressing the idea of the effort required by the action (Latin *parturire,* "to be in labor," from *parere,* "to give birth") (Marouzeau).

concord (concordance) *See* AGREEMENT, CONGRUENCE.

conditional sound change *See* CONDITIONED SOUND CHANGE.

conditional variant *See* ALLOMORPH, ALLOPHONE.

conditioned Occurring only in a particular environment and under fixed conditions; an allomorph may be phonologically conditioned (voiceless /s/ as a plural sign occurring only after voiceless consonants, as in *bits, backs, lips*); or morphologically conditioned (/en/ as the plural suffix for *ox*) (Walsh).

conditioned sound change 1. A change predictable in

terms of other sounds in the environment (the normal palatalization of Latin *c* ([k]) before *e* or *i* in Italian). 2. Sometimes used more specifically to indicate the process whereby a single phoneme splits into two (/s/ [s ~ h] > /s/ and /h/ in Latin America), or two or more phonemes merge into one (Castilian treats written *s* and *z* as two separate phonemes, /s/, /θ/; when Andalusian, an offshoot·of Castilian, merges *s* and *z* into a single phone ([s]), words such as *casa,* "house," and *caza,* "hunt," become homophonous and indistinguishable in speech; whereupon *cacería* is coined to replace *caza* in Cuba). *Synonyms:* COMBINATORY (*also* DEPENDENT, FUNCTIONAL, HETERONOMOUS) SOUND CHANGE. *Opposites:* AUTONOMOUS (*also* SPONTANEOUS, UNCONDITIONED) SOUND CHANGE.

conditioning The influence exerted upon a phoneme or morpheme by surrounding phonemes or morphemes (a preceding voiceless consonant determines that the written -*s* plural suffix of English shall be unvoiced rather than voiced).

configuration *See* PATTERN.

congeneric groups Groups of words with similar meanings and similar forms (*utter : mutter; twig : sprig*); the similarity of form is often due to a process of analogy (Jespersen). *See also* PHONESTHEME.

congruence 1. A feature of selection whereby certain types of finite verbs are assigned to certain actors or subjects ("I am," but "he is") (Bloch and Trager). 2. A type of AGREEMENT whereby the forms used must be of the same subdivision of the form-classes to which they belong (Latin *bonus homo,* where *bonus* is masculine singular nominative to agree with *homo*) (Hall). *Partial synonyms:* AGREEMENT, BONDING, CONCORD-(ANCE). 3. PATTERNED CONGRUENCE (*q.v.*).

conjugation The system of changes in the verb, by means of prefixes, suffixes, internal flection, auxiliaries, etc., in accordance with factors of person, number, tense, mood, voice, etc. *See also* ACCIDENCE, INFLECTION, PARADIGM.

conjunct form A form that is normally used only in given constructions, not by itself (French *je,* normally appearing only as the subject of a verb, and replaced by *moi* if an absolute form is wanted) (Bloomfield). *See also* CONJUNCTIVE.

conjunctive A word used in conjunction with verbs (French *je le* vois; *j'en* ai; *il y* va) (Hall). *See also* CONJUNCT FORM.

connective construction An exocentric construction (*q.v.*) consisting of a connector and a predicate attribute ("is — a big man") (Hockett).

connector Hockett's term for COPULATIVE VERB. *See also* CONNECTIVE CONSTRUCTION, ZERO CONNECTOR.

connotation The special shades of meaning (based on emotional or other factors) that a form has for its individual users (the evil connotation of *profits* for labor leaders, as against its favorable connotation for management executives). *See also* SEMANTIC POTENTIALITIES.

consonance The recurrence of identical or similar consonant sounds unaccompanied by a similar correspondence of stressed vowel sounds at the end of two or more words, syllables or lines of verse (Italian *miglio, meglio, voglio,* at the end of three successive lines of verse). *See also* ALLITERATION, ASSONANCE, RHYME.

consonant A class of speech sounds characterized by constriction accompanied by some measure of friction, or closure followed by release, at one or more points in the breath channel; a generic term for plosives, fricatives, nasals, laterals, trills or flaps, glottal catches or stops, as well as the first (glide) element of a rising diphthong ([p], [g], [n], [s], [l], [r], [w]). *Opposite:* VOWEL. *See also* CONTOID, SONANT, SONORANT, VOCALIC CONSONANT.

consonant cluster A group of two or more consonants in

sequence (*str-* in *stress; -sts* in *pests*). *See also* CLUSTER 1, NUCLEUS 4.

consonantism The study, history or description of the consonantal system of a language or dialect. *See also* VOCALISM.

consonant shift A term used in Germanic philology to refer to two successive sets of regular changes, the first of which (*Erste Lautverschiebung*) differentiated the Germanic from the other Indo-European languages by changing voiceless stops to voiceless fricatives (English *f*oot, *th*ou, *h*orn, corresponding to Latin *p*edem, *t*u, *c*ornu); voiced stops to voiceless stops (English a*pp*le, *t*wo, *k*in, corresponding to Slavic ja*b*luko, Latin *d*uo, *g*enus); voiced aspirate stops to voiced fricatives (English na*v*el, corresponding to Sanskrit nā*bh*i). The second consonant shift (*zweite Lautverschiebung*) differentiated the High German division of West Germanic from the Low German, as well as from the East Germanic (illustrated by Gothic) and the North Germanic or Scandinavian branches, by changing voiceless stops to affricates or voiceless fricatives (High German *pf*e*ff*er, *z*eit, wa*ss*er, ma*ch*en, corresponding to English *p*e*pp*er, *t*ide, wa*t*er, ma*k*e), and from voiced to voiceless stops (High German ri*pp*e, mi*tt*el, e*ck*e, corresponding to English ri*b*, mi*dd*le, Dutch e*gg*e). *Synonyms :* GERMANIC SOUND SHIFT (FIRST and SECOND), GRIMM'S LAW (as modified by VERNER'S LAW), (ERSTE, ZWEITE) LAUT-VERSCHIEBUNG.

constant A functive (*q.v.*) whose presence is a necessary condition for the functive with which it has a function (*q.v.*) (Hjelmslev).

constellation A function (*q.v.*) between two variables (*q.v.*) (Hjelmslev).

constituent 1. The common part of any two or more complex forms or constructs (*gentle* in *gentleman, gentlemanly, ungentlemanly*) (Whatmough).

2. Any word or construction entering into a larger con-

struction ("My English friend — wrote the poem")
(Walsh).

3. One of two or more linguistic forms entering into a
construction or compound that are either immediately
and normally two in number ("He — writes for the
stage") (*See* IMMEDIATE CONSTITUENT); or are ultimate (*See* ULTIMATE CONSTITUENT) and of any number ("He — write — s — for — the — stage") (Webster
III). *Partial synonyms:* COMPONENT, ELEMENT. *See
also* CONTINUOUS (*also* DISCONTINUOUS) CONSTITU-
ENTS (or MORPHEMES), NOUN CLUSTER.

constituent class Those words and groups of words
which have the same PRIVILEGE OF OCCURRENCE (*q.v.*);
namely, may occur in the same construction pattern
(or slot), and may be substituted for one another and
still make sense ("the man who lives there" and "the
dweller"; "at his son's house" and "there") (Hockett).
Synonym: FORM CLASS.

constrictive Marouzeau's term for FRICATIVE or SPIRANT
(*q.v.*).

construct A repetitive identity of order, either of forms
(stem plus suffix; *slow* plus *-ly*) or of words (actor plus
action plus goal: "the dog bit the man"); the former
is a MORPHEMIC, the latter a SYNTACTIC CONSTRUCT
(Whatmough).

constructed language *See* ARTIFICIAL LANGUAGE.

construction A manner of grouping and combining elements of speech; a significant group of words or morphemes among which there is a direct connection ("The
old man who lives there," or simply "the old man")
(Gleason); a pattern for building composite forms of a
specific form-class out of immediate constituents of
specific form-classes (Hockett); any meaningful combination of linguistic forms, other than compounds consisting of free forms (Webster III). *See also* CLOSED
(*also* COORDINATIVE, DIRECTIVE, ENDOCENTRIC, EXO-

CENTRIC, MORPHOLOGICAL, OPEN, PREGNANT, SUBOR-
DINATIVE, SYNTACTIC) CONSTRUCTION.

contact vernacular A language of current use for every-
day contacts between people of different language back-
grounds. *Partial synonyms:* CREOLE, HYBRID LANGUAGE,
LINGUA FRANCA, MAKESHIFT LANGUAGE, MIXED LAN-
GUAGE, PIDGIN, RELATION LANGUAGE, SABIR, TRADE
LANGUAGE, VEHICULAR LANGUAGE.

contamination 1. The combination into a single word or
expression of elements from different words or expressions, or from different languages (*irregardless,* from
the blending of *irrespective* and *regardless; different
than* from the blending of *different from* and *other than;*
Old French *brusler* [modern French *brûler*], from the
blending of Germanic *brennen* and Latin *ustulare*).
Synonyms: BLENDING, CROSSING, TELESCOPED WORD.
2. Sporadic change whereby the form of one morpheme
or allomorph is affected or modified by the form of another morpheme or allomorph with which it is closely
associated; contamination is possible only when there
is such association of two morphemes; regularly, one
form does not replace the other, nor do the two forms
blend, but one is reshaped to become phonetically
more like the other (West Saxon *eom,* "am," with consonant from the root *es* of Indo-European *esmi* and
vowel from the root of *be*) (de la Garza).

content The intrinsic meaning of a language symbol; the
semantic force of a word or expression.

content elements Those elements which result from a
complete analysis of meaning (*mare* may be analyzed
into "horse" plus feminine gender) (Hjelmslev).

contentive *See* CONTENT WORD.

content word A word which has lexical or semantic
rather than functional or grammatical meaning (*apple,
run,* as against *of, the*). *Synonyms:* CONTENTIVE, FULL
WORD, LEXICAL FORM, NOTIONAL WORD, SEMANTEME,
VOCABULARY WORD. *Opposites:* EMPTY WORD, FUNC-

TION WORD, MARKER, PARTICLE, POINTER, STRUCTURE WORD.

contextual variant   *See* ALLOMORPH, ALLOPHONE.

contiguous assimilation   *See* ASSIMILATION.

contiguous dissimilation   *See* DISSIMILATION.

continuant   1. A speech sound in which there is no stoppage of the air stream, and the flow of breath is channeled but not interrupted; this includes fricatives, resonants, and vowels (Walsh).

2. A consonant that may be continued or prolonged without alteration for the duration of an emission of breath; an open consonant; in some classifications, any consonant except a stop or an affricate; in others, any consonant except a stop, affricate, nasal or semivowel (Webster III). *See also* CONSTRICTIVE, FRICATIVE, SPIRANT, STATIC CONSONANT.

continuous constituents   A construction typified by "the man did come," where *did* and *come,* the two constituents of the verbal expression, follow each other directly, as against "Did the man come?", where they are separated (Gleason). *Opposite:* DISCONTINUOUS CONSTITUENTS.

contoid   A non-vocoid; when functioning as a syllable crest (like the *l* or *r* in Czech *pln, smrt*) it is called a SYLLABIC CONTOID; otherwise, it is equal to a consonant. *Opposite:* VOCOID.

contour   A morpheme, not a phoneme; the term applies to a clause, and includes two, three, or four pitch phonemes and a clause terminal (*q.v.*) (Gleason); a sequence of levels of pitch or stress typically extending over several successive words in the utterance (Webster III). *Synonyms:* INTONATION CONTOUR, OUTLINE. *See also* TERMINAL CONTOUR.

contrast   1. Basic American term to differentiate two utterances.

2. *See* CORRELATION, OPPOSITION; but note that Martinet establishes a distinction between CONTRAST and OPPOSI-

TION, defining the first as the syntagmatic and observable relation of each phoneme with the next, the second as a paradigmatic set of mutually exclusive relations, such as exist between *good* and *bad*.

3. Elsewhere, Martinet offers CONTRAST as a term applied to non-distinctive phonetic features (as in /pin/ vs. /spin/) as opposed to phonemic features (as in /pin/ vs. /bin/).

4. Jakobson calls CONTRAST the differences between intrasyllabic or non-contiguous sounds. *See also* FORMAL CONTRAST.

contrastive analysis A study of the differences and similarities in the structures of at least two languages or dialects; a comparison of the learner's language with the one he is studying in order to give special attention to the areas where the contrast is greatest (Walsh). *Synonym:* CONTRASTIVE LINGUISTICS.

contrastive function The role played by a language feature in helping the hearer to analyze an utterance into successive units (in languages that have a fixed accent, like the initial stress of Czech and Hungarian, the position of the stress serves to mark the beginning of a word) (Martinet). *See also* EXPRESSIVE FUNCTION, OPPOSITIONAL FUNCTION.

contrastive grammar The setting up of parallel descriptive grammars of two or more languages for purposes of comparison rather than of translation (Gleason). *Partial synonyms:* CONTRASTIVE ANALYSIS, CONTRASTIVE LINGUISTICS, TRANSFER GRAMMAR.

contrastive linguistics *See* CONTRASTIVE ANALYSIS, CONTRASTIVE GRAMMAR.

contrastive phrasal doublets Linguistic clichés of the type of "salt and pepper," "black and white," where one of the expressions is used in more or less direct semantic contrast with the other (Macdougald).

convergence 1. Martinet's term for DEDIALECTALIZATION (*q.v.*).

2. A new similarity between two related languages, due to recurrent causes (French and Italian, having diverged in their historical development from Latin, borrow a common learned vocabulary from the parent language, or imitate each other's syntactical constructions and phrasal groups) (Whatmough).

convergence area A region in which unrelated languages in contact display identical or similar characteristics, probably borrowed from one another (the use of a postposed article in Rumanian, Bulgarian and Albanian, three Balkan-area languages of different Indo-European subgroups) (Hoenigswald). *See also* LANGUAGES IN CONTACT, PERIPHERAL LANGUAGE.

conversion The transfer of morphemes and words from one grammatical function to another, generally accomplished by means of suprasegmental phonemes, such as stress and juncture (*présent* vs. *presént; líght + hoúse* vs. *líghthoùse*) (Whitehall). *Synonyms:* FUNCTIONAL CHANGE, FUNCTIONAL SHIFT, TRANSMUTATION.

coordination The formation of compounds by the use of two substantives, which receive equal stress (*gold watch*) (Marchand). *Partial synonyms:* COMPOSITION, FORESTRESS.

coordinative construction An endocentric construction (*q.v.*) with two or more heads but no attributes ("butter and milk") (Bloch and Trager). *Opposite:* SUBORDINATIVE CONSTRUCTION.

coordinator A word that joins two or more heads of an endocentric construction (*q.v.*) (*and, or*) (Bloch and Trager); a coordinating conjunction (*and, or, both . . . and;* note ZERO COORDINATOR in "men, women, children") (Hall).

core (common) Features shared by two or more idiolects (*q.v.*) (speakers A and B have a common core in that they both distinguish *can* from *con* and *kin;* but they lack a common core to the extent that one differentiates between *can* meaning "container" and *can* meaning "to be able," while the other does not) (Hockett).

coronal Pertaining to the corona, or blade, of the tongue.

corpus A sample of utterances for analysis (Gleason); a collection of recorded utterances used as the basis for a descriptive analysis of a language or dialect.

correctness The use of a standard as against a sub-standard language; the avoidance of slang and vulgarisms, but not of colloquialisms.

correlation A binary contrast or opposition shared by more than one correlated pair of phonemes (in the pairs /p/ - /b/, /t/ - /d/, /k/ - /g/, there is a universally shared correlation of sonority, with one member of each pair unvoiced while the other is voiced; one exists only by virtue of the other) (Jakobson). *See also* BINARY PRINCIPLE, CONTRAST, OPPOSITION.

correlative words Members of pairs the occurrence of one of which alerts the listener for the appearance of the others ("as . . . as," "either . . . or," "the more the merrier"); they are regularly used together, but typically are not adjacent (Hughes).

correspondence The matching of segments and segment classes of one language with those of another related language (Germanic initial *f-* and Latin, Greek or Sanskrit *p-*) (Hoenigswald). *See also* DISCREPANT CORRESPONDENCE.

countable noun *See* COUNT NOUN.

counter word A word that has a broad and vague range of meaning, through widespread use in many markedly different situations (*awfully, job*) (Webster III).

count noun A noun that can normally be used in both the singular and the plural, that is readily modified by a numeral, an indefinite article, or a word such as *many, few,* and that does not need to be qualified (English *grape, grapes, a grape, few grapes,* as opposed to Italian *uva,* used only as a singular collective).

Synonyms: BOUNDED NOUN, COUNTABLE NOUN. *Opposites:* MASS NOUN, UNBOUNDED NOUN.

covowel   A semi-consonant appearing only in syllabic peaks, but not in marginal positions (the phoneme /w/ in German appears in the diphthong /aw/, as in *Haus,* but not elsewhere) (Hockett).

creativity (by shortening)   *See* STUMP WORD. *See also* SPORADIC CHANGE.

creole   A CONTACT VERNACULAR or PIDGIN (*q.v.*) that has become the sole or primary language of communication of a speech community; it is usually characterized by a morphological simplification of the language of colonization from which it is normally derived (the Creole French of Haiti). *Synonyms:* HYBRID (*also* MIXED) LANGUAGE.

crest (of sonority)   *See* PEAK, SYLLABIC, SYLLABLE.

critical edition   A transcription of an ancient or medieval document in which the transcriber makes adaptations and changes designed to reconstruct a hypothetical original, or present the document in the most comprehensible and logical fashion. *Opposite:* DIPLOMATIC EDITION (or TRANSCRIPTION).

crossing   The play of two elements acting on each other so as to bring about the formation of a third element which partakes of both (French *rendre,* from the blend of Latin *reddere* and *praehendere*) (Marouzeau). *See also* BLENDING, CONTAMINATION, PORTMANTEAU WORD, TELESCOPED WORD, WORD-CROSSING.

cross reference   A specific anticipation or repetition of one element of a construction provided by another element (in French *ton frère, travaille-t-il?,* there is cross reference to *ton frère* in the subsequent *il;* in the obsolete English construction "John his mark" there is similar cross reference to *John* in *his*) (Hall).

culminative function   The function of the accent in distinguishing meanings in words otherwise identical (English *pérmit, permít;* Spanish *termino, término, terminó*)

(Martinet). *See also* CONTRASTIVE (*also* EXPRESSIVE, OPPOSITIONAL) FUNCTION.

cultural language A language learned in school or acquired for social, literary, scientific or business purposes (foreign languages as studied in American high schools and colleges; the literary Italian language as studied in schools by lower-class dialectal speakers).

cultural transmission The learning of a system, linguistic or otherwise, by the young, and the teaching of that system by the adults of the group (Hockett).

culture 1. Artistic, literary, scientific, and other intellectual achievements, of the individual or the social group. 2. In the anthropological sense, the sum total of the beliefs, values, and behavior patterns of a social group.

culture circle *See* DIFFUSION AND MIGRATION THEORIES.

cumul Inflectional affix or other short inseparable form which conveys simultaneously more than two meanings (Latin ending *-us,* which conveys at once, for second-declension nouns, the concepts of nominative, masculine and singular) (Bally).

cuneiform Wedge-shaped; a system of writing produced by pressing a stylus into wet clay tablets, used in Sumerian, Akkadian, Old Persian and other ancient languages of the Mesopotamian area.

cursive A system of writing for rapid use, characterized by a flowing script, with the letters generally joined and the angles rounded.

cybernetics The study of messages which control action, and of the equipment for communication between man and machine and between machine and machine (Wiener); the study of the interaction between situations and individuals in terms of communication (Carroll); the automatic control system formed by the nervous system and the brain, or by mechano-electric communications devices, such as computers and thermostats.

cycles per second (c.p.s.) *See* PITCH.

Cyrillic alphabet A system of writing used in Russian, Byelorussian, Ukrainian, Serbian, Bulgarian and Macedonian, though in slightly divergent forms; it is said to have been originally devised by the Bishops Cyril and Methodius in the ninth century A.D., and is based mainly on the Greek alphabet, with a few contributions from the Hebrew alphabet, and other characters devised by the inventors. Recent studies seem to indicate that Cyril and Methodius were the inventors of the Glagolitic rather than the Cyrillic alphabet. *See also* GLAGOLITIC ALPHABET.

D

damped sound The result of DAMPING (*q.v.*).

damping In acoustic phonetics, the process of reducing the amplitude of one or a series of sound waves, and originating a number of subsidiary frequencies above and below the natural frequency; the quality of a sound is thus changed by damping; the buccal cavity is a damped resonator, whereas glottal tone is undamped (de la Garza).

dark lateral A lateral pronounced with the back of the tongue held down, like the *l* of *milk* (Hockett).

dark vowel Gray's term for BACK VOWEL (*q.v.*).

deceptive cognates *See* COGNATES.

decibel A unit of measurement of sound or of electrical energy arrived at by comparing what is produced at one point with what is produced at another; abbreviation : *db*.

declension 1. The system that appears in connection

with nouns, pronouns and adjectives in the Indo-European and other languages, whereby the form of the word changes in accordance with its function in the word group, as well as with other subsidiary concepts, such as number and grammatical gender.

2. The presentation in a prescribed order of the inflectional forms of nouns, adjectives and pronouns.

3. Classes of nouns or adjectives having the same type of inflectional forms. *See also* ACCIDENCE, INFLECTION, PARADIGM.

decoding 1. Identifying the constituent significant elements of a message.

2. The psychological process whereby a hearer derives meaning from a verbal message (Walsh). *See also* ENCODING.

dedialectalization The tendency of local dialects to merge into a national standard by reason of centripetal, standardizing factors, such as a central government, good lines of communication, education, national sentiment, etc. *Synonym:* STANDARDIZATION. *Opposites:* DIALECTALIZATION, DIVERGENCE.

dediphthongization *See* MONOPHTHONGIZATION.

deep grammar A study of the valence ties between the parts of a sentence (the relationship of *he* and *runs* in "he runs fast," as contrasted with the relationship between the same two words in "he runs a shop") (Hockett).

deep vowel *See* BACK VOWEL.

defective A word lacking one or more of the forms normal for its class (*ought,* which has no past tense; *ethics,* defective in the plural, as against *sheep,* which has a plural with zero modification (Hill). *See also* FORLORN ELEMENTS.

deferred preposition A preposition placed at the end of the sentence or clause ("something I will not put up with") (Charnley).

definition Division of a sign content ("mare" = "horse" +

feminine gender), or of a sign expression ($sto = s + t + o$) (Hjelmslev).

deflection (or **deflexion**) 1. In historical linguistics, the loss of inflection (Spanish merges the six cases of Latin *murus* into the single form *muro*) (Gray). *Synonyms:* COMMON CASE, LOSS OF INFLECTION, SYNCRETISM. *See also* MERGED FORM, OBLIQUE CASE.

2. In synchronic linguistics, what occurs when a completely productive part of a paradigm does not belong to the same class as other members (the morphemic vs. the syntactic comparison of adjectives in English, as illustrated by *slow, slower, slowest* vs. *beautiful, more beautiful, most beautiful;* participles, which belong to a verb class, functioning as adjectives : "the singing fool") (de la Garza).

degeneration (of **meaning**) *See* PEJORATION.

degree of boundness (of a **morpheme**) The degree to which a morpheme may be separated or isolated, as reflected by its uses in other functions (Latin amav*it* vs. French *il* aimait or English *he* loved) (Weinreich).

delabialization Historically, the pronunciation of a formerly rounded sound without lip-rounding; the dropping of an element of speech involving labialization (Latin *quinque* to Vulgar Latin *cinque*). *Partial synonym:* UNROUNDING. *Opposites:* LABIALIZATION, ROUNDING.

demarcative function The use of phonemic and non-phonemic features, including accent, to mark off the boundaries of words and morphemes (the initial word stress of Czech, which gives the listener indication of the beginning of a new word) (Martinet).

demotic 1. The modern Greek vernacular or colloquial form of the language, characterized by a simplification of grammatical forms and by the use of Turkish and other loan words (also spelled *demotike, dhemotike*). 2. An ancient Egyptian style of writing which was a simplification of the HIERATIC.

denasalization The elimination of nasalization or a nasal element (Old French /bɔ̃nə/, *bonne,* to modern French /bɔn/, *bonne;* Latin *mensem* to Italian *mese*). *Opposite :* NASALIZATION.

denotation The meaning which a form has for all who use it (the intrinsic meaning of *water*).

density of communication The extent to which an individual talks to another or others (Hall).

dental A sound made by placing the tip of the tongue against the upper teeth (Spanish *d* and *t* in *dotar*); sometimes loosely used for ALVEOLAR (*q.v.*). *See also* INTERDENTAL, LABIODENTAL.

dentolabial *See* LABIODENTAL.

dependent sound change *See* CONDITIONED SOUND CHANGE.

derivation 1. Historically, the formation of a word from an earlier word or from a base by the addition of a prefix or suffix (*rebuild, boyish*), by functional change (*to* picnic), or by back formation (*to peddle* from an earlier *peddler*); restricted by some linguists only to the first of the three processes.

2. Descriptively, the relation of a word to a base, as expressed in terms of the presence of affixes (*teaches* from *teach*), vowel alternation (*rode* from *ride*), consonant alternation (*spent* from *spend*), difference of accentuation (*presént* from *présent*), suppletion (*better* for *good*), zero suffix (*sheep* from *sheep*); the relation of a word to a base when they are not of the same inflectional paradigm (*song, sing*) (Webster III); Martinet and purely descriptive linguists restrict the term to cases where one moneme exists solely in derivatives and is an affix (*friendly,* where *-ly* is not used by itself, but only as an adjectival or adverbial suffix). *See also* COMPOSITION, PARASYNTHETIC DERIVATION, PRIMARY WORD, SECONDARY WORD.

derivational affix An affix characterized by, used in, or relating to derivation (*re-* in *reorder;* historically, *-sc-*

in *finisco* from *finio*) (Webster III). *Partial synonyms:* BOUND MORPHEME, FORMANT, FORMATIVE. *See also* (and do not confuse with) INFLECTIONAL ENDING.

derivative A word formed from another by DERIVATION (*q.v.*) (*boyish* is a derivative of *boy*). *See also* SECONDARY DERIVATION.

derived primary word A word that contains more than one bound form (*re-ceive, con-tain*).

descriptive Concerned with the description of the structure of a language at a specific point in time, with the exclusion of historical and comparative considerations. *Partial synonym:* STRUCTURAL.

descriptive grammar A grammar that follows descriptive principles, presenting actual usage on different levels, formal and informal, standard and substandard, written and spoken, in the light of actual observation of the facts of usage. *Opposites:* NORMATIVE GRAMMAR, PRESCRIPTIVE GRAMMAR.

descriptive linguistics *See* LINGUISTICS, STRUCTURAL LINGUISTICS.

détente The final phase (or release) in the articulation of a phoneme, when the vocal organs leave the position taken during the emission of the phoneme to fall into a neutral position or prepare for the next phoneme; if the off-glide is abrupt, a glottal stop (*q.v.*) may result (Marouzeau). *Partial synonyms:* ABGLITT, ABSATZ, FINAL GLIDE, OFF-GLIDE, RELEASE. *See also* DIPHTHONGIZATION, DIVERGENT CHANGE.

determinant 1. The differentiating part of a compound, normally placed first in English (*rain* in *rainbow*) (Marchand). *Opposite:* DETERMINATUM.

2. In ideographic writing, a symbol added to another symbol to give an indication of the general connotation of the latter (the symbol for water added to the phonetic characters for *river*) (Hughes). *Synonym:* DETERMINATIVE 2.

3. In sentence structure, a word that usually accom-

panies or marks a given structural element (articles, numerals, demonstrative adjectives for nouns; prepositions for adverbial constructions; coordinating conjunctions for independent exocentric structures) (Hughes). *Partial synonyms:* EMPTY WORD, FORM WORD, FUNCTION WORD, MARKER, PARTICLE, POINTER, STRUCTURE WORD.

determination A function between a constant and a variable (*q.v.*) (Hjelmslev).

determinative 1. A sound or syllable added to the base or stem of a verb, or interpolated between the base and the inflectional ending to modify the aspect of the verb (Dorfman); a suffixal sound or sound sequence added to a root, producing a longer root of the base, often with a modified meaning, to which derivational affixes or inflectional endings may be added (*d in *gheud, "to pour," shown by Latin *fudi* and Gothic *giutan,* but not by Sanskrit *homa* or Greek *cheein*) (Webster III). *Partial synonyms:* FORMANT, THEMATIC MORPHEME, THEMATIC FORMANT.

2. A written symbol used with a noun to indicate morphological or semantic classes, such as plurals, gods, human beings, etc. (Lehmann); a sign attached to a word in some forms of writing to indicate class, number, or other features, thus often distinguishing the word from its homographs (Webster III); in ideographic writing, a semantic but non-phonetic sign added to a basic ideogram to indicate its proper meaning in the context by identifying the category to which the depicted concept or thing belongs (Dorfman). *Synonyms:* CLASSIFIER 2, DETERMINANT 2, KEY, RADICAL, SEMANTIC COMPLEMENT, SEMANTIC INDICATOR.

determinative compound A compound in which a noun or adjective is combined with another noun, adjective, or adverb which determines, modifies or qualifies it (Dorfman); a compound where one component plays

the part of a genitive or other oblique case with respect
to the other (Graff).

determinatum   The grammatically dominant part of a
compound, which normally receives the inflection and
is placed last in English (*bow* in *rainbow*) (Marchand).
Opposite : DETERMINANT.

determiner   An attribute of the type that normally precedes other attributes in the same expressions (*the, this,
that, any, no, some, what, which, my, our, a, each,
either, every, one*) (Bloch and Trager); a generic expression for articles, possessives, demonstratives, etc.
(Francis); a word indicating a noun (*the, this, my*)
(Walsh); a word marking Class I forms (nouns),
which can be substituted for *the* in the frame "(The)
concert is good" (Fries); a limiting noun-modifier (*a,
either, some, whatever,* possessive adjectives, possessive
case forms, such as *John's,* and characteristically occurring before a descriptive adjective modifying the
same noun ("that big yellow house," "his new car")
(Webster III). *See also* BOUNDED NOUN, MARKER.

Devanagari   An alphabet (with characteristics approaching those of a syllabary) with long horizontal strokes
on the tops of most of the characters, used by Sanskrit,
Hindi, and other languages of India, both ancient and
modern.

devoice   To pronounce without vibration of the vocal
cords a sound voiced in other positions, or formerly
voiced (German *Tier* represents a High German devoicing of the originally voiced Proto-Germanic dental
preserved in English *deer*). *Synonyms :* DESONORIZE,
UNVOICE. *Opposites :* SONORIZE, VOICE.

diachronic   Across time; considering linguistic phenomena as occurring over a period of time; a diachronic
description of a language may be built by comparison
of the synchronic descriptions of the same language at
different historical periods (Webster III). *Synonyms :*

DYNAMIC, EVOLUTIONARY, HISTORICAL. *Opposites:* STATIC, SYNCHRONIC.

diachronic grammar *See* HISTORICAL GRAMMAR.

diachronic linguistics The study of words, speech, languages, and language change from the point of view of evolution in the course of time; the study of the chronological changes in a language. *Synonyms:* DYNAMIC (*also* EVOLUTIONARY, HISTORICAL) LINGUISTICS. *Opposites:* STATIC (*also* SYNCHRONIC) LINGUISTICS. *Partial opposite:* STRUCTURAL LINGUISTICS.

diachronic phonetics A branch of phonetics which studies and classifies phonetic laws by explaining and accounting for phonetic changes in the course of time. *Synonym:* (HISTORICAL) PHONOLOGY.

diacritic A mark added to a letter to modify its value; a modifying sign or mark over, under, after or through an orthographic or phonetic character or combination of characters to indicate a phonetic or semantic value different from that of its unmarked counterpart (ç, ć, č, ł, l, ñ, δ, ż) (Webster III). *See also* BREVE, CEDILLA, DIAERESIS, MACRON, MODIFIER 2, QUANTITY MARK, TIL(DE).

diaeresis 1. Phonetically, the resolution of one syllable into two, by separating the vowel elements of a diphthong, or by resolving [j] and [w] into vowels.

2. Orthographically, a diacritic mark placed over one of two adjacent vowels to indicate that it does not form a diphthong with the preceding or following vowel, but is to be given full, independent phonetic value in pronunciation (French *naïve, Noël,* Spanish *averigüe*).

3. Sometimes used for the mark of UMLAUT (*q.v.*).

dialect A specific branch or form of a language spoken in a given geographical area, differing sufficiently from the official standard or literary form of the language in one or all of the levels of the language (pronunciation, grammar, vocabulary, and idiomatic use of words) to be viewed as a distinct entity, yet not sufficiently different from the other dialects of the language to be regarded as a separate language; a dialect often has its own literary form, and the distinction between language and dialect is often difficult to formulate on either literary or political bases; major dialectal areas are somewhat arbitrarily established on the basis of the coincidence of bundles of isoglosses, but the term is often loosely applied to the speech form of a minor locality. *See also* DIA-SYSTEM, PATOIS.

dialectalization　The breaking up of an originally unified language into various dialects or local forms, in accordance with the inherent centrifugal tendency of language when unopposed by centripetal factors. *Synonym:* DIVERGENCE. *Opposites:* DEDIALECTALIZATION, STANDARDIZATION.

dialect atlas　A set of maps marking off the boundaries of selected features of given dialects, such as sounds, vocabulary, grammatical forms, etc. *Synonym:* LINGUISTIC ATLAS. *See also* ISOGLOSS.

dialect geography　The study of local linguistic differences within given speech areas. *Synonyms:* AREA(L) LINGUISTICS, LINGUISTIC GEOGRAPHY.

dialectology　The study of dialects, especially as they differ socially and geographically. *See also* AREA(L) LINGUISTICS, DIALECT (or LINGUISTIC) GEOGRAPHY, GEOGRAPHICAL LINGUISTICS, NEOLINGUISTS.

diaphone　1. All variants of a phoneme occurring in all the utterances of all the speakers of a language (French tongue-trilled as against uvular *r*) (Webster III).

2. A phoneme of one dialect corresponding to but phonetically different from that of another dialect (the British and American sounds of *o* in *not, lot, pot,* or of *r* in *very*).

diaphoneme　1. A category or member of a category consisting of the entire range of dialectal variants of an allophone (Webster III).

2. A phoneme peculiar to the phonemic structure of a dialect (Jones-Hill).

dia-system Lehmann's term for DIALECT (*q.v.*).

dictionary 1. A list of the words of a language, usually in alphabetical order, with their meanings, often their derivations, and occasionally their histories (ETYMOLOGICAL DICTIONARY).

2. A list of the words of a language with their equivalents in a foreign language, or of the words in a foreign language with their equivalents in the native language, or of both (BILINGUAL DICTIONARY).

3. A work listing, alphabetically or by some other convenient method, the terms in a given field of knowledge or study, with definitions, explanations, examples, and occasionally foreign-language equivalents. *Synonym:* GLOSSARY.

differential meaning The difference in meaning between forms used in different contexts (*still* in "he's still" vs. "he's still here") (Faust). *See also* CONNOTATION, DEEP GRAMMAR, DENOTATION, REFERENTIAL MEANING.

differentiation 1. Gray's term for CONTIGUOUS DISSIMILATION (*q.v.*).

2. The development of allomorphs into full separate morphemes or doublets (Latin *deus* and *dīvus* come originally from two alternants, *de-* and *deiv-*, of a single stem meaning "god," "divine") (Hoenigswald).

3. The development from one language to many (Latin branching out into the various Romance languages) (Webster III).

diffuse phoneme The opposite of COMPACT PHONEME (*q.v.*) (Jakobson).

diffusion 1. The spreading of linguistic elements from one group to another, in a culture area where borrowing takes place. *See* GEOGRAPHICAL CLASSIFICATION.

2. Geolinguistically, the migration of speakers of language to other areas, where they come into contact with

another language, with consequent phenomena of language changes. *See also* LANGUAGES IN CONTACT.

diffusion and migration theories These both arose as methodological weapons against nineteenth-century evolutionism, where typological and genetic linguistic features were greatly confused. The DIFFUSION CONCEPT deals with the CULTURE AREA, i.e. areal or geographical linguistics or classification; what is involved is largely BORROWINGS, where the greatest number of resemblances are in sound only, or meaning only, and occasionally in both sound and meaning. The MIGRATION THEORY deals with the KULTURKREISLEHRE, or CULTURE CIRCLE, where genetically related cultures assume importance, and geographical distances become irrelevant; this parallels linguistic GENETIC CLASSIFICATION, where there is usually a convincing number of sound-meaning resemblances in language (the German equivalents for English *sing, sang, sung* are *singen, sang, gesungen,* with both sound and meaning resemblances; when this happens repeatedly in two culture areas, it cannot be due to chance). The DIFFUSION CONCEPT and the MIGRATION THEORY are not to be confused (de la Garza). *See also* GENETIC (*also* GEOGRAPHICAL) CLASSIFICATION.

diffusion concept *See* DIFFUSION AND MIGRATION THEORIES.

diglossia The coexistence in the same area of a colloquial idiom of inferior prestige, side by side with a more learned language; the phenomenon applies to entire communities, while BILINGUALISM is the same phenomenon appearing only in an individual (Martinet).

digraph A two-letter symbol used to represent a single speech sound (*th* in *this, ea* in *each, ng* in *thing*). *See also* COMPOUND GRAPHEME.

dilation Gray's term for INCONTIGUOUS (or NON-CONTIGUOUS) ASSIMILATION (*q.v.*).

diminutive A word or affix indicating smallness, lovability, pity, sympathy, etc. (*Jeanie, Peg, lambkin, -ette, -ling,* German *-chen, -lein*). In the terminology of some languages, a careful distinction is made between the pet name, indicating fondness, and the true diminutive, indicating smallness (Italian VEZZEGGIATIVO, DIMINU-TIVO). *Opposite:* AUGMENTATIVE.

ding-dong theory The belief that there is an inherent or mystic correlation between sound and meaning, or between the SIGNIFIER and the SIGNIFIED (Max Müller). *Synonym:* NATIVISTIC THEORY.

diphoneme A single phoneme which has two values simultaneously; its existence is doubtful (Hindi *me,* which according to some authorities may be pronounced *mē,* as against *mē,* which may not be pronounced *me*) (Entwistle).

diphthong 1. The combination of a syllabic and a non-syllabic vowel; a sound made by gliding continuously from the position for one vowel to that for another (*i*ce, French t*oi,* German h*eu*te, Spanish c*ue*va) (Walsh).
2. A gliding monosyllabic speech item which starts at or near the articulating position for one vowel and goes on to the position for another vowel (Webster III).
3. The term, which according to its etymology means "twice-sounding," was first used to designate two vowels, then extended to designate two consonants ([ks]); today it is used only to designate vowel combinations. Diphthongs may be considered as (a) vowels in which there is appreciable change of quality during the course of their pronunciation; (b) sequences of vowels; (c) vowels plus semi-vowels. Phonetically, the first interpretation is generally the best; phonemically, diphthongs are usually best treated as sequences or as single phonemes, depending upon their distribution, and how this fits into the over-all phonemic structure of the particular language. Thus, there may be a marked difference in the phonetic and phonemic significance of the term diphthong (de la Garza). *Partial synonyms:*

(COMPLEX) VOWEL CLUSTER, VOWEL SEQUENCE, COM-
POUND PHONEME. *See also* FALLING (*also* RISING)
DIPHTHONG, NUCLEUS.

diphthongization Historically, the process whereby a
monophthong changes into a diphthong (Latin *ferrum*
to Spanish *hierro*). *Synonyms:* BREAKING, BRECHUNG,
VOWEL FRACTURE. *Opposites:* DEDIPHTHONGIZATION,
MONOPHTHONGIZATION. *See also* DIVERGENT CHANGE,
OFF-GLIDE, VOWEL SHIFT.

diplomatic edition (or **transcription**) In historical linguistics, a transcription of an ancient or medieval document in which no changes or adaptations are made, but
the text is transcribed precisely as it appears in the
available manuscript or inscription. *Opposite:* CRITICAL
EDITION (or TRANSCRIPTION).

dipodism *See* ISOCHRONISM.

directive Any preposition, postposition or suffix expressing location, direction, time or agency (Bodmer).
Synonyms: DIRECTOR, INDICATOR.

directive construction An exocentric construction consisting of a director and an axis ("on — the table")
(Hockett).

director *See* DIRECTIVE CONSTRUCTION. *Synonyms:* DI-
RECTIVE, INDICATOR.

discontinuous constituents Constituents of the same
construction which are separated in the text from each
other by other linguistic units or phonemes (*"Did* the
man *come?"*, French *ne . . . pas*) (Gleason). *See
also* CONSTITUENT, DISCONTINUOUS MORPHEME, UNI-
VERSAL COMBINATION.

discontinuous formant One of two formants expressing
a single morpheme, which do not occur together within
a word, but as two at least potentially independent
words, which may have other words in between (*drive
. . . home*) (Hughes).

discontinuous morpheme A broken or repeated sequence
(French *ni . . . ni, ne . . . pas,* Latin *-arum . . . -arum*

in *bonarum puellarum*) (Whatmough). *Partial synonym:* DISCONTINUOUS CONSTITUENT.

discourse analysis 1. The study of meanings as verbal equivalences, by distributional analysis (Harris, Carroll).

2. The structural analysis of texts larger than one sentence (Webster III). *See also* LOGOTACTICS, MORPHOTACTICS, PHONOTACTICS.

discrepant correspondence An instance where a given form does not behave in accordance with the phonetic law that should govern it, by reason of learned, dialectal or foreign borrowing, or analogy (Italian *plebe* from Latin *plebem* should have been *pieve,* which actually exists in another meaning, but has been retained in practically unchanged form by reason of learned use) (Hall). *See also* RESIDUE FORMS.

discrete units Those linguistic entities whose value is not affected by variations of detail determined by the context (phonemes; tones in languages where tones are phonemic) (Martinet).

discrimination *See* AUDITORY DISCRIMINATION.

disjunction *See* COMMUTATION, PROCESS, SYSTEM (Hjelmslev).

disjunctive opposition Phonemes in different series and orders opposed to each other (*d* and *p* are opposed not only because they are in different series, one voiced, the other unvoiced, but also because they are in different orders, one dental, the other labial).

dispersion Geolinguistically, the migration of the speakers of a language to different language areas where they constitute a linguistic minority and are eventually absorbed (Italian-speaking immigrants to the United States, Brazil, etc.).

displaced speech An utterance that covers a non-immediate situation (*q.v.*) ("You will see him tomorrow morning at the station"); the use of linguistic signs or words to refer to objects not present in specific situa-

tions ("Dinner will be ready at eight o'clock tonight").
Synonym: REFERRED SPEECH.

dissimilation   Sporadic sound change whereby there is
the development of a dissimilarity between two identical or closely related phonemes (Latin *peregrinum* to
French *pèlerin,* where the first of the two *r*'s is dissimilated to *l*); also, the loss of one of the two phonemes
(*governor* to Cockney *guv'ner*). If the two phonemes
are adjacent, the dissimilation is said to be CONTIGUOUS
(Latin *anima* > *an'ma* > Spanish *alma,* in which the
n is dissimilated from *m,* another nasal, by being turned
into the lateral *l*). *Synonym:* DIFFERENTIATION. If the
two phonemes are not adjacent, the dissimilation is
called INCONTIGUOUS or NON-CONTIGUOUS or DISTANT
(Latin *januarium* > Italian *gennaio*). If the phoneme
that produces dissimilation (DISSIMILATORY PHONEME)
precedes the dissimilated phoneme, the dissimilation is
called PROGRESSIVE DISSIMILATION or LAG (Latin *rarum*
> Italian *rado*). If the dissimilatory phoneme follows
the dissimilated phoneme, the dissimilation is called
REGRESSIVE or RETROGRESSIVE DISSIMILATION or AN-
TICIPATION (Latin *domina* > *dom'na* > Italian
donna). *Note:* Progressive and re(tro)gressive dissimilation are occasionally inverted in the writings of some
scholars. *Opposite:* ASSIMILATION. *See also* HAPLOLOGY
(or SYLLABIC DISSIMILATION).

dissimilatory phoneme   *See* DISSIMILATION, INDUCER.

dissyllabic   Consisting of two syllables (*many, repeat*).

distant assimilation   Assimilation (*q.v.*) of not contiguous (incontiguous) phonemes. *Synonyms:* DILATION,
INCONTIGUOUS ASSIMILATION.

distant dissimilation   Dissimilation (*q.v.*) of non-contiguous (incontiguous) phonemes; this is a sporadic
sound change. *Synonym:* NON-CONTIGUOUS ASSIMILA-
TION. *Opposite:* CONTIGUOUS ASSIMILATION.

distinctive   Capable of distinguishing or differentiating
among meanings; capable of making a segment of ut-

terance different in meaning as well as in sound from an otherwise identical utterance; making a speech item a phoneme rather than an allophone (Webster III); contributing to identifying a language sign from all others (Martinet). *Synonyms:* FUNCTIONAL, OPPOSITIONAL, PHONEMIC, RELEVANT, SIGNIFICANT. *Opposites:* IRRELEVANT, NON-DISTINCTIVE, NON-FUNCTIONAL, NON-PHONEMIC. *See also* ACOUSTIC FEATURES, MARK, PHONOLOGICAL COMPONENTS.

distinctive function The use of phonemically relevant features to distinguish linguistic signs (Martinet).

distribution 1. Descriptively, the occurrence of linguistic items in terms of context or geography (Webster III); the sum of the contexts in which an element may occur, or a set of environments (Walsh); the syntagmatic arrangement of elements in the spoken chain (Martinet). *See also* COMPLEMENTARY DISTRIBUTION. 2. Geolinguistically, the position, arrangement and extent of languages throughout the world, or in given areas.

distribution, law of The theory that words once synonymous tend to be subsequently differentiated, and cease to be interchangeable (Bréal).

distributive A word which refers singly and without exception to all members of a group (*each, every, either, none*); or which refers to a single member of a group (*which* in "which one of them?"); or which indicates division into smaller groups or into individuals (Latin *bini,* "by twos," *singuli,* "one by one").

distributive numeral A numeral referring to units or groups, each consisting of an indicated number of the members considered ("by twos," "by the dozen," Latin *trini,* "by threes").

divergence Martinet's term for DIALECTALIZATION (*q.v.*).

divergent change A change of the acoustic (*q.v.*) variety, where a long vowel breaks into a diphthong (Anglo-Saxon *wīn,* with a pure long vowel, turns into *wein,* ultimately into *wine,* because the original vowel is not begun at the proper height) (Sweet). *Synonym:* DIPHTHONGIZATION.

domal *See* CACUMINAL, RETROFLEX.

domesticated word A word borrowed from one language and adopted for use in another in its original form, at least in writing (*foyer, garage*). *See also* ACCLIMATIZATION, ALIEN WORD, NATURALIZED WORD.

dorsal *See* GUTTURAL, VELAR.

dorso-alveolar A consonant sound produced with the front part of the dorsum against the alveoli (French *s* in *souche*) (Martinet).

dorsum The back part of the tongue, usually coming into contact with the soft palate or velum.

double articulation *See* ARTICULATION.

double bar juncture A question mark juncture.

double consonant 1. Orthographically, a letter occurring twice (tu*nn*el).

2. Phonetically, an acoustic impression apprehended or functioning as two consonants, produced by prolonging the articulation (English bu*s s*eat, Italian a*ss*o), repeating the articulation (Spanish pe*rr*o), or prolonging the interval between occlusion and release (English coa*t t*ail, Italian fa*tt*o). *See also* DOUBLING, GEMINATION.

double cross juncture A period juncture; a terminal juncture, signaling the end of an intonation pattern (Smith).

doublets Alternative forms; two or more words stemming from the same original word, but currently used with different meanings, and often displaying different stages of popular or learned development (*frail, fragile; dish, disc*). MORPHOLOGICAL DOUBLETS are two or more forms of the same word, use of the proper form being determined by phonetic environment or distribution, i.e., how the form functions in context (*a, an;* French *le, l'*). *See also* CONTRASTIVE PHRASAL DOU-

BLETS, MORPHOLOGICAL DOUBLETS, QUADRUPLETS, TRIPLETS.

doubling 1. *See* DOUBLE CONSONANT, GEMINATION.

2. *See* ADDING.

drift The concept of the observed historical direction of linguistic change; an assumed trend toward general change in the structure of a language over a period of time, indicated by specific changes (Webster III); a consistent change in the pattern of a language, or a movement of language down time in a current of its own making (Sapir), eventually resulting in the breaking up into dialects because of specific phonetic tendencies (Dorfman). *See also* PHONETIC CHANGE.

dual A grammatical number indicating two, in addition to the singular and plural (Gothic *wit*, "we two"); in languages that have a dual, the plural normally refers to three or more.

duality of pattern The arrangement of phonemes, but also of morphemes, each of which is represented by an arrangement of phonemes (Hockett).

duration 1. Impressionistic acoustic term indicating the relative length of time during which the vocal organs vibrate in speech or remain in the position required for the articulation of a given sound. *See also* DOUBLE CONSONANT, GEMINATION, LENGTH, MODIFICATION, PROSODIC FEATURES, QUANTITY, SECONDARY PHONEME, VOWEL QUANTITY.

2. One of the dimensions of speech forms, tied up with the TEMPO (ALLEGRO/LENTO) of the utterance, its intonation pattern, accent by stress, and rhythm; it is very difficult to measure, for reasons of fusion or coarticulation (overlap) (de la Garza).

3. A function of the rhythmical structure of language; the assignment of time in rhythm, i.e., the use of time expansion of various sounds (de la Garza).

4. Duration functions as a DISTINCTIVE MARKER in Hungarian (*török*, "Turkish"; *törők*, "dagger"; *törők*,

"breakers"); in English, it is functional in that it differentiates sound quality (de la Garza).

durative *See* IMPERFECTIVE.

dynamic accent Accent depending on the force of expiration or stress. *Synonyms:* EXPIRATORY ACCENT, INTENSITY ACCENT, STRESS ACCENT. *See also* INTENSITY, LOUDNESS.

dynamic linguistics Saussure's term for HISTORICAL LINGUISTICS.

dynamic middle A use of the middle voice (*q.v.*) indicating that the actor is acting for himself or on his own behalf; most Latin deponent verbs are in origin dynamic middles (Greek *lyomai* in the sense of "I am loosing for myself"; in the sense of "I am loosing myself," it is reflexively used) (Gray).

dynamics Historical grammar endeavoring to explain grammatical phenomena which it considers related (Jespersen).

E

echoic (or **echo**) **word** The imitation of a sound heard in nature (*buzz, clang, crash*). *Synonyms:* IMITATIVE (*also* MIMETIC) WORD, ONOMATOPOEIA, ONOMATOPOETIC WORD.

echoism 1. Phonetic assimilation of the following to the preceding vowel. *Partial synonym:* VOWEL HARMONY.

2. Synonym for ECHOIC WORD (*q.v.*).

eclipsis 1. In Celtic grammar, the term for certain phonetic changes, especially nasalization, of initial pho-

nemes of words when they follow directly certain words
or flectional forms.

2. The omission or suppression of words or sounds
(Webster III).

economy   1. The tendency of language to follow the law
of least effort, commensurate with the need for communication (Martinet).

2. Reducing the phonemes of a language to the smallest
possible number consistent with necessary distinctions
of meaning.

3. Reducing the rules in the grammar of a language to
the smallest possible number. *See also* ENERGETICS.

egressive   A sound produced with air coming out from
inside. *Opposites:* INGRESSIVE, SUCTION STOP. *See also*
SECONDARY FEATURES, PRESSURE STOP (de la Garza).

ejective   A voiceless plosive with a simultaneous glottal
stop (Gray); mouth closure and release of the glottis
occurring almost simultaneously (Webster III).

element   A constituent part, or a part of a unit separable
by analysis (Dorfman). *See also* COMPONENT, CONSTIT-
UENT.

elevation (of **meaning**)   *See* AMELIORATION.

elision   1. In poetry, the suppression of a vowel or of an
entire syllable for euphony or meter (*e'er* for *ever*).

2. In grammar, by free variation or for morphological
reasons, the use of a speech form lacking a final or
initial sound that a variant speech form has (*there's,*
French *l'été*). *See also* MORPHOPHONEMIC SYSTEM, PHO-
NETIC MODIFICATION.

-eme   A suffix used in linguistics to indicate a significantly distinctive unit of structure in a language
(Walsh).

emic   Pike's term for FUNCTIONAL (*q.v.*). *Opposite:*
ETIC.

emotive accent   *See* FUNCTIONS OF PITCH.

emphatic articulation   In Semitic, the pressing of the
blade of the tongue against the palate in the formation

of some consonant sounds; the articulation is then velarized or alveolar rather than dental, or pharyngeal
rather than velar (Webster III).

emphatics *See* STYLISTICS. *See also* CHARACTEROLOGY
OF SPEECH, PARALINGUISTICS, RANDOM VARIATIONS.

empty word In Chinese, a word which serves to indicate
or define function or syntactic relationship of a FULL
WORD (*q.v.*); a particle or pointer word. *Partial synonyms:* FORM WORD, FUNCTION WORD, MARKER, PAR-
TICLE, POINTER, RELATIONAL WORD, STRUCTURE WORD.

enclitic A word, usually non-syllabic, pronounced as
part of the preceding word (the abbreviated form of
am in "I'm going home"; Latin *-que* in *senatus popu-
lusque*). *Opposite:* PROCLITIC.

encoding Converting non-linguistic intentions, impulses
and emotions into a system of communication, which
may be language (Walsh). *Opposite:* DECODING.

endocentric construction 1. One whose resultant phrase
belongs to the same form class as one of the constituents (the HEAD, *q.v.*) ("Poor man," which belongs to
the same form class as *man,* the head; *poor* is the AT-
TRIBUTE; in "very fresh milk," *milk* is the head, *very
fresh* the attribute; while in "very fresh," *fresh* is the
head, *very* the attribute) (Bloomfield).
2. A word or group of words fulfilling the function,
respectively, of a noun ("the big red book," "language
and thought in action"); of a verb ("was being told
off," "should have been seen"); of an adjective ("up-
to-date," "down-to-earth"); or of an adverb ("forty-
five years ago," "in a moment or two"). *Opposite:*
EXOCENTRIC CONSTRUCTION. *See also* MULTIVERBAL
ENDOCENTRIC STRUCTURE.

endocentric form A form or construction which contains
its center (or head) within itself (*work*s, un*gentleman*ly, the four handsome French *girls* on the boat)
(Hall).

endocentric phrase A phrase that has the same grammatical function as the one of its immediate constituents which does not modify the other ("fresh milk," which has the same function as "milk" alone) (Bloch and Trager).

endocentric structure *See* ENDOCENTRIC CONSTRUCTION 2.

endophasia Implicit, non-vocal, inaudible, invisible language, conscious or unconscious. *Opposite:* EXOPHASIA.

energetics A theory that language tends constantly toward maximum expressiveness with least effort, with an interplay of opposing demands (the individual seeks ease of expression, while the social consciousness calls for distinctness of communication) (Jespersen). *See also* ECONOMY.

English vowel shift *See* VOWEL SHIFT.

enhancement (of **meaning**) *See* AMELIORATION.

enumerative A numeral adjunct, used in Chinese, indicating the general class of the object that follows (*i-t'iao lu*, "one-twig-length [of] road"; a distant English parallel is *head* in "five head of cattle") (Entwistle). *See also* AUXILIARY NUMERAL, CLASSIFIER 1.

environment The circumstances or surroundings in which a sound or grammatical form is found (Walsh); the surrounding sounds or grammatical forms that influence or modify a sound or grammatical form (the fact that *s* precedes *p* in *spin* causes the *p* to lose the aspiration it would have if it came initially).

epenthesis The interpolation in a word or sound group of a sound or letter which has no etymological justification, but whose usual purpose it is to ease a difficult transition between two other adjacent sounds (Anglo-Saxon *thuner, brēmel* > English thun*d*er, bram*b*le; Latin *camera,* reduced to *cam'ra* by syncopation, > French cham*b*re; Scandinavian *knīf* > French *c*anif); some authorities reserve EPENTHESIS for consonants only, and use ANAPTYXIS (*q.v.*) for vowels; others speak of VOWEL or CONSONANT EPENTHESIS. *See also*

EXCRESCENT (*also* INTRUSIVE, PARASITIC) CONSONANT (or VOWEL).

epicene A noun having a single form that can be of male or female gender (*secretary*).

epigraphy The study, deciphering and interpretation of ancient or medieval inscriptions or records carved or engraved into stone, clay, or other solid materials. *See also* PALEOGRAPHY.

epilegma Any unit of analysis of utterance, such as a word; in polysynthetic languages, a corresponding portion of a sentence-word (Whatmough). *See also* UTTERANCE.

episememe The smallest meaningful grammatical unit; the meaning of a TAGMEME (*q.v.*) (Bloomfield).

epithetologue A form characterized by inflection for case, normally including nouns, adjectives and pronouns (Gray).

eponym A person from whose name, or the name itself, from which the name of a group or country or other geographical or sociological unit is derived (*Washington,* for the city or state of Washington; *Bolívar* for Bolivia).

equalization Gray's term for COMPLETE ASSIMILATION (*q.v.*); a type of assimilation in which the assimilated phoneme is made completely identical with the assimilatory phoneme (Latin *actum, dom'nam,* > Italian *atto, donna*).

equivalent sentences Two otherwise different sentences containing the same combination of equivalent classes, even though they have different combinations of morphemes ("Casals plays the cello" — "The cello is played by Casals") (Harris). *See also* TRANSFORMATIONAL ANALYSIS.

ethnolinguistics The study of the interrelation of linguistics and ethnology, or non-linguistic cultural behavior (Carroll, Olmstead).

ethnophonemic transcription A transcription that makes

concessions to the spelling habits of the users of the language (the use of orthographic *ch* and *j* in French fashion when teaching literacy to Haitian Creole speakers, in order to prepare them for later instruction in standard French) (Hall).

etic Pike's term for NON-FUNCTIONAL (*q.v.*). *Opposite:* EMIC.

etymology The history, sometimes also the prehistory, of a linguistic form as shown by tracing its phonetic, graphic and semantic development from the earliest available records, its course of transmission from one language to another; analyzing its component parts, identifying its cognates in other languages, and tracing it and its cognates back to a common ancestral form in the recorded or assumed parent language (Webster III); that branch of linguistics which deals with the origin and history of words, tracing them back to their earliest ascertainable base in a given language group. *See also* FOLK ETYMOLOGY.

etymon 1. The original form which supplies the etymology of a given word (Latin *caballus* is the etymon of French *cheval,* Italian *cavallo,* Spanish *caballo,* etc.). *Opposite:* REFLEX.

2. A word or morpheme from which other words are formed by derivation or composition (*year* is the etymon of *yearly*).

euphemism The substitution of a word of more pleasant connotations for one of unpleasant or disagreeable connotations (*pass away* for *die; Eumenides,* or "well-disposed ones," for *Furies*).

euphony 1. A pleasing sound or combination of sounds (a usually subjective feature), and the acoustic effect produced by such sound or sounds ("Italian offers euphony for singing purposes"). *Opposite:* CACOPHONY.

2. A tendency to greater ease of pronunciation, leading to regular combinative changes that seem caused by

greater speed and less effort (Webster III). *See also*
ECONOMY, ENERGETICS.

evolutionary linguistics   Saussure's term for DIACHRONIC
LINGUISTICS.

exclusive first person   In some languages, a form of *we*
that excludes the hearer ("he and I," but not "you and
I"). *Opposite:* INCLUSIVE FIRST PERSON.

excrescent consonant   1. The closure of the tongue
against the alveolar ridge before an articulation is completed, which is heard as a stop (Western American
varmin*t* for *vermin,* once*t* for *once*).

2. Any EPENTHETIC, INTRUSIVE, or PARASITIC CONSO-
NANT (*q.v.*), which may be due to FOLK ETYMOLOGY
(*q.v.*) (the second *r* in *bridegroom* from an earlier
guma, "man").

excrescent vowel   *See* ANAPTYXIS.

existential sentence   A sentence affirming or denying the
existence of something ("there is . . . ," "there is
not . . .") (Jespersen).

exocentric construction   A construction whose resultant
phrase belongs to the form class of no immediate constituent (in "John ran," the resultant phrase is neither
a nominative expression, like "John," nor a finite verb
expression, like "ran"; in "with me," the constituents
are a prepositional expression and an accusative expression, but the resultant phrase has a different function from either) (Bloomfield); a syntactical construction which as a unit has a different function or belongs
to a different class from any of its constituent elements
(Dorfman). Basically, what older grammars would
term a COMPLETE SENTENCE ("I am here"). *Opposite:*
ENDOCENTRIC CONSTRUCTION.

exocentric form   A form or construction which has its
center (or head) outside of itself ("on the boat")
(Hall). *Opposite:* ENDOCENTRIC FORM.

exocentric phrase   A phrase that does not have the same
function as any of its immediate constituents ("of our

horses," which is neither a preposition nor a substantive expression, but functions as an attribute of a noun, of a verb, or of an adjective lying outside of the phrase itself) (Bloch and Trager). *Opposite:* ENDOCENTRIC PHRASE.

exocentric structure *See* EXOCENTRIC CONSTRUCTION.

exolinguistics McMillan's term for METALINGUISTICS (*q.v.*).

exophasia Vocal and audible language (Gray). *Opposite:* ENDOPHASIA.

expansion 1. Grammatically, the addition of elements that do not modify mutual relationships and functions (by COORDINATION, "he buys furniture" is expanded to "he buys and sells furniture"; by SUBORDINATION, "he was lying in the dust" is expanded to "he was lying in the dust of the road") (Martinet). *See also* ANTICIPATORY EXPANSION, SEQUENTIAL EXPANSION.
2. What happens to a form when another related form, or a part of that same form's meaning, becomes obsolescent; when the latter becomes obsolescent, and therefore unproductive, the former expands and becomes more productive (Old French *molt,* derived from Latin *multum,* became obsolescent before the inroads of *très,* derived from Latin *trans,* until it was completely replaced by the expansion of the latter; in modern French, the periphrastic future formed with *aller,* as in *je vais manger,* is steadily expanding at the expense of the formal future *je mangerai*) (de la Garza). *Opposite:* OBSOLESCENCE. *See also* PRODUCTIVE, UNPRODUCTIVE.

experiential word A word denoting a thing with which the speaker has had direct, firsthand personal experience or contact.

experimental phonetics The practical study of speech sounds, as to production (PHYSIOLOGICAL PHONETICS), or propagation in the air (ACOUSTIC PHONETICS), without consideration of meaning or semantic content. *Synonym:* LABORATORY PHONETICS.

expiratory accent Accent characterized by varying loudness dependent on the degree of energy with which the vocal cords are vibrated during the expiration or release. *Synonyms:* DYNAMIC (*also* INTENSITY, STRESS) ACCENT.

expletive 1. A syllable, word or group of words inserted in a word or sentence to satisfy some grammatical rule or custom, but the omission of which would not alter the meaning (*"there* are many people here"; *"it* is easy to do that"). *Synonyms:* FLOATING ELEMENT, STRUCTURE WORD.

2. An exclamatory word, often profane or obscene; an interjection ("Hell!" "Ouch!").

explicative linguistics A theory of linguistics that rejects the negative position that the causes of linguistic change are inscrutable, and claims they are ascertainable through a structural explanation of the diachronic process.

explicatory diachronic linguistics That phase of diachronic linguistics in which questions of causation are dealt with (Martinet).

explosion The sudden opening of the closure in the oral air passage, resulting in the sudden, audible exhalation of air (Dorfman); the third phase, or sudden release, of a stop sound; but a stop often has no explosion (final *t* in American [kæt]).

explosive 1. A consonant sound characterized by an explosion of breath in its articulation at the moment of release, when it occurs in certain environments or positions (English initial *p* of *pit*) (Webster III).

2. *See* OCCLUSIVE, PLOSIVE, STOP.

expressive That aspect of language which characterizes the speaker, as opposed to APPELLATIVE (characterizing the hearer) and REPRESENTATIONAL (characterizing the subject of discourse) (Trubetskoi).

expressive features Jakobson's term for CHARACTEROL-

OGY OF SPEECH, EMPHATICS, PARALINGUISTICS, RANDOM
VARIATIONS, STYLISTICS.

expressive function That function of the accent which
informs the hearer of the state of mind of the speaker
(*"You* did this?", betokening disbelief or sarcasm)
(Martinet). *See also* CONTRASTIVE (*also* DISTINCTIVE,
OPPOSITIONAL) FUNCTION.

extension *See* ANALOGY, ANALOGICAL (*also* MORPHOLOG-
ICAL, SEMANTIC) EXTENSION.

extensional meaning *See* ANALOGY, MORPHOLOGICAL
(*also* SEMANTIC) EXTENSION.

external hiatus Hiatus (*q.v.*) between two words (Ital-
ian *la amica,* which becomes *l'amica*). *Opposite:* IN-
TERNAL HIATUS. *See also* AUTOMATIC (*also* MORPHO-
PHONEMIC) ALTERNATION.

externalization The mental act or process whereby sensory data originally considered to be internal are pro-
jected into the outside world.

external linguistics The study of language as interrelated
with factors of history, ethnology, economics, religion,
etc.; to some extent synonymous with HISTORICAL LIN-
GUISTICS (Saussure). *Opposite:* INTERNAL LINGUIS-
TICS. *See also* MENTALISTIC THEORY, NEOLINGUISTS.

external open juncture The transition from a pause to
the first segmental phoneme of an utterance, or from
the last segmental phoneme to the following pause
(Bloch and Trager). *See also* JUNCTURE.

external sandhi A word having, potentially, two forms,
each occurring in different environments; considering
the other paradigms, this type of alternation is predictable; if it did not take place, the phonemic pattern
of the language would be different (French adjectives
which occur before the noun, as *bonne* /bɔn/ ~ *bon*
/bɔ̃/, or *sotte* /sɔt/ ~ *sot* /so/, where the fuller form is
the base form) (de la Garza). *Opposites:* INTERNAL
SANDHI, OPTIONAL INTERNAL SANDHI. *See also* AUTO-

MATIC (*also* MORPHOPHONEMIC, REGULAR) ALTERNA-
TION.

extra-word   Outside the word (syntax deals with relationships among words or larger units). *Opposite:*
INFRA-WORD.

extrinsic meaning (of word or expression)   What is sup-
plied by the additional, or suprasegmental phonemes
("Really?" uttered in a sarcastic or unbelieving tone).
Opposite: INTRINSIC MEANING. *See also* EXPRESSIVE
FUNCTION.

eye dialect   That written form of a spoken dialect which
purports to represent dialectal features or substandard
language (*massa, wuz, sez*) (Gleason).

F

fading   The drop in pitch and volume at the end of an
utterance (Walsh).

falling diphthong   A diphthong where the syllabic or
stressed element precedes the non-syllabic glide, and
where there is less stress on the second than on the first
element (*oi* in *noise*). *Opposite:* RISING DIPHTHONG.
See also GLIDE.

false cognates   *See* COGNATES.

familiar forms   Forms of verbs, pronouns, etc., indicating or implying familiarity, affection, kinship, etc., occasionally also contempt or lack of respect, particularly on the part of the speaker toward the person
addressed (French *tu* as against *vous* in addressing a
single person; Japanese *iku,* "to go," as against *iki-
masu*). *See also* HONORIFIC.

family A large group of related languages (Germanic, Romance, Slavic, as some of the subdivisions of Indo-European; but Indo-European could itself be called a family of languages) (Hall). *See also* STOCK.

family tree theory The belief that innovations spread like branches issuing from a tree trunk, giving rise to the separate branches of Indo-European (Schleicher). *Synonym:* STAMMBAUMTHEORIE. *See also* WAVE THEORY.

faucalization A secondary feature whereby there is an accompanying approximation of the faucal pillars to the tongue root, thus reducing the area of the pharyngeal opening into the mouth, in sound production (de la Garza). *See also* SECONDARY FEATURES.

faucal plosive A stop released through the nasal cavity by a sudden lowering of the velum (*t* in *cotton*) (Webster III).

faucal sounds A cover term for PHARYNGEAL, GLOTTAL and LARYNGEAL sounds, all produced in the area of the throat (Bloch and Trager).

feedback 1. In general, the return to the input of a part of the output.

2. Linguistically, the sound and feel of one's own speech.

3. More specifically, the aspect of sound whereby if one feels and hears what one is doing or saying in speech, one can articulate well and be assured that his speech is not deteriorating. There are five types of feedback : (a) auditory—the distance between mouth and ears is constant, and one hears one's own speech as being more sonorous than it really is; (b) vibratory—this takes place through bone conduction, and is felt only by the speaker (or by the deaf-mute who puts his fingers on the speaker's throat); (c) kinesthetic—the feeling of where one's tongue hits, etc.; (d) tactile sensation—feeling through touch, akin to kinesthetic feedback; (e) intention—the deepest psychological stratum, whereby one knows his own intention, and does

not have to interpret what is being said (this is only slightly accessible to the analyst through speech disorders) (de la Garza). *See also* ASPECTS OF SOUND, AUDITORY FEEDBACK, AKOUSMA, GRAPHEMA, KINEMA, KINESTHETIC FEEDBACK, LEGEMA, ORAMA, TRANSMISSION.

field conditions   The procedure of studying and analyzing a language from the spoken angle, with the aid of native informants, whose utterances are gathered, collated, categorized, and worked by a process of phonemic and morphemic analysis into a complete description of the language under consideration (Gleason). *See also* PHILOLOGICAL CONDITIONS.

figurae   The smallest units of language, having no content of their own, but capable of entering into composition with other figurae to form signs (*q.v.*) (Hjelmslev).

figurae system   A communication system based on analyzable signs, such as language (Hjelmslev). *See also* SYMBOLIC SYSTEM.

final (off-)glide   *See* OFF-GLIDE.

final position   The position of the last sound, or morpheme, or syllable of a word; it is customary, however, to describe a vowel as in final position if it is the last vowel in the word, even if it is followed by one or more consonants (Latin am*a*nt). *See also* AUSLAUT, OFF-GLIDE.

first articulation   The way in which an experience common to all ,of the linguistic community is organized; the combination of meaning and vocal form; the totality of the meaning of a word like *head* plus the three individual phonemes that enter into the spoken word /hɛd/ (Martinet). *See also* SECOND ARTICULATION.

fissure   Entwistle's term for SLIT FRICATIVE or SPIRANT (*q.v.*).

fit   The relationship between a writing system and the language it represents (examples of good fit: *sit, set, rub;* examples of bad fit: *though, women, nation*) (Walsh).

fixation The state of a dead element in a living language, which continues to be used in certain set connections (Old French *oui,* "heard," surviving in modern French *par ouï-dire,* "by hearsay") (Marouzeau). *See also* PETRIFICATION.

fixed stress (or **accent**) 1. Stress which always falls on a specified syllable, regardless of flectional or other changes and of syntactic function (Polish stress, which always falls on the penult syllable).
2. Stress which always falls on a syllable specified in terms of vowel length or consonant combinations (Latin stress, falling on the penult syllable if it contains a long vowel or a diphthong, or a short vowel followed by a consonant in the same syllable; otherwise on the antepenult) (Webster III). *Synonym:* BOUND STRESS (or ACCENT). *Opposite:* FREE STRESS (or ACCENT).

fixed word order A word order which cannot be changed without destroying the meaning of the utterance (English "John sees George," where a reversal of *John* and *George* would alter the meaning, and any other arrangement of the words would be contrary to usage). *Opposite:* FREE WORD ORDER.

flap A sound produced by the very rapid vibration of an articulator; it is often equal to a single vibration of a trill, sometimes to a very short stop (Gleason); an energetic single bouncing of the tip of the tongue against the hard palate (American English Be*tt*y, British English be*rr*y) (Webster III).

flection *See* ACCIDENCE, INFLECTION.

flectional endings Bound morphemes (or formants) which have no independent existence or use, but are combined with free morphemes (or bound morphemes which are roots) to yield declensional and conjugational forms (the *-us, -ī, -ō, -um* of Latin *mūrus, mūrī,* *mūrō, mūrum,* or the *-ō, -ās, -at, -āmus, -ātis, -ant* of the present tense of *amō;* the *-s, -ed, -ing* of *walks, walked, walking*).

flectional language 1. A language which expresses grammatical relations of words and shades or modifications of their meaning by affixing prefixes or suffixes to the roots of the words; this term thus applies both to AGGLUTINATIVE and AMALGAMATING languages (Dorfman).

2. In nineteenth-century linguistics, which dealt with typology on the level of morphology, a language expressing grammatical relations of words and nuances or relations of root ideas by means of affixation, where the root or stem of the word changes shape (de la Garza). *See also* FUSION, INFLECTION, REPLACIVE, SYMBOLISM, SYNTHETIC.

flexion, flexional *See* FLECTION, FLECTIONAL.

floating element An unnecessary or superfluous word in a sentence (*"There* is a book on the table"). *Partial synonyms:* EXPLETIVE 1, STRUCTURE WORD.

flow-chart A diagram indicating the order in which various syntactical forms normally appear in a given language (French *me, te, se, nous, vous; le, la, les; lui, leur; y; en*) (Hall).

fluctuating spelling The orthographic differences encountered at the same period, often in the same document, despite the fact that they represent an identical sound (Old High German *ertha, erdha, erda;* Old French *fradra, fradre* in the Oaths of Strasbourg); when the orthography becomes standardized, these variant spellings are replaced by a standardized form (Saussure).

focal area A region whose characteristic speech features are imitated in neighboring regions, and from which innovations spread (Paris in medieval France). *Synonyms:* RADIATING (*also* PRESTIGE) CENTER. *See also* GRADED AREA, PRESTIGE LANGUAGE, RELIC AREA, TRANSITION AREA.

focal word A specific word in which one is interested, in grammatical analysis (de la Garza).

folk etymology 1. A change in spelling or pronunciation of words to make them look or sound more similar to familiar words, with little regard to similarity in meaning or derivation (*sparrowgrass* for *asparagus; chaise lounge* for *chaise longue; crayfish* from French *écrevisse; Picketwire* from French *Purgatoire;* English *bridegroom* from Anglo-Saxon *brydguma*). *Synonyms:* AS-SOCIATIVE ETYMOLOGY, POPULAR ETYMOLOGY. *See also* METANALYSIS, PHONOSYMBOLISM.

2. A sporadic change akin to METANALYSIS, but distinct from it, particularly in that it has no necessary effect on the pattern of the language; furthermore, although folk etymology need not be accompanied by metanalysis, it underlies almost every instance of metanalysis (de la Garza).

forestress The heavier stress placed on the first part of certain compound words (*workshop, gunman, toothbrush*) (Marchand). *See also* ACCENT, COMPOSITION.

forlorn elements Defective (*q.v.*) parts (English *went,* which has no present form, but must function as the past of *go*) (Hockett).

form 1. A recurrent vocal feature which has meaning, and is made up wholly of phonemes (de la Garza).

2. A meaningful unit of linguistic signaling, smallest or complex, which when uttered always contains grammatical form. The forms of a language are always finite in number (de la Garza).

3. One of the different shapes or aspects a word may take as a result of inflection, change of spelling, or change of pronunciation.

formal amalgam *See* AMALGAM.

formal contrasts Contrasts in the form of words signaling greater differences in function or meaning ("the dog's friend arrived" vs. "the dog's friendly arrival," where the change in the forms of the last two words signals changes of function) (Francis).

formant 1. The reflection in the spectrum of articulated vowel sounds, revealing voice pitch and fundamental frequencies (de la Garza).

2. In the spectrum, a region where the pitch is indicated by the spacing between the harmonics of the formant, and the timbre or quality of the sound is indicated by the number of formants that occur (de la Garza).

3. A characteristic component of the quality of sound; one of the resonance bands which together determine the phonetic quality of a vowel; the harmonics which make up vocoid sounds.

4. A determinative (*q.v.*).

5. A derivational affix, or bound morpheme (Hughes). *See also* DISCONTINUOUS FORMANTS, INTONATION FORMANT, LEXEME.

formative A sound, syllable or group of syllables, usually without a recognized meaning when used by itself, which is added to words to change their meaning or function, or as a means of word formation and derivation (*-ing* in *working*) (Dorfman); an element in a word (prefix or ending) serving to give the word appropriate form, but which is no part of the base (Webster III); a bound form which is a part of a word (*un-* in *unkempt*). *Synonyms:* BOUND MORPHEME, (DERIVATIONAL) AFFIX, FORMANT 4.

form class 1. A part of speech that can be identified by special features of form or ending (English nouns, adjectives, verbs, adverbs) (Walsh); a group into which forms showing recognizable phonetic or grammatical similarity are classified (Dorfman).

2. Words and groups of words that have the same position (or PRIVILEGE OF OCCURRENCE, *q.v.*) in a construction, and one or more morphological or syntactic features in common (in a construction such as "the

— is . . .", any word or word group that would logically fit : *book, hat, going, swiftly flowing stream,* etc.). *See also* MAJOR FORM CLASS.

formless language A non-flectional or isolating language (*q.v.*) (Dorfman).

form word A word not denoting an idea in itself (articles, prepositions, etc.) (Sweet). *Partial synonyms:* EMPTY WORD, FUNCTION WORD, MARKER, PARTICLE, POINTER, RELATIONAL WORD, STRUCTURE WORD.

fortis Of one of two homorganic stops, the one pronounced with stronger articulation and, usually, aspiration (English initial *p, t, k,* as opposed to *p, t, k* after initial *s,* or to *b, d, g*). *Opposites :* LENIS, TENUIS.

Fourier analysis A process whereby one complex sound wave is resolved into several simple waves; of particular importance for the determination of timbre (*q.v.*) (Hughes).

fracture *See* BREAKING, DIPHTHONGIZATION, VOWEL FRACTURE.

fragment An element of speech which may be completive (the answer "home" to the question "Where are you going?", or "yes" to the question "Do you like it?") or exclamatory ("Ouch!", "What the devil!") (Hockett). *Partial synonym:* EXPLETIVE 2.

frame A test sentence or word group, one element or slot of which can be successively replaced or filled by different forms; part of a syntactical or morphological construction that stays unchanged though the rest is altered by the substitution of new items ("The boy is —"). *See also* MULTIPLE SUBSTITUTION FRAME, OVER-ALL FRAME.

free form A morpheme which can be used as an independent word and has a distinct meaning of its own when used alone (*street, walk*) (Bloomfield). *Synonyms:* FREE MORPHEME, MORPHEME. *Opposites:* BOUND FORM (or MORPHEME), DERIVATIONAL AFFIX, FORMANT, FORMATIVE.

free morpheme *See* FREE FORM.

free position Descriptive of a vowel that comes at the end of a syllable (Latin *ca*-nis, *pa*-trem). *Opposite:* CHECKED POSITION.

free stress Stress which may fall on any syllable of a word or expression, according to flectional form or the syntactic function in which it is used (Russian *vodá*, plural *vódy;* Latin *íter,* genitive *itíneris*). *Opposites:* BOUND (*also* FIXED) STRESS (or ACCENT), RESTRICTED STRESS.

free syllable *See* OPEN SYLLABLE.

free variants 1. Non-contrastive variants in the same position (de la Garza).
2. Variants which are not conditioned by their environment, but optional with the individual speaker (final *-t* in *net* may be articulated by the same speaker with aspirated release, or without this non-distinctive, irrelevant feature) (Dorfman). *Synonym:* OPTIONAL VARIANT.

free variation The relation of free variants to one another; the use in the same environment by the same or different speakers of forms perceptually different but semantically the same and idiomatically normal (*with* pronounced with voiced or unvoiced *th*).

free word order Words in an utterance which may occur in any position, according to the discretion of the speaker, without changing the basic meaning of the utterance (Latin *"Paulus amat Petrum," "Petrum amat Paulus," "Amat Paulum Petrus,"* etc.). *Opposite:* FIXED WORD ORDER.

frequency 1. A measure of number per category.
2. In acoustic phonetics, the number of cycles per second of a sound, which indicates its pitch (Walsh).
3. *See* PITCH.
4. The number of occurrences of a given form or phoneme in a given text or period of time. *See also* FUNCTIONAL YIELD, PRODUCTIVITY.

fricative A consonant produced by friction caused by the air moving through a sustained narrow passage somewhere in the mouth; this may be voiceless ([f], [θ], [s], [ʃ]), or voiced ([v], [ð], [z], [ʒ]) (Walsh); a consonant produced by narrowing the air passages, thus producing audible friction as the air is expelled from the lungs. While most linguists use FRICATIVE and SPIRANT as synonyms, Martinet distinguishes a fricative (friction of air clearly perceptible) from a spirant (friction not perceptible). *Partial synonyms:* CONSTRICTIVE, CONTINUANT, CONTINUATIVE, SPIRANT, STATIC CONSONANT.

frontal A sound made with the front part of the tongue, in the area of the hard palate.

fronted A sound produced with the tongue advanced from a given position.

fronting Bringing a sound from the back to the front part of the mouth; in the case of vowels, bringing the bunch of the tongue from the back to the front of the mouth ([u] > [y]). *See also* UMLAUT.

front vowel A vowel whose point of articulation is in the front part of the oral cavity, and which is pronounced with the mass of the tongue pushed toward the front of the mouth and the front part of the tongue arched toward the palate (machine, met). *Synonyms:* BRIGHT (*also* PALATAL, SLENDER) VOWEL. *Opposites:* BACK (*also* BROAD, DARK, DEEP, VELAR) VOWEL.

full voice *See* VOICE. *Partial opposites:* MURMURED VOWEL, WHISPERED VOWEL.

full word In Chinese, any word expressing a concept, idea or image, or designating a person, object or quality; roughly, verbs, substantives and adjectives. *Partial synonyms:* CONTENT WORD, LEXICAL WORD, NAMING WORD, NOTIONAL WORD, SEMANTEME, VOCABULARY WORD. *Partial opposites:* EMPTY WORD, FUNCTION WORD (or FORM), MARKER, PARTICLE, POINTER, RELATIONAL WORD, STRUCTURE WORD.

function 1. A connection between two terms; a linguistic unit has functions or connections in relation to other units, so that certain units presuppose others (a dependent clause presupposes an independent clause, but not vice versa); it also occupies a given place in the chain (Hjelmslev).

2. The part played by a word or ending in a sentence or utterance (Dorfman).

3. A feature of meaning distinguished as characteristic of a type of word (number is a function of nouns, tense is a function of verbs) (Webster III). *See also* CONTRASTIVE (*also* CULMINATIVE, DEMARCATIVE, DISTINCTIVE, EXPRESSIVE, OPPOSITIONAL) FUNCTION.

functional *See* DISTINCTIVE.

functional and structural theory The view that every language is a coherent structure in which the component elements have specific functions to perform; that is, to keep the linguistic signs distinct from one another, thus making human communication through speech possible; variability of speech is thus due to the changing needs of society, reflecting themselves in functions of element, and resulting in the modification of the linguistic structure (Dorfman).

functional change 1. The use of a word, without change in form, in syntactic functions assigned to different parts of speech ("to *contact* someone"). *Synonyms:* CONVERSION, FUNCTIONAL SHIFT, TRANSMUTATION. *See also* SUBSTANTIVAL ADJUNCT.

2. Changes in the phonemic system caused by the need for phonemes to function differently as new conditions arise (Dorfman).

functionalism The STRUCTURALISM (*q.v.*) of the Prague school. *See also* FUNCTIONAL AND STRUCTURAL THEORY.

functional linguistics A study in which phonemes and other linguistic elements are viewed and classified according to their function (i.e., according to what they communicate that is distinctive) in a given language.

functional load The extent to which the contrast between two phonemes is phonemic (Gleason); the measure of functioning of phonemic difference as the sole distinction between two otherwise identical elements (morphemes or words) in a language (Webster III). *See also* FREQUENCY, FUNCTIONAL YIELD.

functional meaning 1. The special meaning of an element (*'s* in "the boy's father," conferring upon *boy's* a genitival value) (Sturtevant). *See also* GRAMMATICAL (*also* LEXICAL, REFERENTIAL, SEMANTIC) MEANING.

2. The meaning of a position; the meaning common to all forms which can occur in a given position, when they are in that position (de la Garza). *See also* CLASS MEANING.

functional moneme Martinet's term for FUNCTION WORD (*q.v.*). *See also* MONEME.

functional shift *See* FUNCTIONAL CHANGE.

functional word *See* FUNCTION WORD.

functional yield The degree of use to which OPPOSITIONS (*q.v.*) are put (there is a large functional yield in the opposition *p/b,* as shown by *pat/bat, cap/cab, clapper/clabber,* etc.; but a low functional yield in unvoiced vs. voiced *th,* as shown by *mouth* (noun)/ *mouth* (verb), *ether/either, thigh/thy*) (Martinet); the number of pairs of words distinguished by a single given feature; the lower the yield, the more possible it is to eliminate the phonemic opposition involved, and reduce the number of phonemes in the language (Hughes). *See also* ECONOMY, FREQUENCY, FUNCTIONAL LOAD.

functions of duration *See* DURATION.

functions of pitch (a) DISTINCTIVE: pitch distinguishes words on the morphological level, and thus acts as a phoneme. *See also* PITCH ACCENT, PITCH LEVELS, TONE LANGUAGES; (b) IN PHRASES: pitch distinguishes phrase, clause, and sentence structures; when a speech measure has two or more different meanings, each is significantly correlated with the different INTONATIONAL PATTERN given it in different utterances (N.B.—intonation alone is not capable of this; the speaker uses all the expressive features at his command). *See also* DURATION, PITCH, STRESS; (c) EMOTIONAL: (phonological); an adjunct to the linguistic signal; this situation borders on that of gesture, and may influence the behavior of the hearer; according to Trubetskoi, this is part of the "procédés phonologiques d'appel ou de déclenchement qui sont fonctionnels, et qui doivent être distingués des manifestations extra-linguistiques" ("phonological processes of appeal or release which are functional, and must be distinguished from extra-linguistic manifestations"). Emotive accent in English may take a number of different forms, thus affecting the stress, duration, intonation, or quality of the utterance. *See also* APPELLATIVE, PARALINGUISTIC (de la Garza).

functions of stress *See* WORD STRESS.

function word An unstressed word in the sentence, expressing primarily grammatical relationship (prepositions, auxiliary verbs, conjunctions, adverbs, interjections, articles, certain pronouns: *a, the, my, who, and, one, do, of, but, may, very*); a word having grammatical rather than lexical meaning, and used primarily to show relationship (Walsh); a word indicating relationship or the function of other words (Schlauch). *Partial synonyms:* EMPTY WORD, FORM WORD, FUNCTIONAL MONEME, FUNCTOR, MARKER, PARTICLE, POINTER, RELATIONAL WORD, STRUCTURE WORD. *Opposites:* CONTENT WORD, FULL WORD, LEXICAL FORM (or WORD), NOTIONAL WORD, SEMANTEME, VOCABULARY WORD.

functives The two terms of a FUNCTION (*q.v.*) (Hjelmslev).

functor 1. A FUNCTION WORD (*q.v.*) (Hall).

2. A word or form of one of the following types:

(a) substitutes (*it, all*); (b) markers (*and, in*); (c) inflectional affixes (*-s, -ed*); (d) derivational affixes (*-y* of *creamy*) (Hockett). *See also* CONTENTIVE.

fundamental pitch *See* PITCH.

fundamental tone *See* PITCH.

fused compound A compound in which the sense of the original individuality of the component parts is largely lost (*offspring, downcast, roadster*) (Schlauch). *Synonym :* SOLID COMPOUND.

fusion 1. Historically, the union of two adjacent sounds or other linguistic elements to form new sounds or elements, where the two component parts are not directly discernible (Latin *amare habeo* > French *aimerai;* Danish *at sige,* "to say," plus *sik,* "self," shortened to *-s,* becoming *at siges,* "to be said") (Martinet). 2. A change in the shape of the stem as root plus affix come together into a word (foul /fawl/ ~ filth /fil + θ/). *See also* FLECTION, INTERNAL MODIFICATION, REPLACIVE, SYMBOLISM (de la Garza). 3. Coalescence between root and affix (Latin *pes* from *ped-s*) (Webster III). 4. Phonetically, *see* COARTICULATION 2. *Synonym :* OVERLAPPING.

G

gap *See* ACCIDENTAL (*also* STRUCTURAL) GAP, HOLES IN THE PATTERN.

gathering The initial process in linguistic analysis of the descriptive type under FIELD CONDITIONS (*q.v.*), consisting in questioning the native informants and recording their responses, which will later be collated, categorized, and analyzed to determine the phonemic and morphemic structure of the language under consideration (Gleason). *See also* COLLATION, LINGUISTIC ANALYSIS.

gemination Doubling or prolonging, especially of consonant sounds; in writing, it is usually indicated by a double letter (Italian *fatto;* Finnish *kuusi*); in speech there is a lengthening of the sound, or of the period of the HOLD, or complete closure preceding the release of a plosive. *See also* DOUBLE CONSONANT, DOUBLING.

gender A grammatical category which may be inflectional or not, and which may or may not come close to a culture's non-linguistic recognition of sex and personality; gender distinction need not agree with anything in the practical world, and this is true in most cases; languages may have from two gender subclasses (as in French) to many (Bantu languages have twenty) (de la Garza). A grammatical distinction or classification of words, appearing chiefly in the Indo-European and Semitic languages (masculine-feminine, or masculine-feminine-neuter, or animate-inanimate); any of two or more subclasses within the grammatical classification of a language (nouns or pronouns or adjectives) that are partly arbitrary, but also partly based on distinguishable characteristics (shape, social rank, sex, animate vs. inanimate), and that determine agreement with and selection of other words or grammatical forms (Webster III). *See also* CASTE, GRAMMATICAL GENDER, NATURAL GENDER.

gender noun A noun which indicates by its separate form the sex of the being designated (*boy, girl; bull, cow*).

genemmic phonetics The study of speech sounds after they are produced. Subdivided into PSYCHOLOGICAL and PHYSICAL (PHONOGENETIC and VIBRATORY) phonetics. *Synonym:* ACOUSTIC PHONETICS. *See also* ARTICULATORY PHONETICS, GENETIC PHONETICS.

general grammar A study of the general principles believed to underlie the grammatical phenomena of all languages (Webster III). *See also* PANCHRONIC (*also* PHILOSOPHICAL, UNIVERSAL) GRAMMAR.

general semantics A philosophy of language-meaning, founded by Alfred Korzybski, and continued by S. I. Hayakawa, Wendell Johnson, and others; the study of language as a representation of reality (Carroll, Korzybski); a study meant to improve the habits of response to environment and of one individual to another by training in the better and more critical use of words and other symbols (Webster III); a science dealing with the effect of the symbol system on man's behavior, whose basic principle is that the word is not to be viewed as the thing, and the event that the word may symbolize is not to be viewed as an isolated happening (Fessenden).

generative grammar The process of producing or generating structures from a KERNEL (*q.v.*) (from "man bites dog" one goes on to "the bad man bites the good dog on the ear") (Hall).

generic grammatical category A whole system of classification (number in English, gender in Spanish, case in Latin) (Hockett). *Opposite:* SPECIFIC GRAMMATICAL CATEGORY.

generous plural A pluralized form of a word already bearing a plural connotation (*you-all, youse, you-uns*).

genetic classification The classification of languages by historical relationship and descent, demonstrable or hypothetic, from a single common ancestor (the Romance languages as the descendants of Latin; Latin, Greek, Sanskrit, Gothic, etc., as the descendants of Indo-European). *See also* AREAL (or GEOGRAPHICAL) CLASSIFICATION, TYPOLOGICAL CLASSIFICATION.

genetic phonetics The study of the production of speech sounds. *Synonym:* ARTICULATORY PHONETICS. *See also* ACOUSTIC PHONETICS, GENEMMIC PHONETICS.

geographical classification 1. Non-technically, a classification based upon the geographical location of languages, without regard for their origin or typology, and often employed as a supplement where comparison and reconstruction for purposes of classification are difficult (American Indian, African Negro, Australian, Papuan languages; Balkan languages).
2. Technically, geographical (or areal) linguistic classification deals with the diffusion and borrowing of linguistic forms in a restricted, geographically continuous culture area. It is based on the effects which one language has on another, whether the two languages be genetically related or not. It is arbitrary within limits, non-exhaustive, and non-unique. COMPARATIVE RECONSTRUCTION and GENETIC CLASSIFICATION are a prerequisite for correct AREAL CLASSIFICATION, and four classes of linguistic contact phenomena must be considered : borrowing, meaningful order, meaning resemblances, and influence of sound systems on one another (de la Garza). *See also* DIFFUSION AND MIGRATION THEORIES, LANGUAGES IN CONTACT.

geographical linguistics *See* AREAL LINGUISTICS, DIALECTOLOGY, LINGUISTIC GEOGRAPHY, NEOLINGUISTS.

geolinguistics The study of languages in their present-day state, with particular reference to number of speakers, geographical distribution, economic, scientific and cultural importance; also their identification in spoken and written form; this term should not be confused with GEOLINGUISTICA, occasionally used by Italian linguists, as a synonym for LINGUISTIC GEOGRAPHY (*q.v.*).

Germanic sound shifts Synonymous with CONSONANT SHIFT (*q.v.*). The First Germanic Sound Shift occurred before the Christian era, and separated Proto-Germanic from the rest of the western Indo-European language families; the Second, or High German, Sound Shift took place between the first and the eighth centuries of the Christian era, and separated the West

Germanic languages into a High and a Low German group. *See also* GRIMM'S LAW.

gestural language *See* PASIMOLOGY. Gesture often accompanies speech, but it is also used alone in certain cases (American Indian tribes that do not know each other's language; Boy Scouts from various language backgrounds; the deaf and dumb).

ghost form (or **ghost word**) 1. A form created by false etymology or other error in writing, printing or pronunciation on the part of a lexicographer, author or scribe (the name of the city of Nome, bestowed as the result of a reader's misinterpretation of the written query "Name?" on a map of the area). *Synonyms:* PHANTOM WORD, VOX NIHILI. *See also* FOLK ETYMOLOGY.

2. The unjustified use of an archaism (*derring-do, forsooth*) (Hall).

gingival *See* ALVEOLAR.

Glagolitic alphabet An old form of writing used by the Slavs, antedating the Cyrillic (*q.v.*).

glide A non-significant sound produced by the passing of the vocal organs to or from the articulating position for a speech sound; the less prominent vowel or vowel-like sound in the articulation of two consecutive vowel sounds unequal in prominence (the brief *i*-sound in *yell*) (Webster III); a transitional sound, articulated rapidly, with constant movement, and swift frequency change; also a non-syllabic vocoid ([j], [w], [r]); the glide may be audible or non-audible, but is generally produced without noise; it is an ON-GLIDE if it precedes the syllabic vowel (*ye*), an OFF-GLIDE if it follows the syllabic vowel (*oy*) (de la Garza).

gloss An interlinear or marginal notation in an ancient or medieval manuscript giving a translation or explanation of a word or passage.

glossary A word list; a brief dictionary, listing terms used in a given field of study or literary work, with explanations or definitions of their meanings. *Synonym:* DICTIONARY 3.

glossematics The quasi-mathematical analysis of language, based on the distribution and inter-relationship of glossemes, devised by Hjelmslev and the Copenhagen school; a theory of the SYSTEM (*q.v.*), or pattern of mutual relationships of linguistic elements; the NORM, a set of rules based on the System and describing the limits of variation for each element; and of USAGE, a set of rules based on the Norm, and describing the limit of variation tolerated in a speech community at any given time (Whatmough).

glosseme The smallest meaningful unit (Bloomfield); the smallest form that linguistic analysis can establish; the irreducible invariants (*q.v.*) (Hjelmslev); that which has meaning, including forms, constructions and zero elements; it may be said to coincide in part with morpheme and with tagmeme (the latter is the smallest meaningful unit of grammatical form); the glosseme may be a word, a stem, a grammatical element, an intonation, or a given word order. *See also* NOEME.

glossolalia Language coined and used by the insane, or by members of certain religious sects (Pentecostists); any form of glossolalia may be meaningful to its individual coiner, but there is no evidence that it has meaning for his hearers.

glott-, glotto- A combining form meaning language.

glottal A sound produced in the larynx by narrowing or constricting the vocal cords ([h], or the catch between the two *o*'s of *coordinate*). *Synonym:* LARYNGEAL.

glottal catch A sound formed by closing the glottis and suddenly releasing air with an explosive effect; a full-fledged phoneme in some Oriental and African languages (New York dialect *bo'l* for *bottle*). *Synonyms:* GLOTTAL STOP, STØD. *See also* IMPULSION, PLOSIVE.

glottalization Secondary feature whereby a sound is accompanied by closure of the glottis.

glottalized Made with pressure applied in the glottis.

glottalized timbre Egressive air sounds produced when the larynx, with closed glottis, is thrust upward, compressing the air beyond it; if the oral or nasal passage is open, pharynx air rushes out; if not, the passage is capped, and a glottalized pressure stop or ejective results (de la Garza). *Opposite:* IMPLOSIVE.

glottal stop The closing, opening, or both, of the vocal cords; it is a voiceless, fortis, impulsive, unaspirated, simple pressure stop. *See also* GLOTTAL CATCH, GLOTTALIZED TIMBRE, STØD.

glottis The opening at the upper part of the larynx, between the vocal cords.

glottochronology A method of deducing, on the basis of statistical comparisons of vocabulary similarities and divergences, the family relationship of languages, as well as the probable date when the branches of a given family were separated from the common parent language (Swadesh). *See also* LEXICOSTATISTICS, TIME-DEPTH.

glottology *See* LINGUISTICS.

glottopolitics Hall's term for governmental policies in regard to language matters (such as the use of dialects for school instruction).

govern To call for a certain case or mood; to demand or take (on the part of the accompanying form) the selected form of the noun or verb. *See also* GOVERNMENT.

government 1. Inflectional forms used to signal the place of a word in a syntactic structure (Gleason).
2. The type of agreement where the subsidiary taxeme of selection has to do with the syntactic position of the form (Bloomfield).
3. The influence exerted by one word, such as a preposition or conjunction, upon the case or mood of another word (in Latin, *cum* governs the ablative case; *nisi* governs the subjunctive mood).

gradation 1. The change from one vowel to another to

accompany a change in the degree of stress (*ford* vs. *Oxford*) (Webster III). *See also* ABLAUT, APOPHONY, MUTATION, QUALITATIVE (*also* QUANTITATIVE) GRADATION.

2. The relative amount of a quality in two or more objects (*fine, finer, finest*); occasionally carried much farther by the use of prefixes, suffixes and different words (degrees of bigness in Latin American Spanish: *requetegrandazo, regrandazo, grandazo, regrande, grande, grandecito, chiconcito, chicón, chico, chiquito, chiquitito, chiquichicho*) (Lenz, Entwistle).

grade *See* NORMAL (*also* REDUCED, ZERO) GRADE.

graded area A region showing characteristic speech features reflecting different degrees of influence from two or more focal areas; an area of spreading or flaring isoglosses. *Synonyms:* TRANSITIONAL ZONE, TRANSITION AREA. *See also* FOCAL (*also* RELIC) AREA.

gradual opposition A more elaborate framework set up by Trubetskoi, whereby oppositions are linear, not binary, and the relations are postulated in a set, by degrees; vowels and consonants are opposed; the gradual opposition of front unroundedness in vowels, done in degrees, appears as

(de la Garza)

grammar 1. That part of the study of language which deals with forms and the structure of words (MORPHOLOGY) and with their customary arrangement in phrases and sentences (SYNTAX) (Walsh).

2. The meaningful arrangement of forms in a language, according to the four taxemes of ORDER, MODULATION, MODIFICATION and SELECTION. In languages which use

bound forms, the grammar consists of SYNTAX and MORPHOLOGY, with the constructions of compound words and phrase-derivatives occupying an intermediate position. The DESCRIPTIVE GRAMMAR of a language consists of PHONOLOGY (PHONETICS and PHONEMICS), MORPHEMICS (MORPHOPHONEMICS, ARRANGEMENT, MORPHOLOGY), SYNTAX, and LEXICOLOGY. Various other classifications within the field of grammar are possible (de la Garza). *See also* CONTRASTIVE (*also* DESCRIPTIVE, NORMATIVE, PRESCRIPTIVE, TRANSFER, TRANSFORM) GRAMMAR.

grammatical alternation A formal alternation which is regular and depends upon grammatical (syntactic or morphological) peculiarities of the underlying forms; it is not automatic, nor does it depend upon the phonetic peculiarities of the underlying forms (in German, plural nouns are derived from singulars by the addition of bound forms, such as *-e, -er, -en,* which differ according to the gender of the underlying form; the alternation is regular and syntactic, but not phonetic or automatic) (de la Garza). *See also* AUTOMATIC (*also* PHONETIC, REGULAR) ALTERNATION.

grammatical analysis The determination of the grammatical categories to which the words in a sentence belong, as well as their functions in the structure of the sentence (Dorfman).

grammatical borrowing The borrowing of whole sets of related loan words, thus bringing about grammatical change in the borrowing language (Hindi borrows, apparently from Altaic, a new system of separate suffixes to indicate number and case, which replace the inflectional endings of Sanskrit). *See also* GRAMMATICAL CHANGE, LOAN WORD (de la Garza).

grammatical categories 1. The classes into which the words of a language are divided according to their formation, nature and functions (nouns, adjectives, verbs, etc.) (Dorfman). *Synonym:* PARTS OF SPEECH.

2. Large form classes which completely subdivide either the whole lexicon or some important form class into form classes of approximately equal size (number, case, gender, tense, mood, aspect, iteration, perfection); they may be inflectional or syntactic in form (de la Garza). *Synonym:* MAJOR FORM CLASSES. *See also* GENERIC (*also* OBLIGATORY, SPECIFIC) GRAMMATICAL CATEGORIES.

grammatical change When a language borrows from another language a large number of loan words containing the same derivational affix, and also many of the underlying forms of these loan words, the recurrent affix, in due time, takes on a distinct function; i.e., it becomes PRODUCTIVE in the borrowing language, thus bringing about a grammatical change (Middle English borrowed many Norman-French adjectives containing the derivational affix *-able/-ible,* as well as the verbs which underlay the adjectives; in due time, the recurrent suffix became functional as a derivational affix in English, leading to such hybrids as *lovable*) (de la Garza). *See also* LOAN WORD.

grammatical devices Word order, inflection, and function words; for writing, punctuation may be added.

grammatical equivalents Words or groups of words whose meaning is so similar that their substitution does not change or affect the meaning of the sentence (*hastily, with haste*).

grammatical form Tactic form (*q.v.*) with its meaning.

grammatical gender The classification of words as to gender regardless of logical considerations, such as natural sex (German *das Mädchen, das Weib, der Fisch*). *Opposite:* NATURAL GENDER. *See also* CASTE, GENDER.

grammaticalization The turning of a notional element into a structural one (Latin ablative singular feminine *mente,* as in *clarā mente,* "with a clear mind," becomes the Romance adverbial suffix *-mente* or *-ment*) (Marouzeau).

grammatical meaning The meaning of a grammatical form (*q.v.*); the meaning expressed by a grammatical ending, word order, or intonation; a grammatical category (plural, interrogative, subject); that part of the meaning which varies from one form of a paradigm to another (*-s, -ed, -ing*). *Partial synonym:* FUNCTIONAL (or STRUCTURAL) MEANING. *Opposites:* LEXICAL (*also* REFERENTIAL, SEMANTIC) MEANING.

grammatical moneme *See* MORPHEME.

grammatical stress The natural emphasis given in spoken language to the principal words in a sentence. *Synonyms:* MORPHOPHONEMIC (*also* SENTENCE) STRESS.

grammatical structure The totality of the grammatical (morphological, syntactical and other) features of a language.

graphema The idea about the writing of a symbol existing in the mind of the individual (one's mental concept of how to write the letter *t*). *See also* AKOUSMA, KINEMA, LEGEMA, ORAMA.

grapheme The smallest unit of writing or printing that distinguishes one meaning from another (English *b, c, d, f*); the components of the grapheme are its ALLOGRAPHS (*q.v.: p* of *help, pp* of *hopping, gh* of *enough*, etc.). *See also* COMPOUND GRAPHEME.

graphemics Carroll's term for GRAPHONOMY (*q.v.*).

graphic shapes All written forms, including not only those with phonetic significance, such as letters of the alphabet, but also those with symbolic significance (Roman and Arabic numerals, marks of punctuation, mathematical and astronomical symbols, etc.) (Fries).

graphonomy The systematic study of writing and writing systems (Hockett). *Synonym:* GRAPHEMICS.

Grassmann's law A phonetic law to the effect that when reduplication or other processes result in two aspirated consonants in one Indo-European root, one, usually the first, is deaspirated (the Greek root *the-* is redupli-

cated in the present tense of the verb "to place," but
thithēmi becomes *tithēmi*).

grave phoneme   A phoneme showing concentration of energy in the lower frequencies of the spectrum (Jakobson). *Opposite:* ACUTE PHONEME.

great English vowel shift   *See* VOWEL SHIFT.

Grenzsignal   "Border sign"; Trubetskoi's term for JUNC-
TURE (*q.v.*).

Grimm's law   A phonetic law describing the regular consonantal sound shifts that occur in languages of the
Germanic family (Indo-European aspirates, *bh, dh, gh,*
become Germanic voiced plosives, *b, d, g;* Indo-European voiced plosives, *b, d, g,* become Germanic unvoiced plosives, *p, t, k;* Indo-European unvoiced plosives, *p, t, k,* become Germanic fricatives, *f, th, h*). *See
also* CONSONANT SHIFT, GERMANIC SOUND SHIFT,
VERNER'S LAW.

groove fricative   A fricative, such as *s,* pronounced with
the tongue grooved by raising the edges (Gleason).
Synonym: GROOVED SPIRANT. *See also* RILL (SLIT)
FRICATIVE.

groove spirant   A sound produced by means of a front-
to-back channel in the tongue. *Synonym:* GROOVE
FRICATIVE. *See also* RILL (*also* SLIT) FRICATIVE (or
SPIRANT).

guttural   *See* VELAR.

H

half-open vowel   A vowel articulated with the arch of the
tongue halfway between the highest and the lowest elevation (*a* of *hat*). *Partial synonyms:* MID- (or MIDDLE)

VOWEL. *See also* CENTRAL VOWEL, CLOSE VOWEL, OPEN VOWEL.

half-rounded vowel A vowel uttered with the lips midway between the spread and the rounded position (*a* of *father*). *See also* ROUNDED (*also* UNROUNDED, NEUTRAL) VOWEL.

half voice *See* MURMURED VOWEL. *Synonym:* SOTTO VOCE.

haplography Omission in writing of one of two consecutive identical sounds or groups of sounds or syllables (author's inadvertent *haplogy* for *haplology* in an earlier work).

haplology Sporadic sound change whereby there is an omission in speech of one of two consecutive identical or similar sounds or groups of sounds or syllables (British *tempo'ry* for *temporary;* American *prob'ly* for *probably*). *Synonym:* SYLLABIC DISSIMILATION.

hard consonant *See* VOICELESS SOUNDS, UNVOICED.

harmonic *See* PITCH.

head (of an intonation) Everything from the center, inclusive, to the end of the intonation (Hockett).

head (of a macrosegment) The immediate constituent of an endocentric compound or construction having the same function as the entire compound or construction (in "a polite old man," the function of head could be assumed by "old man" or "man") (Hockett).

head word The center or base of a cluster; the noun (or verb) in a noun (or verb) cluster (Walsh); a word qualified by a modifier (but the relation between the modifier and the head is not always easy to state) (Fries); a word modified by another word or words in a sentence (Dorfman); the CENTER of a construction (*q.v.*).

heavy base A long vowel in a normal-grade root syllable (Greek *phāmí*). *Opposite:* LIGHT BASE. *See also* ABLAUT.

heavy stress The strongest of the four degrees of stress (as on the initial syllable of *battlefield*). *See also* STRESS.

helper verb   Bodmer's term for AUXILIARY VERB (*q.v.*).

hesitation form   The deliberate or accidental use in conversation of an indeterminate sound or form at the point of hesitation ("er . . . ," "uh . . . ," "whozis").

heterographic spelling   A system in which the same letter or digraph or group of letters stands for different sounds in different words (*gh* in *through, enough, ghost*).

heteronomous sound change   *See* CONDITIONED SOUND CHANGE.

heteronym   1. A word identical with another word of the same language as to written form, but different in sound and meaning ("to *tear* the page," "to shed a *tear*").

2. The literal translation of a word from another language (German *Wasserleitung,* literally translated from Latin *aquaeductus*). *Synonyms:* CALQUE, LOAN-SHIFT, LOAN TRANSLATION.

heteronymous   Having different names or designations ("son and daughter," "parent and child").

heterophemy   The wrong use, generally unconscious, of one word instead of another which it closely resembles in sound or spelling (*tortuous–torturous; cavalry–calvary; principle–principal*).

hiatus   A pause or break in sound between two successive vowels; INTERNAL if within the word (Latin vin*ea*); EXTERNAL if between two successive words (Italian l*o* *a*lbero, which breaks the hiatus by elision of the *o, l'albero*); the position wherein a vowel stands before another vowel, without an intervening consonant, and does not form a diphthong with the following vowel (French *naïve, Noël*).

hierarchy   A system of classes, subclasses and sub-subclasses, each working within the framework of the last (Gleason).

hieratic A cursive form of the ancient Egyptian writing, simpler and less pictorial than the hieroglyphic, used by temple scribes. *See also* DEMOTIC.

hieroglyph A pictographic or ideographic sign for a word or syllable, usually carved on stone.

hieroglyphic The most formal writing system of the ancient Egyptians, carved on stone. *See also* DEMOTIC, HIERATIC.

high vowel A vowel produced with the tongue raised toward the roof of the mouth (mach*i*ne). *Synonym:* CLOSE(D) VOWEL. *Opposites:* LOW (or OPEN) VOWEL.

hiragana The more cursive of the two Japanese kanas or syllabaries; "flat writing." *See also* KANA, KATAKANA, KANJI.

historical grammar That branch of grammar which traces phonological, morphological, syntactic and lexical phenomena of a language back to earlier stages of that language.

historical linguistics *See* DIACHRONIC (*also* DYNAMIC, EVOLUTIONARY) LINGUISTICS.

historical phonology *See* DIACHRONIC PHONETICS.

hold *See* SISTANT. A phase which is absolutely necessary for the utterance of a stop sound; it must be flanked on at least one side by a sudden transition. *See also* HOLDING PERIOD, PAUSE OF SILENCE.

holding period The period of complete closure between the onset or formation of the articulation for a plosive and the release of the breath stream. *Synonym:* PAUSE OF SILENCE. *See also* HOLD, EXPLOSION, IMPLOSION, SISTANT.

holes in the pattern Non-symmetrical features in a phonemic pattern (if the phonemic pattern of a language includes *p, t, k, b, d,* but not *g,* there is a hole in the pattern); the presence of gaps in one or more series of a phonemic paradigm (Martinet). Such "holes" have a tendency to become filled. *Synonym:* CASES VIDES. *See also* ATTRACTION, SYMMETRY.

holophrase A single word expressing an entire sentence or idea (Italian *diluvia*, "it's raining cats and dogs"; Latin *ningit*, "it's snowing").

holophrastic Having identity of word and sentence, as with the POLYSYNTHETIC (*q.v.*) languages (Entwistle). *Synonyms:* INCAPSULATING, INCORPORATING.

holosynthetic Entwistle's term for POLYSYNTHETIC (*q.v.*).

homogram A word resembling another in writing, though of different origin (French *faux*, representing both Latin *falcem*, "sickle," and Latin *falsum*, "false" (Marouzeau). *Partial synonym:* HOMOGRAPH.

homograph A word identical in written form with another, but different in origin, sound or meaning ("a *lead* pipe," "he will *lead* us"; "I am going to the *fair*," "my *fair* lady"). *Partial synonyms:* HETERONYM, HOMOGRAM.

homonym 1. A word identical in written form and sound with another, but different in origin and meaning ("to play *pool*," "to swim in the *pool*").

2. A word that sounds like another word with a different meaning, with or without a difference of spelling ("a *stout* heart," "a *stout* lady"; "fir," "fur").

3. A word pronounced like another, but spelled or capitalized differently (*pole, Pole; calorie, Calorie; read* [past tense], *red*). *See also* HETERONYMOUS.

homophone A word identical in sound with another, but different in written form, origin and meaning (*all, awl; to, too, two; bear*, "to carry," *bear* as the name of an animal, *bare*). *See also* HOMONYM.

homorganic phonemes Two or more different phonemes whose utterance requires the articulation of the same vocal organ (*p, b*, both requiring bilabial articulation); two or more phonemes articulated in the same part of the speech mechanism, but which differ in one or more features of phonation (the bilabials [p], [b], [m]) (Bronstein).

homotopical Articulated at the same point of articulation.

honorific A language form expressing respect, high esteem, etc., in speaking to or about a social superior (German *Sie,* Italian *Lei,* Portuguese *o senhor,* Japanese *gozaimasu* for the familiar *desu*). *See also* FAMILIAR FORM.

hybrid A word composed of elements originating from more than one language (*automobile,* with *auto* from Greek, *mobile* from Latin; *remacadamized,* with *re* from Latin, *mac* from Celtic, *adam* from Hebrew, *ize* from Greek, *-d* from Germanic). *Partial synonyms:* LOAN BLEND, MONGREL WORD.

hybrid language *See* CREOLE, CONTACT VERNACULAR.

hyperbole Overstatement or exaggeration ("a breathtaking panorama," "she was frightfully old").

hyper-correction *See* OVER-CORRECTION. *See also* HYPER-URBANISM.

hyperform A reconstructed form of a word resulting from over-correction, and mistakenly assumed to be more correct than the correct form it replaces (French *Bastille* for earlier *Bastie,* with new spelling caused by self-consciousness of speakers about pronouncing an earlier palatalized *l* as *y*). *See also* FOLK ETYMOLOGY.

hyper-urbanism The pronunciation of a word in an over-elegant or over-correct manner, sometimes because of its written form (*of-ten*), sometimes to avoid provincial or "incorrect" speech ("Whomever is involved in this prank has a poor sense of humor"). *Synonyms:* HYPER-CORRECTION, OVER-CORRECTION. *See also* SPELLING PRONUNCIATION.

hypocorism The use of diminutives, terms of endearment, baby talk ("Uzzums want uzzum's milk?").

hypotaxis Subordination; the use of subordinating conjunctions, relative pronouns, etc., to produce complex sentences ("The man who came yesterday said that

he had been here before") (Entwistle). *Synonym:* EX-
OCENTRIC CONSTRUCTION. *Opposites:* ENDOCENTRIC
CONSTRUCTION, PARATAXIS.

I

IC   *See* IMMEDIATE CONSTITUENT.

iconic   Characterized by a symbolism which purports to
present an image of the object described (Chinese
pictographs).

identification of languages   The study of the distinctive
features (phonemes, phoneme clusters, typical endings,
canonical forms, privilege of occurrence, grammatical
arrangements, etc.) which are peculiar to a given
spoken language, and of the written characters, combinations of characters, diacritic marks, etc., which distinguish a given written language, for purposes of
identification. *See also* GEOLINGUISTICS.

identifying units   Those distinctive, contrastive features
which permit the speaker of a language to distinguish
between two similar utterances which may sound identical to a non-speaker (Fries).

identity   The phonetic or semantic equivalence of two or
more words or expressions, synchronically or diachroni-
cally (Saussure).

ideogram   1. The picture or symbol that symbolizes a
thing or concept, but not the word or phrase for it.

2. The picture or symbol that symbolizes not the object pictured, but something the object is supposed to
suggest (as distinct from a PICTOGRAM).

3. A symbol or group of symbols representing a particular morpheme, word or phrase, but without separate phonetic representation of the phonemes involved

(3, +, $, used in an alphabetic language). *Synonym:*
LOGOGRAM.

4. A composite Chinese chara..or combining two other
characters for words of relate.. ..eaning (Webster III).

ideograph   A graphic character, symbol or figure suggesting the idea of an object without expressing its name,
or symbolizing an abstract idea or quality. *Synonyms:*
IDEOGRAM 3, LOGOGRAM. *See also* PICTOGRAM.

ideographic   Consisting of IDEOGRAMS (*q.v.*).

ideophone   A form that conveys an impression, not a
meaning, and describes a predicate in respect to manner, color, sound, action, etc.; said to appear in some
Bantu languages, and to include such impressions as
the gait of fat persons, a stealthy gait, appearing suddenly, issuing forth in numbers, etc. (Entwistle).

idiolect   1. The individual's use of language, with his own
speech habits and choice of words (Walsh); the individual's personal variety of the community language
system; the speech habit of a single person at a given
point of his lifetime.

2. Term used in American linguistics to describe the
ideal minimum phonemic system (of one individual),
in which there is nothing else than RANDOM VARIATION
(*q.v.*) (de la Garza). *See also* STYLISTICS. *Partial
synonym:* PAROLE (as used by Saussure).

idiom   A word or group of words having a special meaning which is not inherent to or determinable from its
component parts (*white paper* in the diplomatic sense,
as against *white paper* in the ordinary connotation);
an expression peculiar to a language and conveying a
distinct meaning that is not necessarily explicable by,
and may occasionally even be contrary to, the meanings
of its component parts ("to run out of something,"
"Monday week," "look out" in the sense of "be careful"). *Synonym:* LEXICAL CLUSTER.

idiomatic expression   *See* IDIOM.

idiomatic usage   The use of a word or expression with a meaning of its own, sometimes contrary to the principles of grammar or usage. *See also* IDIOM.

idiophoneme A phoneme peculiar to the phonemic structure of the speech of an individual (Jones-Hill).

imitation label The verbal description of a spoken sound ("French *u* is a high, front, rounded vowel sound") (Hall).

imitative word *See* ECHOIC WORD, MIMETIC WORD, ONOMATOPOEIA.

immanent linguistics A science that describes and defines language only on the basis of its own, inner presuppositions (Hjelmslev).

immediate constituent (or **IC**) 1. One of the two or more constituents from which any construction is directly formed (in "my English friend wrote this poem," "my English friend" and "wrote this poem" are the two IC's of the sentence; "my," "English" and "friend" are the IC's of the subject; "wrote" and "this poem" are IC's of the predicate; "this" and "poem" are the IC's of the object of the verb) (Walsh). *See also* CONSTITUENT, ULTIMATE CONSTITUENT.

2. One of the constituents into which a construction can be immediately broken down into successive layers or levels (de la Garza).

immediate speech Speech referring to a present, visible, tangible situation, as opposed to DISPLACED, NON-IMMEDIATE, or REFERRED SPEECH (*q.v.*) ("Take this book") (Hughes).

immigrant language (or **dialect**) 1. The language of another country, spoken in communities composed of immigrants from that country, usually with the admixture of words and constructions borrowed from the language of the host country.

2. The language of the country that is host to the immigrants, as distorted by the immigrants' native speech habits. *Synonyms:* LANGUAGE (or PIDGIN) OF IMMIGRA-

TION. *See also* BORROWING, FOLK ETYMOLOGY, LOAN
TRANSLATION, PIDGIN CREOLE.

immovable speech organs The teeth, alveoli, palate,
velum, pharyngeal walls. *Opposites:* ARTICULATORS,
INITIATORS, MOVABLE SPEECH ORGANS.

imparisyllabic Not having the same number of syllables
in all singular declensional cases (Latin *iter,* genitive
itineris). *Opposite:* PARISYLLABIC.

imperfective A verbal aspect considering the action of
the verb in its progress (continued or repeated), regardless of its beginning or completion (Russian *davat',*
as against the perfective *dat'*). *Synonym:* DURATIVE.
Opposites: MOMENTARY, PERFECTIVE.

impersonal verb A verb denoting action by an unspecified or indefinite agent, normally used only in the third
singular (English *methinks;* Latin *ningit,* Italian *nevica,*
"it is snowing").

impingement (of an immediate situation) The use of
expressions which seem conventional, but have undergone a semantic shift for the purpose of signaling aware-
ness of the other speaker ("*Now,* this man I met yesterday was bald"; "now" in this usage does not mean
"at this time," but is interjected merely to draw the
listener's attention) (Hughes).

implosion A noise heard as a result of the complete
closure of the oral air passage (Dorfman); an inrush
of air leading to a glottalic suction stop, which occasionally accompanies AUSLAUT (*q.v.*) in American English. *See also* CLICK, INJECTIVE.

implosive A stop produced by drawing the air into the
pharynx by closing the vocal cords and pulling the
larynx downward, so as to create a slight vacuum above
it (rarifying the air in that chamber, and thus setting
up an ingressive air stream to fill the gap) (Gleason).
See also INGRESSIVE.

improper compound In flectional languages, a compound
in which the elements are loosely linked, and both or

all are inflected (Old French *mesdames*). *Opposite:*
PROPER COMPOUND.

impulsion   Term used by Marouzeau and Van Ginneken
for GLOTTAL STOP (*q.v.*).

impure marker   1. A connector that has no function but
to connect ("John *is* here"; "*as* a friend") (Hockett).
2. A DIRECTIVE PARTICLE which is itself a constituent
in a construction in which it also has a structure-indi-
cating role (English prepositions *in, on*) (de la Garza).
Opposite: PURE MARKER.

incapsulating language   *See* POLYSYNTHETIC LANGUAGE.

included position   Said to be had by a word, phrase or
other linguistic form when it is part of a larger form
and does not constitute a sentence by itself ("yesterday," or "with my friend" in "I went there yesterday
with my friend") (Dorfman). *See also* ABSOLUTE
FORM, SANDHI FORM.

included sentence (or **utterance**)   One that forms part of
a larger construction, usually by reason of the fact that
it contains some type of sequence signal ("No, he's
not here" in reply to "Is Mr. Smith in?") (Fries-Sledd).
See also SEQUENCE SENTENCE (or UTTERANCE).

inclusive first person   In some languages, a form of *we*
that includes the hearer, as against one that excludes
him. *Opposite:* EXCLUSIVE FIRST PERSON.

incongruity   The meaning differences attached to words
in different languages which are ostensibly equivalent
(Latin *altus* corresponds to English *high,* but also to
English *deep*) (Sturtevant).

incontiguous assimilation   *See* ASSIMILATION. *Synonyms:*
DILATION, DISTANT ASSIMILATION.

incontiguous dissimilation   *See* DISSIMILATION. *Synonym:*
DISTANT DISSIMILATION.

incorporating language   *See* POLYSYNTHETIC LANGUAGE.

incorporating sounds   Sounds and sound combinations
which are taken into one language to which they are
not native from another (initial [ts] in *tsetse fly;* Ger-

man *ach-Laut* [χ] in *Bach;* initial [ʃm] combination in *schmo*).

incorporation *See* ABSORPTION 1.

indeclinable Incapable of being inflected; having only one form, and incapable of showing distinctions of number, gender, case, etc. (English definite article or adjective; Russian *kino*). *Partial synonym:* INVARIABLE.

independent element A word or group of words having no grammatical connection with the rest of the sentence in which it is used (an interjection, such as *Oh* in "Oh, come in!").

indicator *See* PHONETIC INDICATOR.

indigenous language A language native to the region where it is spoken, and not demonstrably imported into it (Hawaiian in Hawaii), or imported in the past, but now the current language of the majority of the population (English in the United States).

indirect spelling The use of a spelling device to indicate something different from its ostensible meaning (the double *l* in German *Teller* does not indicate a lengthened *l,* but shortness of the preceding vowel; the *e* of English *make* does not indicate that it should be pronounced, but that the preceding *a* has the sound of a diphthong (Saussure).

induced *See* INDUCER.

inducer In ASSIMILATION, DISSIMILATION, ANALOGY (*q.v.*), the element that starts the change (in Latin *peregrinum* to French *pèlerin, r* is the inducer, *l* the induced) (Marouzeau). *Partial synonyms:* ASSIMILATING (or ASSIMILATORY) PHONEME, DISSIMILATING (or DISSIMILATORY) PHONEME.

infection 1. Incontiguous retrogressive assimilation (*q.v.*), particularly of the umlaut type (in German *Sätze* from singular *Satz,* the root vowel *a* is said to be infected by the final front vowel) (Gray).
2. The influence on a speech sound of the vowel sound preceding or following (Webster III); this would in-

clude incontiguous progressive assimilation and vowel
harmony (*q.v.*).

infix A formative or type of affix inserted within the
word (the *n* in the present tense of Latin *linquo,*
whose stem is *lic-,* as shown by *liqui, lic-tus;* Arabic
iq-ta-raba, "to cause oneself to come near," from *qariba,*
"to be near"; British colloquial *damn* in *inde-damn-
pendent*).

inflection 1. The addition of certain endings to the base
of a word to express grammatical relationships, functions and aspects; common in synthetic languages, but
little used in analytical tongues. *See also* ACCIDENCE,
CONJUGATION, DECLENSION.

2. Where one stem or underlying form occurs in fixed
order with a paradigmatic set or class of inflections,
all of which differ in syntactic function; only one member of the paradigmatic class can be attached to the
stem, and this closes the construction. Inflection is a
predictable, regular, almost completely productive process, which seldom violates the morphophonemic rules
of the language. Constructions which result from the
process of inflection are endocentric. In these terms,
inflection is very different from the linguistic process
of derivation in language (de la Garza).

inflectional affix 1. A prefix or suffix that has no independent meaning and cannot be used by itself (*-us* in
Latin *murus*) (Dorfman).

2. A bound form which has only grammatical meaning,
and which, when added to a stem, usually follows the
morphophonemic rules of the language, and closes an
endocentric construction (de la Garza). *See also*
CUMUL, INFLECTION.

inflectional ending *See* INFLECTIONAL AFFIX (*also* SUF-
FIX).

inflectional language A language characterized by internal change, prefixes and suffixes to indicate grammatical relations (Sanskrit, Greek, Latin, Russian). *See also*

AGGLUTINATIVE (*also* ISOLATING, POLYSYNTHETIC) LAN-
GUAGE.

inflexion, inflexional *See* INFLECTION, INFLECTIONAL.

informant 1. A native speaker of a language, or a person having near-native command of the language, who
serves as a model for imitation; his function is to il-
lustrate the sounds and forms of the language so that
he may be imitated or recorded, but not to explain the
grammar or structure.
2. A person supplying linguistic or cultural data to an
interrogator.

infra-word Within the word (morphology deals with
grammatical forms which are smaller than the word).
Opposite: EXTRA-WORD.

ingressive Sound produced with air going into the mouth.
Opposites: EGRESSIVE, PRESSURE STOP. *See also* SEC-
ONDARY FEATURES, SUCTION STOP (de la Garza).

initial glide *See* ON-GLIDE.

initial mutation A change in the initial consonant of a
word under given conditions; in the Celtic languages,
initial consonants change in accordance with the original final sound of the preceding word, or with the
position of the word in the sentence. *See also* ASPIRA-
TION, LENITION, NASALIZATION.

initial position Position at the beginning of a word; in the
case of a vowel, it may be said to have initial position
if it is the vowel of the initial syllable, even if it is preceded by a consonant or consonant cluster.

initiator In speech production, the pulmonary tract and
the articulatory tract (i.e., oral-pharyngeal cavity)
function actively; the former is responsible for various
levels of the larger articulatory organization, such as
breath, stress, and syllabic pulses, while the latter ac-
complishes all the great articulatory variations of speech
sounds. During speech, the normally slow-moving air
mass of the vocal tract is set in motion by the muscles
of the articulatory and pulmonary regions; thus, these

muscles act as INITIATORS, and are dealt with in MOTOR PHONETICS. During speech and singing, the air mass in motion is greater than in normal breathing, and the inhalation is short in relation to the exhalation. Exhalation is far more important than inhalation. *See also* ARTICULATORY PHONETICS, EGRESSIVE, INGRESSIVE, MOTOR PHONETICS (de la Garza).

injective A voiced stop during the production of which the glottis is moved downward to produce a rarefaction, so that the release of the oral closure is accompanied by a sudden influx of air from the outside; found in some West African languages. *Opposite:* EJECTIVE. *See also* CLICK, IMPLOSION, SECONDARY FEATURES.

inkhorn terms Words of Latin or Greek origin, borrowed by fifteenth- and sixteenth-century English writers in practically unmodified form, and used in "aureate" English (*furibund, obstupefact, magnificate, armipotent*); most have since dropped out of the language, but a few survive (*inflate*).

inlaut A medial sound or position in a word or syllable. *See also* ANLAUT, AUSLAUT.

inner closure In the formation of stops, the closure that is formed at the bottom of the lungs, with the air chamber extending from the diaphragm to the point where the outer closure is articulated (mouth, larynx, pharynx, etc.) (Bloch and Trager).

innovation A change in sound, word form or meaning, beginning at a certain geographical location and radiating outward to neighboring areas, or starting with an individual and spreading by imitation to other members of the speaking community. *See also* AFFECTIVE LANGUAGE.

inorganic An element which does not essentially and originally belong to the system or form under consideration (*p* in French *dompter,* from Latin *dominare*) (Marouzeau). *See also* ANAPTYXIS, EPENTHESIS.

input In transformational grammar, the term applied to

a construction that is transformed into another (according to certain transform rules) which is called the OUTPUT (input: "he goes"; output: "he does go," "he does not go," etc.).

inspiration   An intake of breath.

integration   1. The fitting of two phonemes into a system of oppositions, despite their low functional yield (*q.v.*) (voiced and unvoiced [θ], [ð] of *ether-either, thigh-thy;* but the two phonemes fit into the general system of voiced vs. unvoiced) (Martinet).

2. The regular use of a borrowed element, and its incorporation into an idiolect, dialect or language (*slip-koba,* used by Puerto Rican immigrants for *slipcover*).

intellectual variations   Trubetskoi's term for EMPHATICS, RANDOM VARIATIONS, STYLISTICS.

intension   *See* FEEDBACK, TRANSMISSION.

intensity   1. The force of utterance given to a phone (initial [p] of English *pat* has greater intensity than that of French *patte;* but the final [t] of the French word has greater intensity than that of the English); in the case of a consonant phoneme, intensity is usually attended by aspiration (*q.v.*) in English (but not in French).

2. Acoustic term, and attribute of sound, which is shown by the degree of darkness of the formants, bursts, etc., on the spectrogram. Intensity relates to the force or stress with which the sound is produced by the speaker, and to the attribute of loudness of the sound to the hearer (de la Garza).

intensity accent (or ACCENT OF INTENSITY)   *See* STRESS ACCENT.

intensive compound   A compound in which the meaning of one component intensifies that of the other (*stone-deaf*).

intensive language course   A type of language course in which there is great concentration of time and effort on the language-learning process, coupled with a methodology of imitation of informants and repetition.

interdental A sound formed by placing the tip of the tongue between the teeth (English *th,* Castilian *c + e, i,* or *z:* [θ]).

interdependence A function (*q.v.*) between two constants (*q.v.*) (Hjelmslev).

interference The negative effect of one speech habit on the learning of another; the transfer of the speaker's own features of sound, structure or vocabulary to the target language (an English-speaking learner who pronounces *h* in Spanish *haber,* or says *quiero a hablar* for "I want to speak") (Walsh); deviations from the norm of either language occurring in the speech of bilinguals as a result of their familiarity with more than one language ("he wants I should go") (Weinreich).

interjectional theory A theory that maintains that human speech originated from ejaculations uttered by primitive man under the influence of pain or emotion. *Synonym:* POOH-POOH THEORY.

interlanguage A generic term for all languages created or suggested for adoption for purposes of international communication; such a language may be natural, like English or French; modified, like Basic English; or constructed, like Esperanto. *Synonyms:* AUXILIARY (*also* INTERNATIONAL, UNIVERSAL) LANGUAGE.

interlinguistics The comparative study of widely known languages to determine the elements they hold in common, usually for the purpose of devising an interlanguage (*q.v.*).

interlude 1. A medial consonant sequence composed of a coda plus an onset (/kn/ of *picnic*) (Hockett).

2. A consonant or sequence of consonants which occur between successive vowels in a single microsegment, and cannot be assigned exclusively either to the syllable that includes the preceding vowel or to the one that includes the following vowel; such a consonant or se-

quence of consonants is said to belong structurally with both the preceding and the following vowel. ZERO INTERLUDES occur also in such forms as (idea /ajdijə/) (de la Garza).

internal change A modification occurring within the word and indicating a change in grammatical function (si*ng,* sa*ng,* su*ng;* goo*se,* gee*se*). *Synonyms:* FUSION, INTERNAL MODIFICATION, REPLACIVE, SYMBOLISM (Sapir). *See also* ABLAUT, UMLAUT.

internal flection Grammatical changes brought about by internal phonemic change or gradation (si*ng,* sa*ng,* su*ng;* Arabic *kitāb, kutub*). *Synonym:* INTROFLECTION. *See also* INTERNAL CHANGE, INTERNAL MODIFICATION, REPLACIVE.

internalize To memorize so thoroughly that what has been learned can be repeated as a ready and automatic response (Walsh). *Synonym:* OVERLEARN.

internal linguistics The pure study of a language in the abstract, without reference to non-linguistic features, such as history or psychology (Saussure). *Partial synonyms:* DESCRIPTIVE (*also* STRUCTURAL) LINGUISTICS. *Opposite:* EXTERNAL LINGUISTICS.

internal modification 1. Descriptively, a morphological process whereby there is an internal alternation of the morpheme to indicate a change in grammatical function (de la Garza). *See also* FUSION, INTERNAL CHANGE, REPLACIVE, SYMBOLISM.

2. Historically, *see* ABLAUT, VOWEL GRADATION.

internal open juncture Open juncture (*q.v.*) occurring as a brief pause of silence between two full vowels in the same word (*cooperate*).

internal pressures Paradigmatic (*q.v.*) forces resulting from types of phonemic opposition operative in a given sound system, which are believed to lead to structural symmetry (*q.v.*) through the addition of special combinations of relevant features or phonemes (the introduction of /ʃ/ into Spanish is facilitated by its sharing the voiceless fricative character with /f/, /s/, /χ/, and palatal articulation with /č/, /y/, /ñ/, /ll/) (Martinet). *See also* HOLES IN THE PATTERN.

internal reconstruction 1. The study of the formal and functional elements of a language for the purpose of determining its origin and previous history, when no related language is available for comparison.

2. The method of internal reconstruction was always used alongside the COMPARATIVE METHOD, even when it did not have a name (see, for example, LARYNGEAL THEORY). Internal reconstruction is possible when working with a given language so long as the conditions of change are the same as the conditions of morphophonemic alternation, and the rule is still phonological. Suppose a regular conditioned sound change becomes productive in a given language; it brings about irregularities in the grammatical system, and creates morphophonemic alternations; then automatic alternation, and allomorphs begin to appear in the paradigm. As long as the phonological conditioning factor is still present, it is possible to reconstruct internally. When, in subsequent sound change, the conditioning phonological factor becomes obsolete, the alternation becomes irregular and non-automatic; it is now strictly a morphological alternation. At this point, only partial internal reconstruction is possible. With time, analogy sets in as a leveling factor, and brings about more and more change to restore regularity in the language, and internal reconstruction becomes even more difficult. At this point, we are forced to have recourse to comparative reconstruction (de la Garza).

internal sandhi A term used to describe the morph in terms of alternations which take place within itself (French /rigurøz/ is in free variation with /rigurœz/, *rigoureuse;* this type of alternation is sporadic and unpredictable, and every French morpheme which ends in /-øz/ has potentially a matching allomorph which

ends instead in /-œz/) (de la Garza). *Opposite:*
EXTERNAL SANDHI.

international language   *See* INTERLANGUAGE.

international phonetic alphabet (IPA)   An alphabet devised for the purpose of representing graphically the
most important sounds occurring in the world's languages; the first successful attempt at an international
phonetic alphabet is attributed to Lepsius, a German
Egyptologist.

intersection (of acoustic allophones)   The confusion of
allophones of two different but similar phonemes (in
certain environments, an allophone of /š/ may be
acoustically identical with an allophone of /s/) (Hockett). *Synonym:* OVERLAP.

intervocalic   Between vowels; said of consonants and
consonant groups.

intonation   1. Features of phonemic accent (*q.v.*) pertaining to the sentence rather than to the individual
word; sometimes called a SUPRASEGMENTAL MORPHEME
(Bloch and Trager); the rise and fall in pitch of the
speaking voice; the modulation of the voice; the pitch,
tone quality and melody of speech, particularly when
used to make a syntactical or emotional distinction
("You went there?" vs. "You went there!"). *Synonyms:* GRAMMATICAL (*also* MORPHOPHONEMIC, SEN-
TENCE) STRESS.
2. The production of significant pitch characteristics in
a speech form (morphemes, clauses) where they are
an integral part of that meaningful unit; thus the term
intonation is applied to the characteristic pitch patterns
themselves (de la Garza). *See also* PITCH.

intonation contour   *See* CONTOUR.

intonation formant   A characteristic intonation pattern
that can turn a statement into a question or an exclama-
tion without any other structural device; counts as one
of the morphemes of a syntactic construction ("You are
writing to him." "You are writing to him!" "You are

writing to him?") (Hughes). *Synonym:* INTONATION MORPHEME.

intonation morpheme *See* INTONATION FORMANT.

intonation(al) pattern A unit consisting of certain pitch or tone variations, which contributes to the total meaning of an utterance (one intonation pattern makes "Leave!" a command, another makes "Leave?" a question). *Partial synonyms:* INTONATION FORMANT, INTONATION MORPHEME.

intrinsic meaning The meaning of a word which is supplied by the basic, or segmental, phonemes (the meaning of the word *really* when uttered in non-committal fashion). *Opposite:* EXTRINSIC MEANING. *See also* CONNOTATION, DENOTATION.

introflection Sweet's term for INTERNAL FLECTION.

intrusive consonant A consonant having no justification in the etymology of the word (*b* in French *chambre,* from Latin *camera*). *Synonyms:* EPENTHETIC (*also* EXCRESCENT, INORGANIC, PARASITIC) CONSONANT. *See also* ANAPTYXIS.

intrusive vowel *See* ANAPTYCTIC VOWEL.

invariable Having only one form; incapable of inflectional or other changes (Russian *kino*). *Partial synonym:* INDECLINABLE. *See also* ISOLATING LANGUAGES.

invariant A concept that shows a formal (and functional) distinction (German *der Mann,* subject; but *den Mann,* object) (Hjelmslev). *Opposite:* VARIANT.

invariant alternation A form represented in all environments by one and the same allomorph (de la Garza).

inverse derivation The formation of a derivative through analogy accompanied by, usually, the loss of a phonetic element (*pea,* derived from a collective borrowed *pease,* interpreted as a plural; *Chinee,* incorrectly formed on the assumption that *Chinese* is a plural (Sturtevant). *See also* BACK FORMATION, FOLK ETYMOLOGY.

inverse spelling An "erroneous" spelling which reflects

uncertainty on the part of the writer by reason of a change in pronunciation (*delight* for an older *deleite,* at a time when *gh* had ceased to be pronounced in words like *light* and *eight* (Bloomfield); a phenomenon of over-correction appearing in writing, as when Latin stonecutters inscribed *diaebus* for *diebus* because they were conscious of the fact that they were prone to use *e* for *ae. Synonyms:* REVERSE SPELLING, UMGEKEHRTE SCHREIBUNG. *See also* OVER-CORRECTION.

inverted Marouzeau's term for CACUMINAL (*also* CERE-BRAL, RETROFLEX, *q.v.*).

IPA *See* INTERNATIONAL PHONETIC ALPHABET.

irregular alternation An alternation which does not occur according to regular or stated conditions (English /mæn/, *man,* alternating with /men/, *men,* in the plural, and /ɔks/, *ox* ~ /ɔksən/, *oxen*), where the English plural morpheme -*s* (/-s ~ -z ~ -iz/) regularly occurs (de la Garza). *Opposite:* REGULAR ALTERNATION. *See also* SUPPLETION.

irrelevant Said of articulatory features of a phoneme which are non-distinctive or non-phonemic; but though playing no part in distinguishing meanings of words, they may be important in clarifying dialect differences and determining foreign accents (Dorfman).

iso- Combining form meaning equal.

isochronism A term applied to verse in which the amount of time between two primary stresses tends to be the same, irrespective of the amount of material between them ("a stitch in time — saves nine"); the effect is often secured by increasing or decreasing the pause which may always accompany a terminal juncture (Hill-Whitehall). *Synonym:* DIPODISM.

isogloss A line separating areas called isogloss areas, where the language differs with respect to a given feature or features; a line marking the boundaries within which a given phenomenon or feature is to be found (Dorfman).

isogrades Lines including isoglosses, but also folklore, cultural traits, etc., to indicate the boundaries of a given culture (Lehmann). *Synonym:* ISOPLETH.

isograph A line on a linguistic map indicating uniformity in the use of sounds, vocabulary, syntax or inflections.

isolate A separate language sound or phoneme (Smith).

isolated opposition The relationship of a set of phonemes whose relevant feature is not shared by other sets (the relationship between *l* and *r* is not paralleled by any other relationship in English) (Dorfman); occurs when a given contrastive feature between two members of a pair does not occur elsewhere in the language (the duration of the trill, which is the contrastive feature between Spanish /r/ and /rr/, does not occur elsewhere in Spanish as a distinctive feature of opposition) (Trubetskoi). *Opposite:* PROPORTIONAL OPPOSITION.

isolating language A language in which each word typically expresses a distinct idea, and is incapable of inflection or formal variation; variations in the parts of speech, and syntactical relations, are determined by word order and by separate particles, so that the sentence consists of a string of formally independent words. *See also* ANALYTICAL LANGUAGE.

isolex A lexical isogloss (*q.v.*) (Migliorini).

isolexic line A line on a linguistic map indicating the approximate boundaries of speech areas where there is uniformity in the vocabulary of the speakers and the use of words (Migliorini).

isomorph A morphemic isogloss (*q.v.*) (Migliorini).

isomorphic line A line indicating the boundaries of uniformity of grammatical forms, inflections, and other morphemic features (Migliorini).

isophone 1. A phonemic isogloss (*q.v.*) (Migliorini).
2. A phonetic feature shared by some but not all speakers of a language, dialect, or group of related languages (Webster III).

isophonic line A line indicating the boundaries of phonetically homogeneous speech areas, where identical phonetic features prevail in the pronunciation of a language (Migliorini).

isopleth *See* ISOGRADE.

isosyllabism A term applied to verse in which all the syllables are of the same length and occupy the same amount of time (French *la cigale ayant chanté tout l'été*) (Hill-Whitehall).

isosyntagmic line A line indicating uniformity in syntactical usage (on the same syntactic level).

isotonic line A line on a linguistic map indicating uniformity in the use of speech tones or tonemes.

isotype A system of writing that uses non-phonetic symbols of universal significance, designed as a medium of education, but also to convey information in ready visual form (the picture of one soldier to indicate an army division).

item-and-arrangement The listing of items and their arrangement (Hall); the static analysis of linguistic forms (the noun *book* plus the suffix -*s* gives the plural).

item-and-process The view of synchronic relationships as involving processes (*books* is formed by the addition of -*s* to the singular *book; men* by the replacement of *a* by *e*); this view requires the selection of one member of a set of forms as basic, with the others derived from it (Hall).

iterative numeral A numeral that answers the question "how many times?" (English *twice,* Latin *ter*). *Synonym :* MULTIPLICATIVE.

J

jamming A special form of SYNCOPATION (*q.v.*) occurring in Vulgar Latin; the elimination of a consonant originally present between vowels (*ego* > *eo; habeo* > *aio*) (Holmes).

Japhetic A hypothetical language family claimed to include North Caucasian, South Caucasian, Sumerian, Elamite, Asianic, Basque, Etruscan, etc. (Marr). The term had been previously used by Leibniz as roughly corresponding to Indo-European. *Synonyms:* ALARODIAN, NOSTRATIC.

Japhetic theory A theory to the effect that the pre-Indo-European languages of Europe were all related to one another and spoken by a single race or group (Marr).

jargon A collective term for words, expressions, technical terms, etc., intelligible to members of a specific group, social circle or profession, but not to the general public. *See also* ARGOT, CANT, CLASS LANGUAGE, JOBELYN, SLANG, SOCIAL STRATIFICATION, SUBSTANDARD LANGUAGE.

jobelyn The underworld cant (*q.v.*) used by the Paris lower classes in medieval times, illustrated in the writings of Villon.

junction A grammatical unit formed by qualified and qualifying terms (*the red barn*) (Webster III). *See also* NEXUS 2, RANK.

juncture 1. A bundle of sound qualities which accompany pauses in speech (Bloch and Trager).

2. The way sounds are joined together (*a name* vs. *an aim*); modifications of sound at word boundary or end of utterance (*nitrate,* with CLOSED JUNCTURE, as against *night rate,* with OPEN JUNCTURE; the quality of both *t* and *r* changes (Walsh).

3. Stress and pitch patterns end in certain characteristic ways, and thus automatically achieve phrasing by means of pauses, called JUNCTURE. Since no fusion takes place across the boundaries of these patterns, juncture belongs rather to the level of phonology, for the prosodic features of stress, pitch, and duration automatically take care of it. Trubetskoi holds that the pos-

sibility of a pause is always present, and that phonetic peculiarities with delimitative functions and with culminative functions serve as substitutes for these pauses. Harris introduced juncture to replace "syllabification" features, in order to account for the difference between *a name* and *an aim*. Haugen replied that juncture cannot account for all such divisions. Bloomfield accounts for juncture as a difference in stress (de la Garza). *Synonym:* TRANSITION. *See also* CLOSED (*also* DOUBLE BAR, DOUBLE CROSS, EXTERNAL OPEN, OPEN, PREPAUSAL) JUNCTURE.

Junggrammatiker *See* NEOGRAMMARIANS.

juxtaposing language A language that expresses grammatical relations and accessory concepts by prefixing classifiers to the words that denote the main concept (the Bantu languages) (Marouzeau).

K

kana A Japanese system of syllabic writing, originating in the eighth or ninth century and used, normally, only for word endings or to give a phonetic explanation of the KANJI (*q.v.*); a Japanese syllabary. *See also* HIRAGANA, KANA MAJIRI, KATAKANA.

kana majiri The Japanese system of using Chinese ideograms with small hiragana characters to the right of each ideogram to give its phonetic value.

kanji The Japanese system of writing, based mainly on Chinese ideograms.

katakana A Japanese system of syllabic writing, derived from standard Chinese ideograms, squarer and more angular than HIRAGANA (*q.v.*), and used mainly in scientific and official documents, telegrams, etc.

katharevousa Modern literary Greek, as opposed to the colloquial DEMOTIC or DHEMOTIKE (*q.v.*); it generally conforms to Classical Greek usage and rejects non-Greek vocabulary.

kernel 1. The basic part of a word, expressing the principal concept, idea or meaning; that portion of a paradigm which is a common element of all variants of that paradigm (*hipp-* in Greek *hippos,* "horse"; it is opposed to the stem, *hippo-,* which is used as a deriving or compounding form, as in *hippo-tes,* "horseman," or *hippo-kantharos,* "horse beetle") (Bloomfield). *See also* NUCLEUS 5, ROOT 1, STEM.

2. The simplest possible fundamental structure ("man bites dog") (Hall).

key *See* DETERMINATIVE 2, RADICAL 2.

kine The smallest unit of perceptible action, analogous to the phone (Birdwhistell).

kinema The idea about the motion of the speech organs existing in the individual's mind. *See also* AKOUSMA, CENTER OF BROCA, GRAPHEMA, LEGEMA, ORAMA.

kineme The unit of gestural expression; the range of kines which may be substituted for each other without changing the general interactional sequence; analogous to the phoneme (Birdwhistell). *See also* ALLOKINE.

kinemic description A description in technical language derived from microkinesic and macrokinesic recording (*q.v.*) (Birdwhistell).

kinemics The study of units of gestural expression (Birdwhistell). *See also* KINESICS.

kinemorph A complex of abstract motion particles from more than one body area; analogous to the morph (Birdwhistell). *See also* ALLOKINEMORPH.

kinemorpheme A class of mutually substitutable kinemorphs; analogous to the morpheme (Birdwhistell).

kinesics The study of non-vocal bodily movements used

in communication (Birdwhistell-Carroll); the systematic study of non-vocal, non-linguistic body motion playing a part in communications (hand gestures, raised eyebrows, shoulder shrugs, pursed lips, changes in stance, etc.) (Walsh). *See also* KINEMICS, PARALINGUISTICS.

kinesthetic feedback The feeling of one's own speech movement (such as where one's tongue hits). *See also* ASPECTS OF SOUND, AUDITORY FEEDBACK, FEEDBACK, INTENTION, KINEMA, TACTILE SENSATION, TRANSMISSION, VIBRATORY FEEDBACK.

kinetic consonant A consonant the pronunciation of which cannot be prolonged without change in quality. *Synonyms:* OCCLUSIVE, PLOSIVE, STOP. *Partial opposite:* STATIC CONSONANT.

koine 1. The form of Greek used during the Hellenistic and Roman periods, and resulting from a compromise or merger of the ancient Greek dialects.
2. A branch of language commonly used by a unified group in a self-contained area within a larger linguistic area, usually the result of a compromise among several dialects of the language (literary Italian, Bahasa Indonesia); it differs from CREOLE, PIDGIN and CONTACT VERNACULAR in being a deliberately sought sublimation of the constituent dialects rather than an unconscious and accidental merger. *Partial synonyms:* COMPROMISE LANGUAGE, UMGANGSSPRACHE.

Kulturkreislehre *See* DIFFUSION AND MIGRATION THEORIES.

kymogram *See* KYMOGRAPH.

kymograph An old mechanical device for recording oscillographic-type visualizations of sound, called KYMOGRAMS; its stylus was activated by a membrane, and it scratched lines upon a sooted scroll of paper, which was unrolled to the sensitive cathode ray oscilloscope; it recorded variations in the total amount of air pressure during articulation, while oscilloscopic vibrations traced single air particles. It involved linguistically ir-relevant data, such as phase, relative pitch and stress, yet insufficient linguistic data. Sound spectography, which is in harmony with human auditory and nervous centers, has superseded it (de la Garza). *See also* SPEC-TROGRAPH.

L

labial   A consonant produced with one or both lips, or a vowel for which the lips are rounded ([p], [b], [m], [f], [v], [w], [y]); a sound in which the lower lip touches the upper lip (BILABIAL), or the upper teeth (DENTOLABIAL).

labialization   1. Lip rounding; pursing or protrusion of the lips (Bloch and Trager).
2. Secondary feature of lip rounding added to the sound (de la Garza).
3. Historical process whereby an unrounded sound be-comes a labial. *Synonym:* ROUNDING. *Opposites:* DE-LABIALIZATION, UNROUNDING.

labialized velar   A velar (*q.v.*) sound pronounced with accompanying lip rounding ([kw-] in *quality*). *See also* SECONDARY FEATURE.

labiodental   A consonant sound produced with the lower lip touching the upper front teeth ([f], [v]). *Syno-nym:* DENTOLABIAL.

labiopalatalization   A SECONDARY FEATURE (*q.v.*) whereby a combination of labialization and palataliza-tion is added to the sound (de la Garza).

labiovelar   A consonant sound produced with the lips

rounded and the back of the tongue coming into contact with the soft palate ([w]).

laboratory phonetics *See* EXPERIMENTAL PHONETICS.

lag 1. Progressive assimilation (*q.v.*), usually of an accidental variety ("short-sleeved shirts of sheer-shucker") (Sturtevant). *Opposites:* ANTICIPATION, RETROGRESSIVE ASSIMILATION.

2. *See* COLONIAL LAG.

lambdacism Substitution of the phoneme [l] for another, usually [r] (Chinese immigrant dialect *chelly* for *cherry;* Tuscan dialectal *poltare* for Italian *portare*). *Opposite:* RHOTACISM.

laminal Pertaining to the blade (upper front surface) of the tongue; sometimes applied to palatal phonemes ([ʃ], [ʒ], [č] or [tʃ], [ǧ] or [dʒ], [j]).

Landsmål The modern Norwegian language, a consolidation of various indigenous dialects. *Synonyms:* New Norwegian, Nynorsk. *See also* RIKSMÅL.

language A tool of communication by which human experience is analyzed differently in each community into units (monemes), each of which has semantic content and phonic expression (Martinet); a system of communication by sound, operating through the organs of speech and hearing, among members of a given community, and using vocal symbols possessing arbitrary, conventional meanings.

language boundary An imaginary line drawn around a speech community, usually but not always enclosing a number of small circles indicating various speech islands (*q.v.*). The line is often thickened by sizable bilingual areas. *See also* ISOGLOSS.

language engineering The application of scientific knowledge to any sphere of human experience, specifically language, for the purpose of obtaining greater productivity and efficiency, whether machines are involved or not (Hughes-Miller).

language family A group of languages derived from the

same parent language; Hall distinguishes between FAM-ILY (group of rather closely related languages, such as the Romance tongues) and STOCK (group of language families, such as Indo-European, composed of the Germanic, Romance, Slavic and other families). *See also* AFFILIATION.

language identification *See* IDENTIFICATION OF LANGUAGES, GEOLINGUISTICS.

language of colonization The language of a politically, economically or culturally superior or stronger nation imposed upon the conquered or dependent nation, or adopted by the latter, as the language of official dealings, business, and as a cultural medium, parallel with or replacing the native language (English in India during the nineteenth and early twentieth century). *Synonyms :* COLONIZING (*also* SUPERIMPOSED) LANGUAGE.

language of immigration *See* IMMIGRANT LANGUAGE.

language shift The change by an individual who is bilingual from the use of one language as his sole or principal medium of everyday communication to another language.

languages in contact Two or more languages coexisting in contiguous areas, and constantly influencing one another in their development, despite the fact that they may not be genetically or typologically related (Rumanian, Albanian and Bulgarian, all Balkan area languages, but of different Indo-European families, seem to have developed in common the feature of a postposed definite article) (Weinreich). *See also* ADSTRA-TUM, CONVERGENCE AREA, DIFFUSION 1, PERIPHERAL LANGUAGE.

language strata The different vocabularies used by a single individual, for colloquial, professional or trade use, or for formal speech and writing (Emerscn).

language system *See* LANGUE.

langue That part of the language system which is inherited or institutional; a complete and homogeneous grammatical system used by an entire community, as against an individual's verbal message or PAROLE (*q.v.*) (Saussure).

laryng(e)al 1. A phonetic term which refers to sounds whose production originates at the glottis, and which involve a constriction of the larynx. *Synonym:* GLOTTAL.

2. Any of a set of three or four phonemes reconstructed, on the basis of indirect evidence, for Indo-European (Kuriłowicz). *See* LARYNGEAL THEORY.

laryngeal theory In 1881–1882, de Saussure, the structuralist later to be known as the father of modern linguistics, wrote his doctoral dissertation on the Indo-European vowel system. He was puzzled by the fact that the *schwa* ([ə]) showed up in a set of correspondences that was irregular, with all corresponding members showing the loss of a sound (Indo-European $e\underset{.}{i} >$ i, $e\underset{.}{u} > u$, $er > r$ [in Sanskrit], $\bar{e} > ə_1$). By comparison and internal reconstruction, Saussure set up the hypothesis that something must also have disappeared in $\bar{e}$ to yield [$ə_1$]; that this sound must have been a laryngeal [h]; and that the change [e + (h)] > [$\bar{e}$] > [ə] must have taken place. This was viewed as very speculative, until Kuriłowicz discovered that in Hittite the laryngeal did occur in this position. The theory that the laryngeals had been lost thus became accepted as certain (de la Garza). *See also* TRILITERAL THEORY.

laryngoscope An instrument for examining the interior and movements of the larynx.

lateral A consonant sound produced with complete closure in the front of the oral cavity, but incomplete closure at one or both sides of the tongue, to permit the escape of air ([l]). *See also* APICO-DENTAL LATERAL.

lateral areas The outer fringes of an imaginary circle surrounding a center of radiation, where innovations have not yet replaced archaic forms. *Synonym:* MARGI-

NAL AREAS. *See also* AGE-AREA THEORY, PERIPHERAL THEORY.

Lautgesetz *See* PHONETIC LAW, SOUND LAW.

Lautverschiebung 1. *See* CONSONANT SHIFT, GERMANIC SOUND SHIFT, GRIMM'S LAW.

2. Occasionally used for MUTATION (*q.v.*).

law of distribution *See* DISTRIBUTION, LAW OF.

lax 1. A vowel sound pronounced with lesser muscular tension in the speech organs ([ɪ], [ɛ], vs. [i], [e]). *Synonyms:* OPEN (*also* WIDE, LOOSE) VOWEL. *Opposites:* TENSE 1 (or NARROW) VOWEL.

2. A sound produced with weaker breath pressure, less vigorous action of the lips or tongue (i.e., less muscular strain and deformity of the vocal tract), and correspondingly lesser concentration of energy in the spectrum and in time. *Opposite:* TENSE 3. *See also* SECONDARY FEATURES (de la Garza).

leap An assumed sudden change in phonetic or semantic development rather than a product of slow evolution; such changes are assumed to be due to imperfect hearing and reproduction on the part of new-generation speakers (/f/ in *enough* from an earlier /enouwγ/) (Jespersen).

learned word A word or form which did not develop popularly, in accordance with the phonetic laws of change of the language, but was introduced by clerical or scholarly use from the Classical lexicons (*episcopacy* vs. *bishopric*). *Synonym:* BOOK WORD. *Opposite:* POPULAR WORD. *See also* SEMI-LEARNED WORD.

legema The idea about movements made, consciously or unconsciously, by the vocal organs when we read, audibly or silently. *See also* AKOUSMA, GRAPHEMA, KINEMA, ORAMA.

lengthening *See* COMPENSATORY LENGTHENING.

lenis (or **lene**) A stop produced with weaker, laxer articulation and, usually, no aspiration (English /b/, /d/, /g/). *Opposite:* FORTIS. *See also* TENUIS.

lenition 1. A phonetic change in the Celtic languages, undergone by a consonant when between vowels, as well as the change of an initial consonant under the influence of the final sound of the preceding word; the replacement of a consonant by a phonetically related voiced consonant requiring less energy of articulation ([k] > [g]). *Partial synonyms:* INITIAL MUTATION, SONORIZATION, VOICING.

2. The maintenance of an opposition between two phonemes on distinct levels which tend to merge, by a change in one to correspond with the change in the other (if originally there is opposition between a geminated and a single consonant, such as *atta — *ata, with separate meanings, and if the geminated consonant becomes simple, so that the two phonemes would merge, the original *ata may become *atha, so that where originally the opposition was between double and single, now it is between plosive and spirant) (Hughes).

lento forms Full forms of words, spoken with full stress (*mistress* vs. the current pronunciation of *Mrs.;* French *moi* vs. *me,* both from Latin *mē*) (Gray). *Synonym:* STRONG FORMS. *Opposites:* ALLEGRO FORMS, WEAK FORMS.

leveling Regularization by analogy of irregular forms; a change of one form to conform with another though related form (Middle English *sang,* singular, and *sungen,* plural, both become Modern English *sang;* Old French *aim, aimes, aimet, amons, amez, aiment* become Modern French *aime, aimes, aime, aimons, aimez, aiment,* with extension of *ai* throughout the entire tense). *Synonym:* ANALOGY.

levels of articulation The level of content or meaning (morphemes) and the level of expression (phonemes) (Martinet).

lexeme A meaningful spoken form (word or stem) that is an item of vocabulary, abstracted from sentence

words; a complete grammatical form. *Synonym:* LEXI-
CAL MONEME. *See also* FORMANT 4.

lexical   Relating to the total stock of linguistic signs or
morphemes in a language; relating to words, word formatives and vocabulary, as distinct from grammatical
forms and constructions (*book, run*) (Saporta).

lexical category   A class of signs expressing ideas des-
tined to be linked or combined in discourse by grammatical link words or particles (Bally).

lexical change   Change in the vocabulary, or total word
stock, of a language, through the processes of derivation, composition, functional change, borrowing, coinage, loss of words, etc. *Synonym:* VOCABULARY CHANGE.

lexical cluster   A combination of two or more words,
usually a verb and a preposition, or a verb and an
adverb, with a special meaning that is not evident from
any component of the cluster ("to call up," "to bring
up," "to carry on") (Anthony). *Partial synonyms:*
IDIOM, IDIOMATIC EXPRESSION.

lexical collocation   *See* COLLOCATION.

lexical form   A linguistic form considered merely in its
purely lexical character as a vocabulary item. *Synonyms:* CONTENT WORD, FULL WORD, SEMANTEME. *Opposites:* EMPTY WORD, FORM WORD.

lexical meaning   The vocabulary meaning of a term such
as *boy,* even though used in a functional manner, as
in *boy's* or *boys* (Sturtevant). *Synonyms:* REFERENTIAL
(*also* SEMANTIC) MEANING. *Opposites:* FUNCTIONAL
(*also* GRAMMATICAL) MEANING.

lexical moneme   Martinet's term for LEXEME (*q.v.*).

lexical word   *See* LEXICAL FORM.

lexicography   The listing and describing of the words or
morphemes of a language, particularly from the standpoint of meaning, with the possible addition of derivation and history.

lexicology   The semantic or morphological study of the
linguistic stock of a language, particularly as to con-

tent, meaning, or use of the individual forms; the study of the words in a language, their meaning and use, their derivation and history.

lexicon The total stock of linguistic signs (words or morphemes or both) in a given language; the list of all the words in a language.

lexicostatistics A technique for estimating from a statistical comparison of vocabulary samplings of two languages the amount of time during which they have diverged from a common parent language. *See also* GLOTTOCHRONOLOGY, TIME-DEPTH.

lexis The grammarian's interest in words; those aspects of linguistic form which grammar cannot handle (the organization of vocabulary; the restrictions which vocabulary items impose on each other; the tendency of one lexical item to go with another, as in "spick and span," "hale and hearty," "auspicious occasion"; etc. (Crystal).

liaison In traditional grammar, linking or ligature; the pronunciation of an otherwise silent final consonant of a word when the following word begins with a vowel sound, for the sake of maintaining the canonical form representative of that language; the two words are thus pronounced as a unit, with common syllabic division (French *les hommes* [le + zɔm]; New England *far off* as against *far cry* [fa + rɔf], [far + kraj]). *See also* SANDHI, EXTERNAL SANDHI.

ligative article A form of the article repeated before the adjective when the latter follows the noun, thus acting as a discontinuous morpheme (*q.v.*) (Greek *ho kyōn ho megas*, "the big dog," literally "the dog the big"; French *le garçon le plus intelligent*, "the most intelligent boy," literally "the boy the most intelligent") (Gray).

light base 1. A short vowel in the root syllable (*e* in Greek *pétomai*).

2. A reflex of the reduced grade of a long vowel, rep-

resented in Indo-European construction by the shwa [ə]. *Opposite:* HEAVY BASE. *See also* ABLAUT.

light syllable An unaccented or unstressed syllable that is obscured in pronunciation (British *int'resting*).

light vowel An unaccented or unstressed vowel, pronounced more or less obscurely and indistinctly, to the point of syncopation (the last two vowels of *general* [ˈdʒɛn-r-l̩]). *Synonym:* ATONIC VOWEL.

linear opposition *See* GRADUAL OPPOSITION.

linear phoneme *See* SEGMENTAL PHONEME.

linear writing A system of writing using signs which are linear designs, or other signs not recognizable as pictures of objects. *Opposite:* PICTOGRAPHIC WRITING.

lingua franca 1. A contact vernacular (*q.v.*) used during the Middle Ages and Renaissance in the Mediterranean area and based primarily on Italian, but with heavy admixtures from Arabic, French, Spanish, Greek, etc. *Synonym:* SABIR.
2. A tongue of common intercourse among people of different language backgrounds (English among people from different parts of India). *Synonym:* VEHICULAR LANGUAGE.

linguistic analysis The scientific analysis of the phonemic and grammatical structure of a language or group of languages, with determination and classification of phonemes and allophones, morphemes and allomorphs, etc. *See also* COLLATION, GATHERING.

linguistic areas Different vocabularies used by individuals at different periods of their lives, as well as those used by different social strata (Emerson).

linguistic atlas A set of maps recording dialectal variations of pronunciation, vocabulary, inflectional forms, and idioms. *Synonym:* DIALECT ATLAS. *See also* LINGUISTIC GEOGRAPHY.

linguistic distribution Geolinguistically, the geographical location of the world's languages, together with relevant information concerning number of speakers, economic and cultural status, etc. *See also* DISTRIBUTION 2, GEOLINGUISTICS.

linguistic form Any phonetic form that has meaning; a meaningful unit of speech (allomorph, morpheme, word, phrase, clause, sentence). *Synonym:* SPEECH FORM.

linguistic geography The study and classification of the geographical extent and boundaries of linguistic phenomena; the study of language differences in a given speech area, and the mapping or charting of their distribution. *Synonyms:* AREA LINGUISTICS, DIALECT GEOGRAPHY, GEOGRAPHICAL LINGUISTICS. *See also* DIALECTOLOGY, NEOLINGUISTS.

linguistic island *See* SPEECH ISLAND.

linguistic minority A group of persons, usually a racial or ethnical minority, whose native tongue and language of everyday use are different from those of the majority of the inhabitants of the country (Pennsylvania German speakers in the United States).

linguistic norm The usage of the majority of the speakers of a language, which determines the standard form of the language, or the NORM (de la Garza).

linguistic norm (doctrine of the) The belief that language is responsible to an expressive ideal, and that such confusions as *uninterested/disinterested, imply/infer,* should be repressed, because they bring about a loss in precision without a corresponding gain (Richards-Hartung). *Opposite:* USAGE (DOCTRINE OF).

linguistic ontogeny *See* ONTOGENY.

linguistic replacement *See* REPLACEMENT.

linguistics 1. In general, the study of man's speech habits; the descriptive analysis of the structures or systems in language—PHONEMICS, MORPHEMICS, MORPHOPHONEMICS, SYNTAX (de la Garza).

2. The study of human speech in its various aspects (units, nature, structure, modifications of language, languages or a language, including phonetics, phonology,

morphology, accentuation, syntax, semantics, general or philosophical grammar, the relation between speech and writing (Webster III).

3. The systematic study of language, or of one or more languages and dialects; linguistics attempts to describe languages and dialects, not to prescribe correct usage (DESCRIPTIVE LINGUISTICS); it analyzes the structure of a language (STRUCTURAL LINGUISTICS); HISTORICAL or DIACHRONIC LINGUISTICS deals with chronological changes in languages, SYNCHRONIC LINGUISTICS with one or more languages at the same point of time; COMPARATIVE LINGUISTICS may be synchronic, dealing with relationships at one point in time between different languages having a common origin; or diachronic, comparing different forms of one language at different points in time; APPLIED LINGUISTICS refers to the use by language teachers of the findings of linguists; CONTRASTIVE LINGUISTICS (or CONTRASTIVE ANALYSIS) compares the natural language of the learner with the target language, to give special attention to areas of maximum contrast (Walsh). *Synonyms:* GLOTTOLOGY, LINGUISTIC SCIENCE, SCIENCE OF LANGUAGE. *See also* EXPLICATIVE (*also* EXPLICATORY, EXTERNAL, FUNCTIONAL) LINGUISTICS, PHILOLOGY.

linguistic science *See* LINGUISTICS.

linguistic sign *See* SIGN.

linguistic typology 1. The classification of languages according to their structural features (not to be confused with AREAL or GENETIC CLASSIFICATION, *q.v.*). *See also* AGGLUTINATIVE (*also* INFLECTIONAL, ISOLATING, POLYSYNTHETIC) LANGUAGE.

2. A type of linguistic classification now done for the purpose of arriving at certain variables in language which are UNIVERSALS. In the nineteenth century linguistic typology was done on the grammatical level; linguists at the time thought that typology would supply a deeper understanding and knowledge of genetic re-

lationships; but the criteria were never well stated or applied, and great confusion between typological and genetic classification resulted. In the twentieth century, PHONOLOGICAL TYPOLOGIES have been done by Trubetskoi, Jakobson and Hockett, who worked with vowels, and by Vogelin, who worked with consonantal systems. Sapir and Greenberg have also done some work with typology, on the grammatical level. The criteria for setting up typological classes may be based on sound only, meaning only, or both. Typology is an arbitrary, unique, exhaustive classification, where some classes may be left empty. No historical implications are involved, though genetically related languages often tend to share many features; geographical discontinuity is irrelevant; and discrepancies in methodology may lead to errors (de la Garza). *See also* SYNTHETIC INDEX.

linkage The connecting of words or phrases in a construction by the use of special form classes ("black cat"; adjective plus noun); of markers ("cats and dogs"; conjunctions); or of inflections ("man's hat"; possessive ending) (Hockett).

linking A phenomenon occurring when a speech sound that has an analogue in spelling is pronounced without pause before the vowel-initial word that follows, but not before a following consonant-initial word or a pause (French *les autres,* vs. *les livres:* [le + zo:tʀ] ~ [le + livʀ]). *Synonym:* LIAISON.

link word Bodmer's term for CONJUNCTION.

lip position One of the three factors important in the articulatory description of vowels. *See also* TONGUE ADVANCEMENT, TONGUE HEIGHT.

liquid A sound type, articulated with only partial closure, that is frictionless, and capable of being prolonged like a vowel; it can, on occasion, be syllabic ([l], usually [r], occasionally [n], [m], [ŋ]).

list The complete set of a language's phonemes or morphemes; said to be CLOSED in the case of phonemes, which are definitely limited in number for each language, to the point where their precise number can be stated; OPEN in the case of morphemes, which are practically infinite (Martinet).

listening discrimination   *See* AUDITORY DISCRIMINATION.

literacy   The ability to read and write one or more languages.

literacy coefficient   Geolinguistically, the percentage of speakers of a language who are able to read and write the language, with possible subdivisions according to their degree of proficiency.

literary language   That dialect of a language regarded as the best, and used for literary purposes; the formal language of literature as opposed to the colloquial language or vernacular. *Partial synonyms:* NATIONAL (*also* STANDARD) LANGUAGE.

litotes   Understatement ("senior citizen" for "old man").

liturgical coefficient   The degree of influence exerted upon one language by another that is used for liturgical purposes in the religion of the majority of speakers of the first tongue (Latin upon Italian; Arabic upon Persian).

liturgical language   The language used in religious services, and occasionally as a means of communication among its religious users (Latin for Roman Catholics, Classical Arabic for Moslems).

loan   *See* LOAN WORD.

loan blend   A new idiom which develops in a language as a result of borrowing, and of which one element is borrowed, the other native, but adapted to the loan original (*chaise lounge* for French *chaise longue*) (Hockett). *See also* HYBRID, LOAN-SHIFT, LOAN WORD.

loan-shift   1. The adoption from another language of a word similar to one that already exists in the borrowing language, with the form of the borrowing language and the meaning of the lending language (Portuguese-American *grosseria,* used with the meaning of "grocery"; in Portuguese the word exists, but means "gross act") (Hockett). The only change directly entailed is semantic.

2. The adoption of a borrowed meaning or culture item, but using for it a word already existing in the language (Italian *piede,* "foot" in the literal sense, used also in the sense of twelve-inch measure under influence of English *foot; gallone,* similarly used for "gallon" where its original Italian meaning is "braid"; *quarto,* used for the liquid measure, where the original meaning is "fourth"). Loan-shifts involve lexical and semantic change, and may also give rise to grammatical change. *Partial synonyms:* CALQUE, LOAN TRANSLATION.

loan translation A compound, derivative or phrase brought into one language through translation of the constituent parts of the term in another language ("reason of state" for French *raison d'état*) (Webster III). *Synonym:* CALQUE. *See also* LOAN-SHIFT.

loan word (or **loan**) 1. A borrowed or adopted word from another language (English *very* from Old French *verai; chic* from Modern French *chic*). *See also* ACCLIMATIZATION, ALIEN WORD, BORROWING, DOMESTICATED WORD, NATURALIZED WORD, PHONEMIC LOAN (or TRANSLATION).

2. A new form in the borrower's speech adopted from the donor along with the object or practice it represents. It is almost always a free form. The acquisition of a loan word in a language constitutes a lexical change; it often constitutes or entails a semantic change; it may even entail a shape change; also, other types of phylogenetic change, such as grammatical changes, alternation changes, phonetic and phonemic changes, may come about as a result of borrowing a group of loan words from one single source (de la Garza). *See also* ALTERNATION CHANGE, FREE FORM, GRAMMATICAL (*also* LEXICAL, PHONEMIC, PHONETIC, SEMANTIC, SHAPE) CHANGE.

localism A word, idiom, grammatical or syntactic construction restricted and peculiar to the speech of a given geographical area or community (New York *boid* for *bird*).

localization *See* POINT OF ARTICULATION.

logical conjunction (or **disjunction**) *See* COMMUTATION, PROCESS, SYSTEM (Hjelmslev).

logogram 1. A written sign representing symbolically one or more words of a given language or of several languages ($, &, 3).

2. Sometimes used to cover IDEOGRAM, PICTOGRAM, or both. *See also* WORD SIGN.

logograph *See* LOGOGRAM.

logos Greek word meaning "meaningful word."

logosyllabic A system of writing whose symbols represent either complete words or complete syllables of words, like later Egyptian or the modern Japanese *kanji*. *See also* LOGOGRAM.

logotactics The study of the area that lies between the word and the phrase or clause (Hill). *See also* DISCOURSE ANALYSIS.

loose vowel Bloomfield's term for LAX or WIDE VOWEL (*q.v.*).

loss of inflection *See* DEFLECTION, SYNCRETISM.

loss of words The disappearance of a word from the language, either because of the disappearance of the object it betokens (*sparking light*), or replacement by a new or borrowed word (Latin *galea* replaced by Germanic *helm* in the Romance languages), or for other, often obscure reasons (Latin *igitur, enim*). *Synonym:* AMORPHOUS CHANGE. *See also* ARCHAISM, OBSOLESCENCE.

loudness The perceptual attribute of the amount of sound a given speech articulation makes; this relates to the STRESS, or quantum of muscular energy which goes into every articulatory movement, and to the acoustic attribute of intensity (de la Garza). *See also* INTENSITY, STRESS.

Low Latin *See* VULGAR LATIN.

low vowel A vowel produced with the tongue in the lower half of the mouth, which is relatively wide open ([ɔ] of *awful*, [ɛ] of *met*). *Partial synonym:* OPEN VOWEL. *Opposites:* CLOSED VOWEL, HIGH VOWEL.

M

machine translation The production, by a high-speed computer, of an equivalent text in a second language on the basis of a text in a first language.

macrokinesic recording A system abstracted from MICRO-KINESIC RECORDING (*q.v.*), for KINEMIC DESCRIPTION (*q.v.*) (Birdwhistell).

macrolinguistics The whole field concerned with language, science and the sciences; its three subdivisions are: METALINGUISTICS, MICROLINGUISTICS and PRE-LINGUISTICS (*q.v.*) (Trager). *See also* PARALINGUIS-TICS.

macron A diacritic mark over a vowel, diphthong or syllable, to indicate length or duration (*mūrī*). *Opposite:* BREVE.

macrosegment A stretch of material spoken with a single intonation (Hockett); a construction consisting of MICROSEGMENTS (*q.v.;* smaller units), spoken with a single intonation (de la Garza); a continuum of speech between two perceptible pauses (Webster III).

major form class Any one of the parts of speech of traditional grammar (nouns, adjectives, verbs, etc.). *See also* FORM CLASS.

majuscule Large letter (capital or uncial). *See also* MINUSCULE.

makeshift language Jespersen's term for CONTACT VERNACULAR (*q.v.*). *See also* PIDGIN, RELATION LANGUAGE, VEHICULAR LANGUAGE.

malapropism 1. The deliberate or accidental substitution of one word for another more or less similar in sound ("she was a lymphomaniac"; "the pies are all occupewed"). *See also* SPOONERISM.
2. RESHAPING (*q.v.*), when the form intended was a learned one ("I'm simply ravishing" for "I'm simply ravenous") (de la Garza).

malformation The process or result of improper or unapproved formation of words by prefixes, endings, etc., from root words, by analogical extension (*five-thirtyish*).

manner (or **mode**) **of articulation** One of the three variables in a traditional phonetic classification of speech sounds, which refers to the type of sound-producing or sound-modifying mechanism in the mouth or larynx (de la Garza). *See also* AFFRICATE, FRICATIVE, LIQUID, NASAL, POINT OF ARTICULATION, SEMI-VOWEL, STOP, VOICE, VOWEL.

margin In a syllable, the onset, coda, or interlude (*q.v.*) (Hockett).

marginal Martinet's term for SUPRASEGMENTAL (*q.v.*).

marginal archaism An archaism occurring in a lateral area (*q.v.*) (Entwistle).

marginal area *See* LATERAL AREA.

marginal sounds Sounds occurring infrequently as phonemic forms, or but rarely in certain sets of speech (initial *shm-, shl-, shn-* in English: *schmo, schlemiel, Shnozzola*). *See also* PHONESTHEME.

margin of security The range within which variants of a phoneme or allophone may move without encroaching upon the sound range of another phoneme (Martinet).

mark The relevant feature which opposes two phonemes

to each other (voice in [p] ∼ [b], labial vs. dental quality in [p] ∼ [t]) (Dorfman). *See also* DISTINCTIVE.

marked member   That member of a bilateral opposition (*q.v.*) which is characterized by the presence of a relevant feature which marks the opposition (in the opposition *pin-bin,* [b] is marked by the presence of the voice feature, absent in [p], the unmarked member of the opposition; but if the opposition is viewed as tense-lax instead of voiced-unvoiced, then [p] is the marked member, [b] the unmarked.) (Dorfman).

marker   1. A special constituent or signal determining the function of a phrase; a word, morpheme, or combination of morphemes indicating the form class or grammatical function of the word that accompanies or includes it (Webster III).

2. A structural signal (*and, or*) which marks the relationship between two or more constructions without itself being one (prepositions such as *in* are IMPURE MARKERS, since they could be viewed as parts of constructions) (Hockett). *Opposite:* PURE MARKER.

3. A linguistic signal marking grammatical categories (*-s* added to a noun marks plurality, added to a verb marks third person singular; *sheep* has a zero marker in the plural, though plurality may also be marked by a numerical adjective ["five sheep"] or by a plural verb form ["the sheep are white"]) (Dorfman).

4. A word that identifies the function of another word (the determiner *the* identifies a noun, the auxiliary *will* or *must* identifies a verb, the intensifier *very* identifies an adjective or an adverb) (Walsh). *Partial synonyms:* DETERMINER, EMPTY WORD, FORM WORD, FUNCTION WORD, PARTICLE, POINTER, SIGNAL, STRUCTURE WORD.

mark of correlation   A relevant feature present in one series, absent in another, holding the two series together in a correlation (the feature of voice, characterizing [b], [d], [g], as against absence of voice in [p], [t], [k]) (Dorfman). *See also* MARKED MEMBER.

mass noun A noun not readily modified by a numeral (*music, bread, milk, oxygen*) (Walsh); a noun denoting a homogeneous substance or concept not subject to subdivision (*sand, butter,* as against "a pile of sand," "a pat of butter"); a noun that is used normally only in the singular, although it indicates numerous units, is readily accompanied by *some,* but not by *a* or *an,* and that needs to be qualified in order to indicate a single unit (*rice* vs. "a grain of rice"; *rices* is not ordinarily used, except to mean various kinds or types of rice) (Gleason). *Synonyms:* QUANTIFIABLE NOUN, UNBOUNDED NOUN. *Opposites:* BOUNDED FORM (or NOUN), COUNT NOUN.

mass word Concepts, properties or things not ordinarily separable into distinct component units (Jespersen). *Synonym:* MASS NOUN.

material content A concept or idea signified by a word which remains the same despite morphological changes (*dog, dogs* have the same material content) (Dorfman). *Opposite:* MODAL CONTENT.

matronymic A name derived from that of one's mother or maternal ancestor (*Nelson, Olafsdatter*). *See also* PATRONYMIC, TEKNONYMY.

maximum silence Any interruption of speech by a period of silence on the speaker's part which is either indefinite or longer than any of the other pauses observed during the course of the speech (Fries-Hughes).

mechanistic theory 1. The view that variability in human speech is the result of complex causes based on man's physiological structure, and particularly his nervous system (Dorfman).

2. An approach to language and linguistics based on objective methodology in recording and classifying language phenomena on the basis of observable forms

(Webster III). *Opposite:* MENTALISTIC THEORY. *See also* NEOGRAMMARIANS, NEOLINGUISTS.

mechanistic theory of change A theory that holds that the variability of human conduct, including speech, is due only to the fact that the human body is a very complex system, and that human actions are part of cause-and-effect sequences exactly like those we observe in physics or chemistry (Bloomfield).

medial 1. Situated between the extremes of initial and final in a word or morpheme (dee*d*ed).

2. As applied to stops in ancient Greek, synonymous with VOICED (*q.v.*) (Webster III).

medial accent Accent falling on a syllable other than the initial or final (prec*a*rious).

medial consonant *See* MIDDLE CONSONANT.

medial position Non-initial or non-final position of a sound or sound cluster within the word or word group unit (be*t*, fre*sh ch*eese).

median resonant 1. One of the vowels and semi-vowels pronounced with the mouth passage open at the midline ([r], [w], [j]) (Gleason).

2. A sound produced without occlusion along the lengthwise middle line of the tongue (Webster III). *Opposite:* LATERAL.

mediopalatal A sound produced at the middle third part of the hard palate, or of the palate as a whole.

medium vowel A vowel halfway between spread and rounded (b*u*t) (Gray). *Synonym:* NEUTRAL VOWEL.

melioration 1. A semantic shift undergone by certain words, involving and producing improvement in meaning (*bravo* from *pravus; knight* from *cniht*). *Synonyms:* AMELIORATION, ENHANCEMENT (OF MEANING).

2. The addition of a meliorative suffix, giving the word a more favorable connotation (*steward* from *sty-ward*).

melody *See* PITCH.

mentalistic theory The view that the variability of human speech is the result of complex causes based on the mental processes of individuals, and that specific factors of the mind must be assumed in order to analyze, classify and explain some or all of the phenomena of language. *Opposite:* MECHANISTIC THEORY. *See also* NEOGRAMMARIANS, NEOLINGUISTS.

merged form   The single form resulting from the merger of various inflectional variants; declensional, such as case forms, or conjugational, such as verb forms (Italian *muro* is a merged form resulting from the merger of Latin *mūrus, mūrō, mūrum*). *Synonyms:* DEFLECTION, SYNCRETISM.

merged verb   A verb combined with an adverb or other separable suffix (*blow up*) (Laird).

message information   A lexical item which is meaningful and not structural (Cheyenne "him not know road," where only message morphemes appear, and all structural morphemes are omitted) (Hughes).

metalanguage   Language used to speak or write about language (Hjelmslev); language used to describe the structure of another language; any language whose symbols refer to the properties of symbols of another language (Dorfman). *See also* OBJECT LANGUAGE, SYNTAX LANGUAGE.

metalinguistics   1. The science relating to METALANGUAGE (*q.v.*) (Hjelmslev).

2. The relations of language to other patterned systems of society, or to the rest of culture-determined behavior (Lloyd); the study of what people talk or write about and why, how they react to it, covering those aspects of linguistics which deal with the relation of language to the rest of the culture (Smith and Trager). *Synonym:* EXOLINGUISTICS. *See also* PARALINGUISTICS.

3. According to Hilbert's theorem, the use of technical language to make logical (philosophical) and scientific statements in mathematics and philosophy; i.e., using

language to make statements about language (de la Garza).

4. According to Trager, all that is left over after the forms, structures, or systems of language (i.e., MICRO-LINGUISTICS) have been abstracted from the PRELINGUISTIC phonetic substance (de la Garza). *See also* MACROLINGUISTICS, MICROLINGUISTICS, PARALINGUISTICS, PRELINGUISTICS.

metanalysis 1. The individual's interpretation or analysis of a preexisting form, including cases of FOLK ETYMOLOGY (*q.v.*) and MISPLACED JUNCTURE (*q.v.*), as well as the creation of new singulars from supposed plurals (*sirloin* for *surloin; an adder* from *a nadder; pea* from *pease; Chinee* from *Chinese*) (Jespersen); replacement of a previous form by a new form that makes better sense to the speakers (*Welsh rabbit* from *Welsh rarebit;* French *ma mie* from *ma amie*) (Hockett). *See also* AFFIX CLIPPING, NUMERICAL METANALYSIS.

2. A sporadic sound change whereby a form of unusual shape is reinterpreted as though it consisted of a sequence of more familiar morphemes represented by more familiar shapes. A boundary change thus takes place, whereby what was formerly part of one morpheme becomes part of another morpheme. This not uncommon process thus affects the morphological pattern of the language involved. Metanalysis potentially involves FOLK ETYMOLOGY, but it need not involve RESHAPING. Examples of metanalysis are the longer forms *peas* and *cherries,* originally singulars, which were reinterpreted as *pea* and *cherry* plus the noun plural morpheme /z/ (de la Garza). *See also* BACK FORMATION.

metaphone A free allophonic variant chosen in preference to another because regarded as more suitable to the type of speech used (*tomahto, eyether,* used in a given situation instead of the more customary pronunciations of *tomato, either*).

metaphony Internal vowel change of an anticipatory nature. *Synonym:* COMBINATIVE CHANGE. *See also* (VOWEL) MUTATION, UMLAUT.

metaphor The expression of an abstract concept by means of a physical analogy (*concord,* literally "with-heart"); the use of one word for another; likening one thing to another by referring to it as if it were the other one ("big drink" for *ocean*); a suggested analogy ("the ship *plowed* the sea"); a compressed simile of an implied comparison ("marble brow" for "brow white as marble"); a figure of speech in which one object is likened to another and given its name (*crane,* the name of a long-necked bird, applied to a machine that faintly resembles the bird). *See also* TRANSFERRED MEANING.

metaphrase A literal translation from one language to another (French *regardez dehors* for English "look out!"). *See also* PARAPHRASE.

metaplasm Any change in a standard or accepted linguistic form, whether by the addition or the omission of a sound or syllable, by the transposition of sounds or sound groups, or by any other phonetic or morphological modification.

metathesis 1. On the syntactical level, change of word order in the sentence.

2. Historically, sporadic sound change whereby there is a transposition of the order of sounds within the word or between words (Anglo-Saxon *wæps, bren* > Modern English *wasp, burn;* Latin *miraculum* > Spanish *milagro*). *See also* TRANSPOSITION.

metonymy Substitution for a word of another word of related meaning ("the deep" for "the sea"). *See also* CATACRESIS.

microkinesic recording A minutely detailed recording system using a notation whose symbols approximate the parts of the body and their movements (Bird-whistell).

microlinguistics 1. Structural linguistics proper (Lloyd); the formal analysis of language structure, laying the foundation for METALINGUISTICS (*q.v.*).

2. That part of MACROLINGUISTICS (*q.v.*) which involves the descriptive analysis of the structures or systems in language (PHONEMICS, MORPHEMICS, MORPHOPHONEMICS, SYNTAX) (de la Garza).

microsegment A stretch of material not broken by a plus juncture (Hockett). *See also* MACROSEGMENT.

middle consonant 1. Saussure's term for TENUIS (*q.v.*). 2. A mute in ancient Greek. *Partial synonyms:* MEDIAL (*also* SOFT, VOICED) CONSONANT.

middle voice A verbal form expressing that the action denoted by the verb is DYNAMIC (performed by the agent for himself, or generally affecting the agent); or REFLEXIVE (with the agent and the object the same) (Greek *lýomai,* "I loose for myself," "I loose myself"). *See also* DYNAMIC (*also* REFLEXIVE) MIDDLE.

middle vowel *See* MID-VOWEL, MIXED VOWEL. Occasionally used as synonym for CENTRAL VOWEL (*q.v.*).

mid-vowel A vowel in the phonation of which the tongue height is at a middle position in the mouth, i.e., at a point between the highest and the lowest elevation. *Synonyms:* HALF-OPEN (*also* MIDDLE, MIXED) VOWEL.

migration theory *See* DIFFUSION AND MIGRATION THEORIES.

mimetic word A word formed to imitate a natural sound (*buzz, crash*), or another word (*litterbug,* on the analogy of *jitterbug*). *Partial synonyms:* ECHOIC WORD, IMITATIVE WORD. *See also* ANALOGY, FOLK ETYMOLOGY, ONOMATOPEIA.

minimal language Jespersen's term for PIDGIN (*q.v.*).

minimal pair Two words sounding alike in all but one feature, and used to identify phonemes and allophones (*back-pack*; German *schon-schön;* French *mon-ton*). *See also* SUBMINIMAL PAIRS.

minuscule An ancient and medieval form of writing derived from the MAJUSCULE (*q.v.*), with simpler and smaller forms.

minus juncture *See* MUDDY TRANSITION.

mixed language A term connected with the spreading of innovations, in geographical linguistics, and the influence of one language on another; so far, there is no definite proof of any language having been so influenced by another that we cannot tell its own particular line of descent. Notions of mixed languages may arise in three ways : (a) by confusion of criteria in LINGUISTIC TYPOLOGY; it must be remembered that such criteria and classification are arbitrary, and not genetic; (b) by confusion between notions of genetic relationship and geographical factors, such as borrowing; (c) by reason of the existence of PIDGIN LANGUAGES (*q.v.*), which have a basis in some existing language, are used as auxiliary tongues, and are nobody's first language (de la Garza). *See also* CONTACT VERNACULAR, CREOLE, GENETIC CLASSIFICATION, GEOGRAPHICAL CLASSIFICATION, TYPOLOGICAL CLASSIFICATION.

mixed-relational element A word halfway between FULL FORM and EMPTY FORM (*q.v.*); a word having a certain amount of dictionary or lexical meaning (*is,* French *de*) (Sapir).

mixed vowel Migliorini's term for MIDDLE VOWEL (*q.v.*).

mixture *See* MIXED LANGUAGE.

mock-form A form deliberately created to produce a humorous effect (*discombobulate, rambunctious*) (Hall).

modal content The functional relationship of a word, as indicated by morphological changes (the singular and plural forms of the same noun have different modal contents). *Opposite :* MATERIAL CONTENT.

modal predicate A form that consists of or includes a

verb, and serves as the second part of a subject-predicate construction (Hockett).

model The shape of a loan word in the language from which it is borrowed (*foyer* in French as against its spoken form in English).

mode of articulation *See* MANNER OF ARTICULATION.

modification *See* PHONETIC MODIFICATION.

modified language A language deliberately changed in spelling, pronunciation or grammatical structure, usually for the purpose of making it easier to learn or of using it as an international language (English with simplified spelling, Basic English, Latino Sine Flexione). *See also* CONSTRUCTED (*also* INTER-) LANGUAGE.

modifier 1. A word, expression or clause qualifying or limiting the meaning of another word or expression.

2. Occasionally used as a synonym for DIACRITIC (*q.v.*).

modulation A feature of grammatical arrangement, or TAXEME, which involves the use of SECONDARY PHONEMES that convey grammatical meaning in the actual utterance of any morpheme (in English, the abstract morphemes *John* [ğɑn] or *run* [rʌn], in actual utterance, are always accompanied by some secondary phoneme of final pitch (! ? .); also, difference in the position of stress distinguishes *cónvict* from the verb *convíct*) (de la Garza). *See also* SECONDARY PHONEME.

molecule *See* SYNTACTIC MOLECULE.

momentary aspect *See* PERFECTIVE ASPECT.

moneme Martinet's term for MORPHEME, free or bound (he uses morpheme in the sense of bound morpheme only, and lexeme in the sense of free morpheme or formant, *q.v.*); one of a series of successive meaningful signs. The AUTONOMOUS MONEME implies not only a reference to an element of experience, but also a definite relationship to the other elements of experience to be communicated (*yesterday, quickly*); the FUNC-

TIONAL MONEME serves merely to indicate the function of another moneme (*to* in "he gives the book to John").

mongrel word   *See* HYBRID.

monogenesis theory   The view that all languages in the world originated and developed from one common parent tongue (Trombetti). *Opposite:* POLYGENESIS THEORY.

monoglot   A person speaking, understanding and using only one language. *Synonyms:* MONOLINGUAL, UNILINGUAL. *Opposites:* BILINGUAL, TRILINGUAL, PLURILINGUAL, POLYGLOT.

monolingual   *See* MONOGLOT.

monophone   A single sound, or the letter or written sign representing that sound. *See also* POLYPHONY.

monophthong   A phoneme produced as a single sound, and with one emission of sound; a vowel sound that throughout its duration has a single, constant articulatory position and acoustic structure, and whose boundary on either side is a consonant or a syllabic boundary (*father*) (Webster III).

monophthongization   The change of a diphthong into a single vocalic sound (Latin *au*ricula > Vulgar Latin *o*ricla). *Synonym:* DEDIPHTHONGIZATION. *Opposite:* DIPHTHONGIZATION.

monosyllabic   Consisting of a single syllable (*yes*).

monosyllabic language   A language in which all or most of the words consist of a single syllable; usually of the ISOLATING type (*q.v.*).

monosyllable   A word of a single syllable (*no*).

monotony test   A test devised for the analysis of tones in tonal languages; words believed to have the same tone are repeated one after the other, producing a monotonous effect; if a word with a different tone is inserted into the sequence, the monotony is broken, and there is acoustic assurance of the tonal difference (Gleason).

mora 1. In tone languages, several parts of the phoneme which may receive divergent tonal treatment (rising-falling, level-rising, etc.) (Dorfman).

2. The minimal unit of quantitative measure in linguistic analysis, especially for vowel quantities (Webster III).

morph A pronounceable series of phonemes which could function as a morpheme in a given language (in English, *pum,* but not *kvulpf*); any phonemic shape or representation of a morpheme (Hockett); in connection with any given morpheme, morph is equivalent to allomorph; any linguistic unit that may convey meaning.

morpheme A minimal unit of speech that is recurrent and meaningful; it may be a word or part of a word (*un-friend-ly, sit-s*); it is a FREE MORPHEME if it can stand alone (friend, sit), a BOUND MORPHEME if it cannot be used by itself (*un-, -ly, -s*) (Walsh). A distinct linguistic form, semantically different from other phonetically similar or identical linguistic forms, and not divisible or analyzable into smaller forms (Dorfman); a linguistic form that is not further divisible without destruction or alteration of meaning, and is the minimal meaningful unit; it may be monosyllabic or polysyllabic (*ant, rhinoceros*); it is relatively constant in a given environment, while the phoneme is realized only through its allophones (Fowkes); Martinet and Hughes reserve the term MORPHEME for BOUND MORPHEME (*-ons* of *travaillons*); Martinet further defines it as a GRAMMATICAL MONEME (*q.v.*). *Synonyms:* GLOSSEME, MONEME, MORPHOME.

morpheme types FREE MORPHEME; BOUND MORPHEME; STEM; ROOT; PREFIX; INFIX; SUFFIX; REDUPLICATIVE MORPHEME; REPLACIVE MORPHEME; SUPPLETIVE MORPHEME; PORTMANTEAU MORPHEME; CUMUL; REPETITIVE MORPHEME; SOCIATIVE MORPHEME; DISCONTINUOUS MORPHEME. *See also* PHONESTHEME (de la Garza).

morpheme word   A word that consists of a single free form or morpheme (*boy, man*).

morphemically conditioned alternation   A type of alternation which is conditioned by another morpheme, and which is always non-automatic (the alternation between /wajf/ *wife* and /wajv/ in *wives,* in English; the shape /wajv/ is required when the noun-plural morpheme /-z/ follows). *Opposite:* PHONEMICALLY CONDITIONED ALTERNATION. *See also* NON-AUTOMATIC ALTERNATION (de la Garza).

morphemic alternant   *See* ALLOMORPH.

morphemics   The study of the distribution and classification of morphemes, and the ways they combine to form words.

morphemic writing system   A writing system that symbolizes morphemes, not sounds or phonemes; roughly equivalent to LOGOGRAPHIC WRITING (*q.v.*) (Hockett).

morpho-   Combining form meaning "shape," "form," "structure."

morphological assimilation   The change of the number, case, gender, etc., of a word, resulting in its deviation from the regular form, and due to the influence of another word in the same sentence ("these kind of books"). *Synonym:* ATTRACTION 2.

morphological construction   A sequence of morphemes forming a complex or compound word (*unlike, baseball*). *See also* CONSTRUCTION, SYNTACTIC CONSTRUCTION.

morphological doublets   1. Two or more forms of the same word (MORPHEMIC ALTERNANTS), the choice of the proper form being determined, systematically and predictably, by its phonetic or morphological environment (*a* before consonants, *an* before vowels; French *le, la* before consonants, *l'* before vowels). *See also* AUTOMATIC (*also* MORPHEMICALLY CONDITIONED, MORPHOPHONEMIC, NON-AUTOMATIC, PHONEMICALLY CONDITIONED, REGULAR) ALTERNATION.

2. Cases of SPORADIC ALTERNATION, whereby some speakers of the same dialect acquire different habits of pronunciation for the same form (having the same meaning), using now the one, now the other in a random and unpredictable way; both forms may be defined as being phonemically similar shapes. Doublets could also exist as a result of ALTERNATION CHANGE, PRONUNCIATION BORROWING, and in LINGUISTIC ONTOGENY (*q.v.*) (de la Garza).

morphological extension 1. A form of ANALOGICAL EXTENSION, consisting of the formation of new words by the addition of suffixes, prefixes, omission of endings, on the analogy of well-known words.
2. The process whereby a part of a word is isolated to be used for the formation of new words, in the manner of a suffix (French *port-ier, lait-ier,* give rise to a false suffix *-tier* later extended to *clou-tier, ferblan-tier, bijou-tier*) (Marouzeau). *Synonym :* RECUTTING. *See also* ANALOGY, BACK FORMATION.

morphological processes AFFIXATION, REDUPLICATION, INTERNAL MODIFICATION, PORTMANTEAU MORPHEME, SUPPLETION, ENDOCENTRIC CONSTRUCTION (compounds), DISCONTINUOUS MORPHEMES, SYNCRETISM, BIFURCATION (de la Garza).

morphological relic A crystallized morphological form, surviving from an earlier stage of the language (Italian *diamine,* a cross of Latin *domine* and *diabole,* which preserves the Latin vocative ending) (Migliorini).

morphological word A word consisting of two or more semanto-phonetic elements consciously interpreted as such, or of two or more semanto-phonetic elements of which at least one does not correspond to an independent word or radical in the system of the language concerned (Graff).

morphology The science and study of the smallest meaningful units of language, and of their formation into words, including INFLECTION, DERIVATION and COMPO-

SITION, and distinct from SYNTAX; the study of the ways and methods of grouping sounds into sound-complexes, or words, of definite, distinct, conventional meaning (Dorfman); the study of constructions in which bound forms appear among the constituents (Bloomfield); the study of infra-word grammatical forms (de la Garza).

morphomatic Whatmough's term for MORPHEMIC.

morphome Whatmough's term for MORPHEME.

morphophoneme A class of phonemes belonging to the same morpheme (/-s/, /-z/, /-iz/ of *kits, kids, kisses;* /f/, /v/ of *knife, knives*); an arbitrarily chosen member of such a class as its representative (base form) in morphological description (plural /s/); one of the phonemes which interchange or replace each other in corresponding parts of various members of a morpheme (Harris).

morphophonemic Of or relating to a class of phonemes belonging to the same morpheme, or to relations among them and conditions determining their occurrence (Webster III).

morphophonemic allomorph An allomorph whose form is dictated by the phonetic environment (*in-, il-, im-, ir-* are allomorphs of a negative prefix or morpheme, whose basic form may be taken to be *in-;* the changes appearing in the other allomorphs are dictated by the initial sound of the following word with which the negative prefix is combined: *illegal, impassable, irrespective;* historically, this type of allomorphic variation may also be described as a series of phenomena of RETROGRESSIVE ASSIMILATION, *q.v.*). *See also* MORPHOLOGICAL DOUBLETS, MORPHOPHONEMIC ALTERNATION.

morphophonemic alternation Alternations in the phonemic shape of alternants of morphemes, pertaining to the sequence-structure of words in terms of phonemes, and conditioned by the surroundings of morphemes. Trubetskoi considers these alternations part of phonology. Hockett considers this a branch of grammar which deals with the phonemic shape of morphemes, words, and constructions, without regard to their meaning; a linguistic level between phonemics and morphemics (de la Garza).

morphophonemic economy This is efficiently manifested when a language uses, or "inhabits," a very high percentage of the favorite canonical forms. On the other hand, the morphophonemic economy of a language shows low efficiency if it "inhabits" only a relatively small percentage of the favorite canonical shapes available. *See also* LOAN WORD (de la Garza).

morphophonemics That branch of morphology which deals with the phonemic aspects of the constitution of the morphemes in the language, and with phonemic variations in morphemes appearing in different grammatical structures (Dorfman); the study of the phonemic differences between the allomorphs of the same morpheme, thus concerning the phonemic shape of morphemes (*ee* of *sleep* vs. *e* of *slept*) (Carroll); the distribution in one morpheme of alternants (/d/ of *played* vs. /t/ of *baked; o* of *wrote* vs. *i* of *write; -t* of *built* vs. *-d* of *build*), and of zero features (*let,* both present and past), regardless of whether the assigned members have any phonemes in common (Webster III).

morphophonemic stress That form of stress which distinguishes *black bird* from *blackbird* (Marchand). *See also* FORESTRESS, GRAMMATICAL STRESS, INTONATION, SENTENCE STRESS.

morphotactics The study of the sequences of morphemes, intermediate between morphemics and the word (Hill). *See also* DISCOURSE ANALYSIS.

motor phonetics The active aspect of ARTICULATORY PHONETICS (*q.v.*) (de la Garza).

movable speech organs The lips, tongue, lower jaw, buccal walls, uvula, epiglottis, and vocal cords. *Synonym:*

ARTICULATORS. *Opposite:* IMMOVABLE SPEECH ORGANS.

mucker pose The affectation of substandard features of speech for the purpose of currying favor with lower-class speakers (Marckwardt).

muddy transition (or **juncture**) Hockett's term for CLOSED JUNCTURE (*q.v.*).

multilateral opposition 1. A group of phonemes in a series, having the same relevant feature (voice, aspiration, occlusiveness, etc.) (Dorfman).

2. Two phonemes that differ in many respects (/a/ and /i/ are alike only to the extent that both are vowels; /t/ is opposed to /v/ by the features of voicelessness, dentality and plosiveness, as against voiced quality, dentolabiality and spirant quality) (Trubetskoi). *See also* BILATERAL OPPOSITION, CONTRAST, GRADUAL OPPOSITION.

multilingual Speaking and understanding several languages. *Synonyms:* PLURILINGUAL, POLYGLOT. *Opposites:* MONOGLOT, MONOLINGUAL, UNILINGUAL.

multilingualism The state of being MULTILINGUAL.

multipartite A language system in which some stems are used in only one part-of-speech function, while others may function as nouns, adjectives, verbs, etc. (Hockett). *See also* BIPARTITE, TRIPARTITE.

multipartite system A morphological system where there are three or more basic parts of speech (English, where nouns are inflected in a given way, verbs in another, and adjectives are uninflected; *fancy* in "fancy dresses" is an adjective and invariable; in "strange fancies" it is inflected as a noun; in "he fancied himself a singer," it is inflected as a verb (Hockett).

multiple substitution frame An arrangement of words in a construction in which each part (slot) is replaceable ("John gives Mary a book," with substitution of all parts, becomes "He wrote her two letters"). *See also* FRAME.

multiplicative numeral A numeral showing how many

times (*single, twofold, triple,* Latin *ter*). *Synonym:*
ITERATIVE NUMERAL.

multiverbal endocentric structure   An expression consisting of more than one word which fulfills the function of a nominal, an adjectival, a verbal, etc. ("The big old house [burned down]" where the first four words fulfill the function of subject, or noun; "[They arrived] in great haste," where the last three words fulfill the function of an adverb) (Hughes).

Murmelvokal   *See* MURMUR VOWEL.

murmur (or **murmured) vowel**   1. A whispered or neutral vowel (*e*-mute in French *demi* [də'mi], *u* in Japanese *desu* [dɛs]) (Dorfman).

2. An unstressed or voiceless shwa when morphemically incidental to the articulation of a consonant (Webster III).

3. A compromise between full voice and whisper, produced when the vocal bands are less elastic (more relaxed) than for normal voicing, and the interarytenoid margins of the glottal opening are kept slightly apart to allow a slight flow of breath; subglottal pressure of the breath stream is lower than for fully voiced or whispered vowels. Vowels of weakly stressed syllables are sometimes murmured (reduced vowels), and they tend to lose their identity, contrary to fully voiced and whispered vowels; this is especially due to laxity of the larynx and all other articulatory muscles in murmured speech, thus failing to provide modulation of the cord tone. Various degrees of murmur are possible; some languages (Madi dialects of the eastern Sudan) use a murmur in which the flow of the breath stream produces a noticeable fricative hiss in addition to reduced cord tone; this is also called BREATHY VOICE. *Synonyms:* HALF VOICE, SOTTO VOCE. *See also* (FULL) VOICE, WHISPER (de la Garza).

musical accent   One of Marouzeau's terms for PITCH AC-

CENT (*q.v.*). *Opposites:* EXPIRATORY ACCENT, INTENSITY ACCENT (ACCENT D'INTENSITÉ), STRESS.

mutation 1. For the Celtic languages, the change of an initial consonant under SANDHI conditions. *Synonym:* LENITION.

2. A generic term for phonological change, particularly of the UMLAUT and ABLAUT varieties (*q.v.*). Marouzeau equates mutation with LAUTVERSCHIEBUNG (*q.v.*) when it occurs in consonants, with UMLAUT when it occurs in vowels. *See also* METAPHONY.

mutation vocalique French term for VOWEL MUTATION (*q.v.*).

mute 1. *See* PLOSIVE, STOP.

2. Orthographically, a consonant which contributes nothing to the pronunciation of a word; a silent consonant (*b* in *plumb, b* in *doubt*).

3. A vowel which contributes to the pronunciation of a word, but does not represent a syllable nucleus (*e* of *mate;* French mute *e,* sounded in some environments, silent in others, or subject to FREE VARIATION (*q.v.*) : *cheval, ch'val*).

N

name word Sweet's term for PROPER NAME.

naming word A word that denotes or symbolizes a person or thing (substantive), an act or happening (verb), or a quality (adjective or other modifier) (Dorfman). *See also* FULL (*also* NOTIONAL) WORD.

narreme A minimal unit of relevant narrative (Dorfman).

narrowed meaning A more restricted meaning of a word which may be used with a broader application (*doctor* as physician; but, more broadly, anyone with a doctoral degree). *See also* WIDENED MEANING.

narrow transcription A careful representation of all identifiable features of a phonetic utterance. *Opposite:* BROAD TRANSCRIPTION.

narrow transcription symbols Additional symbols of IPA (*q.v.*) not generally used for broad or general transcription purposes, but representing variant forms of sound as we hear them (symbols for the glottal stop, nasalization, lip over-rounding, etc.) (Bronstein).

narrow vowel *See* CLOSED VOWEL, TENSE 1. *Opposites:* LAX (*also* OPEN, WIDE) VOWEL.

nasal (sound) 1. A sound produced with open velic cavity, and the oral cavity acting as a secondary resonator; a sound produced with the uvula lowered, allowing the air to escape through the nose, so that the nasal cavity acts as a resonator (hi*m*, ra*n*) (Dorfman).
2. A sound uttered: (a) with nose passage open by reason of lowered velum, and mouth passage occluded at some point (lips for [m], tongue tip for [n], back of tongue for [ŋ]; (b) with mouth open, velum lowered, and nose passage producing phonemically essential resonance (French [ã], [ɔ̃]; Portuguese *ã, õ, um*); (c) with mouth open, velum partly open, and nose passage producing phonemically non-essential resonance, or NASAL TWANG, with nasalization as a secondary feature (Webster III). *Opposite:* ORAL SOUND.

nasal consonants Those consonants which have a resonance chamber in the mouth, although the breath stream is forced to flow through the nasopharynx and the nasal cavities to escape at the nose rather than at the lips. They are classified according to observable peculiarities of their oral articulation, as the major acoustic differences among them are due to differences in the character of the oral resonator, which has the lowest range frequencies for [m], the highest for [ŋ], and an intermediate range for [n]. There are three phases to their normal articulation : onset, hold, and release. The hold involves the production of a controlled opening, which may be of rather brief duration; the release is most prominent, due to its acoustic prominence, duration, and movement pattern. The nasal consonants may be voiced or voiceless, and they may require distinctive forms by virtue of the nature of the release of their oral occlusion; i.e., they may be released with aspiration or with affrication (de la Garza).

nasalization 1. Lowering of the velum so as to leave the nasal cavity accessible to the air stream (Bloch and Trager).

2. A secondary feature, whereby there is added a vigorous lowering of the velum, plus some constriction of the palatopharyngeal arch, to the articulation peculiar to an oral sound. This so-called NASAL TWANG may act as a secondary feature, becoming part of a general basis of articulation. Note that this is distinct from the "nasal" characteristic which is used to mark one or a class of sounds from others which are otherwise like them. *See also* NASAL CONSONANTS, NASAL VOWELS, SECONDARY FEATURE (de la Garza).

nasalized Pronounced with the breath flowing through both nose and mouth (French *en, on, un;* Portuguese *um, são*) (Walsh).

nasal twang *See* NASALIZATION.

nasal vowels Vowels produced by adding the vigorous lowering of the velum, plus some constriction of the palatopharyngeal arch, to the usual movements of the articulation peculiar to the analogous oral vowels. There are degrees of vigor (French nasal vowels are much more vigorously nasalized than those of Danish, German, or Portuguese). Acoustically, the distinguishing feature of these nasal vowels is a characteristic lowering in pitch, plus the addition of at least two frequency components to the vowel spectrum, a high-pitched tone and a low-pitched tone. The characteristic lower pitch of nasal vowels is due to the coupling of the nasal cavities to the pharynx and mouth cavities when the nasals are produced. The additional high-pitched tone is produced by standing vibrations set up in the small space behind the velum and below the posterior nares. The additional low tone seems due to selective transmission of one of the cord tone partials through the nasal fossae (Heffner, de la Garza).

nationalistic (or **nationalism**) **coefficient** The proportion and extent to which a language is regarded as symbolic of nationhood, and used to represent and spread the feeling toward national unity; conversely, the degree to which the national consciousness is reflected upon the language.

national language The official, standard tongue of a political division, used in government documents, and taught in the nation's schools; it usually coincides with the LITERARY LANGUAGE (*q.v.*). *Partial synonym:* STANDARD LANGUAGE.

native word A word belonging to the original linguistic stock of a language, or which historical linguistics cannot identify as a borrowing from another language. *See also* ALIEN (*also* BORROWED, DOMESTICATED, NATURALIZED) WORD.

nativistic theory The view that a mystic harmony or connection exists between sound and meaning, and that human speech is the result of an instinct of primitive man which made him give vocal expression to every external impression (Max Müller). *Synonym:* DING-DONG THEORY. *See also* BOW-WOW (*also* POOH-POOH, YO-HE-HO) THEORY.

natural gender A category in language that is based on natural sex, or the distinction between animate (male and female) and inanimate, so that males are described as masculine, females as feminine, objects as neuter (the use of *she* to refer to a girl). *Opposite:* GRAMMATICAL GENDER. *See also* CASTE, GENDER.

naturalization, language of The language acquired by immigrants to a foreign country after they have resided in it for a time, and passed on to, or independently acquired by, their first-generation descendants. *See also* IMMIGRANT LANGUAGE, INDIGENOUS LANGUAGE.

naturalized word A borrowed word that has been in the borrowing language long enough to take on the borrowing language's phonemic pattern, stress and orthographic form (*very* from Old French *verai; bishop* as opposed to *episcopal*). *See also* ACCLIMATIZATION, ALIEN (*also* DOMESTICATED, NATIVE) WORD.

neatness of pattern Symmetrical pattern or configuration in which the phonemes of a language arrange themselves. *See also* HOLES IN THE PATTERN, PATTERN CONGRUITY, SYMMETRY.

Neogrammarians A linguistic school of the late nineteenth century which included Brugmann, Osthoff, Paul, Leskien and others, and which taught and believed in the universal and absolute validity of phonetic (sound) laws (LAUTGESETZ, *q.v.*); they advocated more exact formulation of the phonetic laws, and their more rigid application to linguistic phenomena, maintaining that "phonetic laws admit no true exceptions," and recognizing the residue as ANALOGY, BORROWING, and CONDITIONED SOUND CHANGE, all normal factors in linguistic change. *Synonyms:* JUNGGRAMMATIKER, REGULARISTS. *See also* NEOLINGUISTS, MECHANISTIC THEORY.

Neolinguists A school of linguistics which included Vossler, Schuchardt, Bartoli, Bertoni, Spitzer and others, which arose in opposition to the NEOGRAMMARIANS (*q.v.*) and their belief in the cogency of sound laws, believing rather in the primacy of the affective and esthetic aspects of language, and maintaining that linguistic change is the result of individual creations which spread and become assimilated on an ever increasing scale. They rejected the exceptionless sound laws, and based their conclusions largely on AREAL LINGUISTICS (*q.v.*); frequency, meaning, sporadic occurrence, non-occurrence, or deviation of sound change, were accepted as explanations. The argument was largely a matter of terminology. *See also* MENTALISTIC THEORY, NEOGRAMMARIANS.

neologism A newly coined word or expression; a use of an old word in a new sense. *See also* COINAGE, PORTMANTEAU WORD, SEMANTIC CHANGE.

nervous system *See* TRANSMISSION.

nesting The arrangement of words within a construction, with the presence of some precluding the placing of others in positions in which they normally could go ("this fresh milk"; "fresh this milk" is prevented by the presence of "this," though "fresh milk" would be possible) (Hockett).

neutralization The temporary suspension, in some position or environment, of an otherwise functioning difference or distinction (/t/ and /d/ are definitely opposed in *tie, die;* but for many American English speakers *wetting* and *wedding* are pronounced identically; since /t/ and /d/, systematically distinct, are not different in this one position, Trubetskoi says the difference is NEUTRALIZED). According to many linguists, we have the ACTUALIZATION of the ARCHIPHONEME (*q.v.*), said to occur when two sounds are distinct in some positions, but the distinction ceases to exist in others (German /t/ and /d/ are neutralized in final position, but not elsewhere; Spanish /r/ and /rr/ contrast only between vowels : *pero, perro*). *Synonyms :* AUFHEBUNG, PARTIAL COMPLEMENTATION.

neutral vowel 1. A vowel produced with the tongue in a position of rest, and not of strongly defined quality;

not too open or closed, front or back, retracted or rounded (*but*). *Synonym:* MEDIUM VOWEL.

2. In Finno-Ugric, [i], which may occur with either back or front vowels. *See also* VOWEL HARMONY.

New Norwegian *See* LANDSMÅL.

nexus 1. A group of words, one of which is a verb, forming a sentence (Jespersen).

2. A predicative relation or construction consisting of grammatical elements that are related or felt to be related. *See also* JUNCTION, RANK.

noa word 1. A word charged with little or no supernatural power, and free of taboo (Webster III). *Opposite:* TABOO WORD.

2. A word used to replace a tabooed word (*gosh, darn*) (Laird).

noeme The meaning of a GLOSSEME (*q.v.*) (Bloomfield).

noise 1. Linguistically, that part of a received message which is extraneous to the original message (Carroll).

2. *See* PITCH.

nomic spelling The traditional, conventional, or orthographic spelling of a language (Sweet). *Opposite:* PHONETIC SPELLING.

nominal A word or group of words fulfilling the function of a noun ("That grand old man [finally died]") (Hughes). *See also* ENDOCENTRIC CONSTRUCTION.

non-automatic alternation A form of alternation where, under specific conditions, the base form of the morpheme is replaced by more than one other form, unpredictably (French adjectives ending in /-øz/, such as /ørøz/ *heureuse,* are quite regularly replaced by a similar form ending in /-ø/ in the masculine: /ørø/, *heureux;* however, a few French adjectives ending in /-øz/ behave irregularly, and are instead replaced by a masculine form in /-œʀ/: /mātøz/, *menteuse,* /mātœʀ/, *menteur;* another example is English /wajf/, *wife,* with its morphophonemically conditioned plural

alternant /wajv/ of *wives*). *See also* AUTOMATIC (*also*
IRREGULAR, REGULAR) ALTERNATION (de la Garza).

nonce-form   Any grammatical form larger than a lexeme,
coined and recoined as needed by the speaker ("a new
hat") (Hockett).

nonce word   A word coined for a special occasion, but
not generally adopted (Coleridge's *mammonolatry* for
"worship of money"; a newspaper's *ringday* for a day
on which four girls became engaged).

non-contiguous assimilation   *See* DISTANT ASSIMILATION.

non-contrastive distribution   1. Allophones of one phoneme, or allomorphs of one morpheme, occurring in
specific environments, so that one does not occur in the
environment of another (English /p/ with aspiration
in the initial position, without aspiration after /s/).
Synonyms: ALTERNATION, COMPLEMENTARY DISTRIBU-
TION, COMPLEMENTATION.
2. Hockett extends the definition to cover allophones
and allomorphs that are: (a) in COMPLEMENTARY
DISTRIBUTION, (b) in PARTIAL COMPLEMENTATION,
(c) in FREE VARIATION.

non-functional feature   A phonic feature which is not
phonemic (does not serve to distinguish one meaning
from another), but may convey some (paralinguistic)
information concerning the speaker's personality, social
position, place of origin, age, even sex (the phoneme
/c/ in some languages of northeast Asia, manifested
as [tš] among men, as [ts] among women) (Martinet).
Synonyms: IRRELEVANT (*also* NON-DISTINCTIVE, NON-
PHONEMIC, PARALINGUISTIC) FEATURE (or VARIANT).
Opposites: DISTINCTIVE (*also* FUNCTIONAL, OPPOSI-
TIONAL, PHONEMIC, RELEVANT, SIGNIFICANT) FEATURE.
See also CHARACTEROLOGY OF SPEECH.

non-immediate situation   A state of affairs which is beyond the range of current time, place, vision, hearing,
etc., and to which linguistic reference is made ("I shall
meet him at the office tomorrow"; "I met him last year

in Paris," vs. "I see him before me now"). *See also* DISPLACED (*also* REFERRED) SPEECH.

non-linear   *See* SUPRASEGMENTAL.

non-nasal   *See* BUCCAL, ORAL.

non-phonemic   *See* IRRELEVANT, NON-DISTINCTIVE, NON-FUNCTIONAL, NOISE.

non-productive   *See* OBSOLESCENT, UNPRODUCTIVE.

non-syllabic   1. In a syllable, any sound other than the SYLLABIC (*q.v.*).

2. A vowel less prominent than another vowel in the same syllable (the second vowel of a falling diphthong, such as bo*i*l).

3. Not constituting a syllable or the nucleus of a syllable (a consonant accompanying a vowel in the same syllable, such as *do*g). *Synonym:* ASYLLABIC.

norm   *See* GLOSSEMATICS, LINGUISTIC NORM.

normal grade   Said to be had by a vowel showing the form *e* or *o* in its primitive stage. *See also* ABSTUFUNG.

normative   *See* PRESCRIPTIVE, STATICS. *Partial opposite:* DESCRIPTIVE.

Nostratic   *See* JAPHETIC.

notional word   A word that carries a full meaning ("he *has* luck" vs. "he *has* gone"). *Synonyms:* FULL (*also* NAMING) WORD. *Opposites:* EMPTY (*also* RELATIONAL) WORD.

noun cluster   A noun with its modifiers. *See also* CONSTITUENT, ENDOCENTRIC CONSTRUCTION.

nucleus   1. The peak of energy in the utterance of a syllable (do*g*); a sound articulated with a peak of sonority (Hall).

2. The syllable with maximum stress in a stress group (*gen*eral).

3. A sequence consisting of a vowel and a semi-vowel, or vice versa (Walsh). *Synonym:* DIPHTHONG.

4. A CONSONANT CLUSTER (*q.v.*).

5. Dorfman's term for KERNEL (*q.v.*).

numeral classifier   *See* AUXILIARY NUMERAL.

numerative classifier A word inserted between a numeral and a substantive, or between a demonstrative and a noun. *See also* CLASSIFIER 1.

numerical metanalysis A phenomenon occurring when, in borrowing, a word originally regarded as a singular comes to be analyzed as a plural, or vice versa (*cherries* from *cerise; peas* from *pois*) (Jespersen). *See also* BACK FORMATION, METANALYSIS, RECUTTING.

Nynorsk *See* LANDSMÅL.

O

object language The language whose structure is described in terms of a METALANGUAGE (*q.v.*). *See also* SYNTAX LANGUAGE.

obligatory categories Grammatical notions which must be expressed to a varying degree (gender in English, fully represented in *he, she, it,* but not in *they*).

oblique case 1. In Classical languages, a collective term for all declensional cases other than the nominative and vocative.

2. In Old French and Provençal, the single declensional form which represents a merger of Latin genitive, dative, accusative and ablative, and is opposed to the nominative case, which is extended to cover vocative functions as well. *See also* MERGED FORM, SYNCRETISM.

obscuration The change of unstressed vowels into shwa or high front *i* (as in the unstressed syllables of gen*e*ral, speak*i*ng).

obsolescence *See* OBSOLESCENT.

obsolescent Falling into disuse; in the process of becoming obsolete (*trolley car,* in cities where local transportation is now exclusively by bus). *Synonym:* UNPRODUCTIVE.

obsolete No longer in general, current use (*sparking light*). *Partial synonym:* ARCHAIC.

obstructive *See* OBSTRUENT.

obstruent (or **obstructive**) A term used to include stops and spirants, both of which are characterized by some degree of obstruction (Hockett); a consonant where the flow of breath is obstructed either in part (FRICATIVE, SPIRANT) or completely (STOP) (Walsh). AFFRICATES, if considered as a distinct type of sounds, also belong to the larger class of OBSTRUENTS. *Opposite:* RESONANT (LIQUID, NASAL).

obtrusion The quality of startling contrast produced by an innovation in the minds of the speakers; an innovation is said to be unobtrusive when it draws little attention, by reason of the fact that it fits into a preexisting pattern (Hockett).

occlusion The complete obstruction of the breath passage in the buccal cavity in the articulation of a stop, oral or nasal. *Synonym:* HOLD. *See also* NASAL CONSONANT, STOP.

occlusive A consonant that momentarily stops the flow of sound; sometimes applied to a nasal. *Synonyms:* PLOSIVE, STOP.

occurrence, privilege of *See* PRIVILEGE OF OCCURRENCE.

off-glide 1. According to Sweet, the final phase in the articulation of a phoneme, in which the vocal organs go back to their normal, neutral position, or assume a position preparatory to forming another sound (Dorfman). *Partial synonyms:* ABSATZ, ABGLITT, AUSLAUT, DETENTE, FINAL GLIDE, RELEASE. *See also* ON-GLIDE. 2. According to Heffner, a modification of the normal release of speech sounds, which results in an adventitious sound peculiar to the fusion within the speech measure; thus, the off-glide is a transitional sound produced during the release of a speech movement. *Opposite:* ON-GLIDE. *See also* GLIDE, TRANSITIONAL SOUND (de la Garza).

3. A vowel added to another vowel, turning it into a diphthong (*day — day-ee; two — to-oo; go — go-oo; fail — fay-ull*) (Walsh). *Partial synonyms:* PEAK SATELLITE, SEMI-VOWEL.

official language The language or languages prescribed or authorized as recognized, usually by a national government; it generally coincides with the NATIONAL and the LITERARY LANGUAGE; a geolinguistic unit may have more than one official language (French and Flemish in Belgium; English and Afrikaans in South Africa; English and French in Canada; German, French and Italian in Switzerland).

old (or **older**) 1. Representing an original or primitive state of affairs, insofar as it can be determined; but this can be only a relative, not an absolute concept (*Old Germanic*). *Synonyms:* PRIMITIVE, UR- (*Primitive Germanic, Urgermanisch*).

2. Indicating a state of the language which is prior to another in point of time (*Old French* vs. *Modern French; Old English* vs. *Modern English*).

3. Indicating a language that continues to present an archaic state of affairs (Lithuanian among the Indo-European languages; Icelandic among the Scandinavian tongues) (Saussure).

omnipotent vowel A vowel that can function as a PEAK, NUCLEUS, PEAK SATELLITE or MARGINAL (Mandarin /i/ is the peak in /bĭ/, "pen"; the satellite in the complex peak /bái/, "white"; marginal in /biău/, "watch" (Hockett).

on-glide 1. According to Sweet, the initial phase in the articulation of a phoneme, in which the vocal organs occupy the position necessary for the formation of that sound, moving from an inactive position, or from the articulating position of the immediately preceding phoneme to the articulatory position for the sound desired. *Synonyms:* ANLAUT, INITIAL GLIDE, ONSET 2. *See also* OFF-GLIDE.

2. According to Heffner, a modification of the normal onset of speech sounds, which results in an adventitious sound peculiar to the fusion within the speech measure. Thus, this glide is not a phenomenon of onset, but a transitional sound produced during the attack of a speech movement. *Opposite:* OFF-GLIDE. *See also* GLIDE, TRANSITIONAL SOUND (de la Garza).

onomasiology 1. The study of the meaning and derivation of names.

2. The study of words and expressions having similar or associated concepts and a basis for being grouped together (Webster III).

onomastics The study of the origin and form of proper names of persons and places, including surnames (Webster III). *Synonym:* ONOMASIOLOGY 1.

onomatology *See* ONOMASTICS.

onomatopo(i)eia The coining of a word on the basis of a real or fancied resemblance to a sound in nature (*baa* to denote the bleating of a sheep). *See also* ECHOIC (*also* IMITATIVE, MIMETIC) WORD.

onomatopo(i)etic theory The view that human speech arose as the result of the imitation of sounds produced in nature. *Synonym:* BOW-WOW THEORY.

onset 1. The beginning (initial phase) of an occlusion (Bloch and Trager); the beginning (initial phase) of a contoid (Hall). *See also* STOP.

2. The movement of the speech organs from a state of rest to the position necessary for the articulation of a given sound; getting into position for utterance (Sweet, Hall). *Partial synonyms:* ANLAUT, INITIAL GLIDE, ON-GLIDE.

3. A consonant or sequence of consonants in the initial position; an initial consonant cluster (*pr-* of *premium*); the consonant or sequence of consonants at the begin-

ning of a microsegment (Hockett). *See also* OFF-GLIDE.

ontogeny (linguistic) The study of the speech habits of a single person from birth to death (Hockett). *See also* IDIOLECT, PAROLE.

open-class words Crystal's term for LEXICAL WORDS.

open construction A construction susceptible of development by substitution or addition of further elements (Hall).

opening sound A sound attended by an explosion or release of breath (Saussure). *Synonyms:* OCCLUSIVE, PLOSIVE, STOP.

open juncture The juncture between two consecutive spoken sounds having less mutual assimilation than close juncture, and less hiatus than terminal juncture (Webster III); a term usually applied to juncture phenomena within the word (OPEN INTERNAL JUNCTURE) or between words (OPEN EXTERNAL JUNCTURE); it is indicated in phonemic transcription by / + / (in "The word is God," open external juncture exists between *the* and *word, word* and *is, is* and *God*). *Synonyms:* OPEN TRANSITION (Gleason), PLUS JUNCTURE, SHARP TRANSITION (Hockett). *Opposites:* CLOSED (or MUDDY) JUNCTURE (or TRANSITION), MINUS JUNCTURE.

open list *See* LIST.

open repertory A productive system of imitation in language-learning by a child, starting when the process of ANALOGY comes into play; if the child has learned by direct imitation *dog, boy* and *dogs,* and it occurs to him that if he wants to refer to more than one boy he may do so by making the same shift he makes from *dog* to *dogs,* he may be said to be acquiring an open repertory instead of the CLOSED REPERTORY he has had up to that moment (Hockett).

open stress The accentual phenomenon that occurs when the consonant is heard just as the intensity of the preceding vowel has begun to decrease (Sweet).

open syllabification A syllabic system where the majority of syllables end in vowels (Italian, Japanese, Indonesian). *Opposite:* CLOSED SYLLABIFICATION.

open syllable   A syllable ending in a vowel sound (Spanish *to*-ro). *Synonym:* FREE SYLLABLE. *Opposites:* BLOCKED (*also* CHECKED, CLOSED) SYLLABLE.

open transition   A normally suprasegmental phoneme (occasionally segmental in some languages), often marked / + /, marking the break between words and parts of words. *Synonyms:* OPEN (*also* PLUS, SHARP) JUNCTURE (or TRANSITION). *Opposites:* CLOSED (*also* MINUS, MUDDY) JUNCTURE (or TRANSITION).

open vowel   *See* LOW VOWEL, WIDE VOWEL.

operator   One of the verbal forms, prepositions, articles, etc. (about one hundred in number) in Basic English (Richards).

opposition   1. The relationship of partial differences between two partly similar elements of language (oral vs. nasal in /b/, /m/; singular vs. plural in *man/men* (Webster III).

2. Every phoneme in a given language is opposed to every other phoneme, since a shift from one to the other in the chain of speech gives either a new or an unintelligible form (Dorfman). *Synonyms:* CONTRAST, CORRELATION; but note that Martinet uses CONTRAST in the sense of the relation of each phoneme with the next in the sequence, defining CONTRAST as syntagmatic and observable, while he reserves OPPOSITION for relations that are mutually exclusive and paradigmatic (*good* vs. *bad*).

3. Europeans define opposition (where only one term is inherent) as a minimal contrast in some one position; i.e., it is a differentiation only between two phonemes, where only one term of the polarity occurs (in the opposition /p ∼ b/, the distinction is voice, and in the opposition /f ∼ p/, the distinction is friction) (de la Garza). *See also* BILATERAL (*also* BINARY, DISJUNC-

TIVE, ISOLATED, LINEAR, MULTILATERAL, PRIVATIVE, PROPORTIONAL) OPPOSITION (or CONTRAST).

optional   Said of something that may or may not occur.

optional external sandhi   Similar to EXTERNAL SANDHI (*q.v.*), but not morphophonemic (/jɔnz goiŋ / ~ / jɔn iz goiŋ/, "John's going," "John is going"; these vary freely, and there is no grammatical difference between them) (de la Garza).

optional variants   *See* FREE VARIANTS.

oral sound   A sound produced with closed velic cavity, so that the mouth alone acts as a resonator; a sound produced with the air stream directed into the mouth, not the nose. *Synonym:* BUCCAL SOUND 2. *Opposite:* NASAL SOUND.

orama   The visual idea of the movement of the speech organs. *See also* AKOUSMA, GRAPHEMA, KINEMA, LEGEMA.

order   1. According to Martinet, the vertical listing of rows of phonemes according to the place of articulation (labial order: /p/, /b/, /m/, etc.). *See also* LINEAR OPPOSITION, SERIES.

2. Grammatical feature, or taxeme, which deals with the structural order of constituents in an utterance. *See also* TAXEME, WORD ORDER (de la Garza).

order class   *See* SUBSTITUTION CLASS.

organic shifting   Failure to hit the desired mark, through carelessness, indolence or indifference; this may lead to language change when it is widespread or widely imitated (*sangwich* for *sandwich*) (Sweet).

organs of speech   *See* SPEECH ORGANS.

orthography   *See* SPELLING.

oscillogram   A record made by an OSCILLOGRAPH (*q.v.*).

oscillograph   A device for making a visual representation of the oscillations of sounds, by locating their point of origin and recording the sound waves on a time scale. *See also* KYMOGRAPH (de la Garza).

oscilloscope   A cathode-ray oscillograph of low voltage for recording wave forms on a fluorescent screen; used in sound-ranging devices and in radio (de la Garza).

outer closure *See* INNER CLOSURE.

outline *See* CONTOUR.

output *See* INPUT.

over-all frame A symmetrical arrangement of the total possibilities of phonemic contrast in the speech community, from which each individual and each dialect selects some, but not all of the possibilities (the phoneme /i/ exists potentially in the speech of all American English speakers, as illustrated by "jist a minute," but not all of them use it) (Hill). *Synonym:* OVER-ALL PATTERN.

over-all pattern The array of phonetic categories necessary and sufficient to account for all the phonemes of all the dialects of a language (Webster III). *Synonym:* OVER-ALL FRAME.

over-correction The tendency, when a pronunciation "error" is widespread, to change back to the supposedly correct form even words which are not involved (by reason of a widespread dialect change from /a/ to /i/ in such words as *sofa,* the tendency creeps in to use *Missourah* and *Cincinnatah* for *Missouri* and *Cincinnati;* because "it is me" is viewed as incorrect for "it is I," the tendency arises to say "between you and I" instead of "between you and me"). *Synonym:* HYPER-URBANISM. *See also* HYPER-CORRECTION, INVERSE SPELLING, SPELLING PRONUNCIATION.

over-differentiation The imposition of phonemic distinctions from a primary system on sounds of a secondary system when they are not required (Weinreich); the natural tendency of a linguistic analyst to read more phonemic differences into the language he is analyzing than actually exist, because in his own language those differences appear (Gleason). *Opposite:* UNDER-DIFFERENTIATION.

overlap 1. The phonetic phenomenon, observable in

the spectrograph, whereby the representation of one phoneme continues after the next one has begun (Hockett). *Synonyms:* CO-ARTICULATION, FUSION.

2. Where the same sound can belong to two different phonemes, i.e., where two formally different sounds converge in one case. Such a sound must be definable or identifiable positively and exclusively (French /sã/, *cent* and *sans*) (de la Garza).

3. Syntactically, where two formally different forms converge in one construction ("flying airplanes": adjective plus noun, or verb plus object). *Synonym:* INTERSECTION (de la Garza).

overlearn *See* INTERNALIZE.

oxytone A word where the final syllable bears the main accent. *See also* PAROXYTONE, PROPAROXYTONE, TERMINAL STRESS.

P

palatal 1. Any type of consonant sound formed by placing the front, or blade, of the tongue against the hard palate (English *sho*re, plea*s*ure, *ch*urch, *J*ohn; German i*ch;* French a*gn*eau; Italian fi*gli*o; in certain languages, such as Russian and Polish, the palatals are often CACUMINAL or RETROFLEX, with tongue cupped and tip of tongue touching the hard palate). *See also* LAMINAL.

2. Of a vowel, *see* BRIGHT (*also* FRONT) VOWEL.

palatalization 1. In diachronic phonetics, the change from a non-palatal to a palatal sound (Latin *centum,* with velar [k], > Italian *cento,* with palatal [č]).

2. Descriptively, a secondary feature added to a normal

stop consonant, whereby the blade of the tongue is brought into close contact with a considerable area of the arc of the hard palate near its forward slope and in the pre-palatal region. *See also* SECONDARY FEATURES (de la Garza).

3. Palatalization of a sound may also occur by assimilation of a point of occlusion or constriction; i.e., an adaptive change affects the exact point at which a fricative or stop is articulated (in English, the occlusion of [k] in *king* is much further forward than that of [k] in *cling*) (de la Garza).

palatalized consonant   1. A consonant accompanied by the timbre of [i] (Russian govori*t'*).

2. *See* PALATALIZATION.

palatal law   A shift whereby Indo-European velars became palatals (i.e., fronted) in Indo-Iranian, by assimilation due to anticipation of a following palatal vowel *i,* or of an *ą* which was the equivalent of Latin or Greek *e;* but remained velars when followed by *u* or by an *a* which was the equivalent of Latin or Greek *o,* thus establishing *a, e* and *o* found in the European languages as the original Indo-European vowels. This was an allophonic change.

palatal vowel   *See* FRONT VOWEL.

paleography   The study of ancient and medieval ways of writing, including the decipherment and interpretation of texts painted or traced with ink or colors on paper, parchment, fabrics, or other soft materials. *See also* EPIGRAPHY.

panchronic grammar   UNIVERSAL GRAMMAR (*q.v.*), applicable to all languages and at all historical stages of their development (Gray). *Synonyms:* GENERAL (*also* PHILOSOPHICAL, UNIVERSAL) GRAMMAR.

panchronic laws   Universally valid principles in linguistics (there is no known language in which a word may not end in a vowel) (Jakobson).

P and Q Celtic   The designation of the two extant

branches of Celtic: the Brythonic, including Welsh, Cornish and Breton, where Indo-European *qu* (**kw*) becomes *p;* and the Goidelic, including Irish, Scots Gaelic and Manx, where it turns into *k* (Welsh *pedwar, pump,* "four," "five," vs. Irish *ceathair, cúig*).

paradigm 1. A series of forms having a common element (*drive, drives, drove, driving, driven*); a complete set of all the various conjugational or declensional forms of a word (*man, man's, men, men's, manly, manfully,* etc.); a set of related words containing a common base and all the affixes that may be attached to it (the complete declension of Latin *mūrus*) (Bloch and Trager). *See also* ACCIDENCE, CONJUGATION, DECLENSION.

2. In phonemics, the listing of all the phonemes of a language in series, orders, and isolated elements; from the paradigm, individual phonemes are selected as they are needed for the chain of speech (Martinet).

3. *See* COMMUTATION, PROCESS, SYSTEM (Hjelmslev).

paradigmatic economy The avoidance of new language elements by forming combinations of existing ones (French *machine à laver*, "washing machine," as against *Bendix,* the name of a brand applied to all washing machines, representing a case of SYNTAGMATIC ECONOMY (*q.v.*) (Martinet).

paradigmatic pattern The general, typical system of declension or conjugation of a given language (English *book, book's, books, books'*).

paradigmatic sound change *See* INTERNAL PRESSURES, SPONTANEOUS SOUND CHANGE.

paragoge The addition of a sound, letter or syllable to the end of a word, without etymological justification, for the sake of pattern congruity, and without change of meaning in the word (Latin *amant* to Italian *aman,* then to *amano*). *Opposite:* APOCOPE. *See also* PATTERN.

paralinguistics 1. The study of the vocal qualifiers con-

veyed by the voice, but not through words or pitch level
or intonation (tone of voice, tempo, humming, snort-
ing, drawling, etc.) (Walsh). *See also* KINESICS, VOCAL
QUALIFIER.

2. The study of tone-of-voice signals, excluding intonation contours, which are described as within the linguistic system (Birdwhistell).

3. Term coined by Trager, which refers to certain aspects of METALINGUISTICS (*q.v.*); it thus also refers to
that part of a speech event which is not linguistically
structured; i.e., to such VARIANTS as social mannerisms,
gestures, facial expressions, voice qualifiers, etc. (de
la Garza).

paraphrase A statement of the contents of a passage
or text in the same or another language, without following the original text verbatim. *See also* META-
PHRASE.

paraplasm The replacement of an established form by
a newly coined one (*skidoo* of the 1920s replaced by
the later *scram*).

parasitic vowel A vowel which inserts itself between two
consonants to simplify a consonant cluster (*fillum* for
film, atheletic for *athletic*). *Synonyms:* ANAPTYCTIC
(*also* EPENTHETIC, EXCRESCENT, INTRUSIVE) VOWEL.

parasynthetic derivation The formation of derivatives
involving both prefixes and suffixes (Italian *incasellare*
from *casella,* "pigeonhole") (Migliorini).

parataxis 1. The use of independent sentences ("The
man came yesterday. He said: 'I have been here before.'", as against "The man who came yesterday said
that he had been here before.") (Entwistle). *Synonym:*
ENDOCENTRIC CONSTRUCTION. *Opposite:* HYPOTAXIS.

2. Two or more clauses, with non-final intonation contour on all but the last ("You're sick, you'd better go
to bed") (Hall).

parisyllabic Containing the same number of syllables in

all or most inflectional forms (all the singular case-forms of Latin *mūrus*). *Opposite:* IMPARISYLLABIC.

parole An individual's use of language to convey messages (Saussure). *Partial synonym:* IDIOLECT. *See also* LANGUE.

paronym 1. A word derived from the same primary word as 'a given word, similar in form, but different in meaning (*manhood, mannish,* both derived from *man*).
2. A word formed from a word in another language (*foyerlike*).
3. A word having a form similar to that of a foreign cognate word (*occasion,* in English and French) (Webster III).

paroxytone A word with its main stress on the penult syllable (*occurring*). *See also* OXYTONE, PROPAROXYTONE.

partial complementation Said to occur when two phonemes are in complementary distribution in some positions or environments, but not in others (Spanish /r/ and /rr/ are in complementary distribution initially, where only /rr/ can occur, and finally, where only /r/ can occur; but medially they are in opposition, as indicated by *pero,* "but," *perro,* "dog") (Martinet). *Synonyms:* AUFHEBUNG, NEUTRALIZATION. *See also* ARCHIPHONEME.

particle *See* EMPTY WORD, FORM WORD, FUNCTION WORD, MARKER, POINTER.

parts of speech In traditional and descriptive grammars, the maximum word classes into which the words of a given language may be classified, either according to morphological construction or syntactic function (nouns, adjectives, verbs, prepositions, etc.). *Synonyms:* MAJOR FORM CLASSES, WORD CLASSES.

pasigraphy A system of writing using signs of universal significance, such as mathematical symbols or musical notation.

pasimology The art or study of communication by gestures, as practiced by American Indian tribes, deaf-mutes, Boy Scouts, etc. *See also* GESTURAL LANGUAGE.

patois The popular unwritten speech in a given locality; the local dialect of the lower social strata, normally unwritten. *See also* DIALECT.

patronymic A name describing the paternity or ancestry of the bearer, and usually derived from the name of a father or ancestor (The *Atreides,* "sons or descendants of Atreus"; *Johnson, Williams, Ivanovich, McHugh, Fitzgerald, O'Sullivan). See also* MATRONYMIC, TEK-NONYMY.

pattern 1. Phonemically, the paradigm of all the phonemes in the language; the phonemic system of a language (Dorfman).

2. The manner in which the smaller units of the language are grouped into larger units (sounds into sound classes; the voiceless-voiced stop pattern in bilabials is paralleled by a similar pattern in the alveolars and velars) (Webster III).

3. Morphologically, the way in which the morphemes of a language group themselves into classes (FREE and BOUND; FULL and EMPTY; nouns, adjectives, verbs, etc.).

4. Phonemically, the inner configuration or structure which consists of all the phonemes in the language; it is a self-contained phonemic system, thus making it impossible to identify any phoneme with a non-linguistic sound. *Synonym:* CONFIGURATION (de la Garza).

5. The name used by linguists to indicate the fact that regular relations exist between linguistic elements, and that regular classification of linguistic elements is possible at various levels (de la Garza).

pattern congruity 1. Hockett's term for NEATNESS OF PATTERN (*q.v.*).

2. Particular formulations of phonemes must be analyzed as being congruous with the general phonemic pattern of the given language, according to their distri-

bution and behavior in clusters; there must be structural parallelism; i.e., like function, like structure. *See also* SYMMETRY (de la Garza).

patterned congruence Grouping language sounds together with respect to various kinds of environment, noting the congruence in behavior of partly similar sounds (Carroll). *See also* PATTERN CONGRUITY.

pattern pressure Pressure exerted by parts of the pattern to preserve distinctions lost in other parts (Italian *cantavo* for an earlier *cantava,* to preserve the distinction between first and third person, and formed by borrowing the ending of the first person of the present tense (Hall).

paucal number A grammatical form indicating a few, as against singular, dual, or the regular plural (the idea conveyed by French *quelques*) (Hockett).

pause of silence The period of complete occlusion before the release of a stop in geminated or "double" plosives. *Synonym:* HOLDING PERIOD. *See also* HOLD, SISTANT.

pause pitch The rise of pitch before a pause in the sentence. *Synonym:* SUSPENSION PITCH.

peak (of sonority) The most sonorous part of a syllable (as a vowel, or syllabic consonant) (Webster III). *Synonyms:* CREST, SYLLABIC, SYLLABIC PEAK.

peak nucleus The main vowel in a diphthong (*o* in *boy*).

peak satellite The glide in a diphthong (*y* in *boy*). *See also* OFF-GLIDE.

pedigree theory The view that the parent Indo-European language split into two branch languages, each again bifurcating, as branches from a tree trunk to smaller branches and twigs (Schleicher). *Synonyms:* FAMILY TREE THEORY, STAMMBAUMTHEORIE. *See also* WAVE THEORY, WELLENTHEORIE.

pejoration 1. A semantic shift undergone by a word, involving a lowering in meaning (Spanish *alguacil,* "constable," Italian *aguzzino,* "hangman's helper," from Arabic *al-wazir,* "vizier"). *Synonym:* DEGENERATION. *Opposites:* AMELIORATION, ENHANCEMENT, MELIORATION.

2. The addition of a pejorative suffix (*poet-aster,* Italian *libr-accio*).

pejorative   *See* PEJORATION.

pendant   All that precedes the head of a macrosegment (Hockett).

penult (or **penultimate**)   The next to the last syllable in a word (capil*lar*y).

perfective   A verbal ASPECT (*q.v.*) expressing a non-habitual or one-time action, or an action considered from the standpoint of its completion, conclusion, or result (Russian *dat',* as opposed to *davat'*). *Synonym:* MOMENTARY. *Opposites:* DURATIVE, IMPERFECTIVE.

peripheral language   A language showing characteristics typical of another language group, supposedly acquired as a result of early separation from its own speech community and contact with the other group (Meillet). *See also* CONVERGENCE AREA, LANGUAGES IN CONTACT.

peripheral theory   The view that languages at the extreme ends of the Indo-European area retained certain features in common by reason of the fact that they broke off earlier than the rest from the parent language (Meillet). *See also* LATERAL AREAS.

petrification   The process by which a complete phrase is combined into a single word (the Moslem battle cry "Ya Hasan! Ya Hussein!" turning into *Hobson-Jobson;* the hypothetical Vulgar Latin *ad illum diurnum de hoc die* becoming French *aujourd'hui*) (Entwistle). *See also* FIXATION.

petroglyph   A primitive pictogram carved on a rock.

phantom word   *See* GHOST WORD.

pharyng(e)al   1. A consonant phonated at the pharynx; formed with the base of the tongue near the back of the pharynx, and the pharyngeal walls strongly contracted (Arabic *ghain*).

2. Distinctive pharyngeal fricatives, emphatic consonants which are characteristic of the Semitic and Ham-
itic languages, are produced by a raised larynx and a
vigorous constriction of the pharynx slightly below and
behind the extreme edge of the velum. Such constriction is made by drawing the body of the tongue back
toward the posterior wall of the pharynx with considerable force. Voiceless [ħ] is thus produced; for voiced
[ʕ], there are very vigorous vibrations of the ventricu-
lar bands. These sounds may also be called PRESS-
LAUTE; the type of squeezed voicing used for [ʕ] is
called PRESSTIMME (de la Garza).

pharyngealization   Secondary feature which involves compression of the larynx.

phememe   The smallest (and meaningless) unit of linguistic signaling; it is subdivided into PHONEME and
TAXEME (*q.v.*) (Bloomfield).

philological conditions   The study of languages and linguistic forms from historical documents, inscriptions,
and other written materials. *See also* FIELD CONDITIONS.

philology   1. The science and scientific study of language, words, and linguistic laws. *Synonym:* LINGUIS-
TICS.

2. The above, with the inclusion of literary, particularly the older, texts of the language, with the study of
the language itself regarded as a means to an end. *Partial synonym:* HISTORICAL LINGUISTICS. *See also* COM-
PARATIVE LINGUISTICS.

3. The study of a language and its entire literary output.

philosophical grammar   *See* GENERAL (*also* PANCHRONIC,
UNIVERSAL) GRAMMAR.

phon(o) or **phon(e)**   Combining form meaning sound,
voice, speech, tone. Derived from Greek word meaning
"articulated sound." *See also* LOGOS.

phonation   The production of speech sounds by the vocal
organs (Bloch and Trager).

phone   Any objective speech sound, considered as a

physical event, and without regard as to how it fits into the structure of any given language. *See also* PHONEME.

phonema Greek word meaning "what has been said." *See also* PHONEME.

phonematic *See* PHONEMIC; preferred by many European linguists (Entwistle).

phonematics 1. Term used by purists to mean PHONEMICS or PHONOLOGIE.

2. Analysis of utterances into phonemes, their classification and combination (Martinet). *Synonyms:* PHONEMICS, PHONOLOGIE, SEGMENTAL PHONEMICS.

phoneme 1. The minimal unit of distinctive sound-feature (Bloomfield).

2. The smallest unit of speech distinguishing one utterance from another, in all the variations it displays in the speech of one person or in one dialect as a result of modifying influences, such as neighboring sounds or stress (Webster III).

3. A single speech sound or group of similar or related speech sounds functioning analogously in a language, and usually represented in writing by the same letter, with or without diacritic marks (Dorfman).

4. The minimal bundle of relevant sound features. A phoneme is not a sound; it can be realized only through one of its allophones; it is a class of sounds, actualized or realized in a different way in any given position by its representative the allophone; it is an ideal toward which the speaker strives, while the allophone is the performance he achieves; it occupies an area within which the various allophones move and operate; its outer limits may approach but not overlap those of other phonemes, and it cannot invade the territory of another phoneme without loss of phonemic distinction (Fowkes). *See also* ALLOPHONE, OVERLAP, PHONE.

phonemic *See* DISTINCTIVE, RELEVANT.

phonemically conditioned alternation An alternation that occurs when a morpheme changes phonetic shape if the nature of the first phoneme of the next word so requires in the given language (the English indefinite article has the shape /ə/, *a,* if the first phoneme of the next word is a consonant, but /æn/, *an,* if the first phoneme of the next word is a vowel; thus the alternation is phonemically conditioned, though non-automatic. AUTOMATIC ALTERNATION (*q.v.*) is always phonemically conditioned, but phonemically conditioned alternations are not always automatic). *Opposite:* MORPHEMICALLY CONDITIONED ALTERNATION (de la Garza).

phonemic analysis *See* LINGUISTIC ANALYSIS.

phonemic change 1. Can occur historically, when UNCONDITIONED PHONETIC CHANGE (*q.v.*) plays havoc with the whole phonemic system of a language, changing the form (significant features), function, distribution, and relative frequency of the phonemes in the system, but nevertheless maintaining a regular PHONEMIC PATTERN. With such change, there may or may not be a change in the number of phonemes in the PHONEMIC CONFIGURATION (e.g., Proto-Germanic). *See also* DRIFT, GRIMM'S LAW.

2. There may be change in the PHONEMIC PATTERN of a language as a result of unconditioned merger of some phonemes, resulting in a reduction in the number of phonemes in the phonemic structure, and change of frequency and distribution of the phonemes in the new structure.

3. A phoneme in a system could also be lost if every word in which it occurs becomes obsolete. Phonemic change would thus be due to a frequency factor.

4. Sporadically, a phoneme could be added to a system if someone invented one, and many followers carried it through (unvoiced [l] in English). *See also* HOLES IN THE PATTERN.

5. The most common type of phonemic change would probably result eventually from a structural allophonic

change which is regular and conditioned in a given language; when the conditioning factor in the allophonic change merges with another sound, and thus ceases to exist. The two sounds which were previously allophones in this conditioned environment (complementary distribution) come to exist in the same environment, and thus become two distinct phonemes, causing addition of a phoneme in the phonemic pattern. *See also* ALLOPHONIC ANALOGY, ALLOPHONIC CHANGE, COMPLEMENTARY DISTRIBUTION, REGULAR SOUND CHANGE.

6. There can be addition of one or more phonemes in a structure due to the influence of another language, whereby, through borrowed forms, new sounds enter the language (English, borrowing such forms as [gəraž], "garage" and [ruž], "rouge," from French, brought into its phonemic structure [ž] which corresponded with [š], and [ž], though infrequent, became part of English phonemic structure). *See also* HOLES IN THE PATTERN (de la Garza).

phonemic loan The introduction of a foreign phoneme in a position where it would not normally occur in the borrowing language (initial /tm/ in *tmesis,* /ts/ in *tsetse fly,* /šm/ in *schmo*) (Sturtevant).

phonemic phrase An utterance or a part of an utterance containing extra strong stress (*"Shut up!"*) (Hall).

phonemics 1. The study of sound features that are pertinent or relevant in a language system (written *p* of *pit, spit, sip,* represents three different phones, but a single phoneme, and the differences among them are automatic) (Fowkes).

2. The classification of the sounds of a language into phonemes, or the study of the phonemic system of a language.

3. The study, analysis and classification of phonemes, their relationships and changes, and their allophones (Dorfman).

4. The linguistic analysis (social and cultural evaluation) of PHONETICS. Phonemics is called PHONOLOGIE in Europe, and PHONEMATICS by Martinet and other purists (de la Garza).

phonemic shape *See* SHAPE.

phonemic stress Accentuation of a different syllable in two words otherwise phonemically identical; stress must thus be considered a SEGMENTAL PHONEME, as it constitutes the minimal contrast, accounting for the only difference in meaning or function between two forms (MINIMAL PAIR, *q.v.*) (Nouns *pérmit* and *óverflow* vs. verbs *permít* and *overflów*) (de la Garza).

phonemic substitution The replacement of a phoneme in a loan word by its nearest equivalent in the borrowing language (a Frenchman's *dees* or *zees* for *this*) (Hoenigswald). *See also* PHONE SUBSTITUTION.

phonemic transcription The written representation of the phonemes in an utterance, with the symbols excluding all irrelevant features (Dorfman). *See also* BROAD (*also* NARROW, PHONETIC) TRANSCRIPTION.

phonemization The structural change in the sound system whereby allophones are raised to phonemic status (historically, the development of an opposition between English *f* and *v* in the initial position; Anglo-Saxon, using only *f* in its orthography, probably pronounced it [f] initially and [v] between vowels, so that the two sounds were in complementary distribution, or allophones of a single phoneme; when Norman influence brought in the sound of [v] in the initial position, [f] and [v], now in opposition, became two distinct phonemes).

phonestheme 1. A seemingly meaningful consonant cluster that may eventually be proved to be a morpheme (/sn-/ for things pertaining to the nose : *snot, snort, snuff, snuffle, sniffle,* etc.); a common feature of sound in a group of symbolic words (Webster III). 2. A phonemic cluster with sound symbolism which begins sporadically and tends to spread (becomes productive) for no ascertainable reason; there is a partial phonetic-semantic resemblance in all forms containing a particular phonestheme; there is more than ordinary relationship between sound and meaning, and the relationship does not seem to be strictly arbitrary, yet phonesthemes are not real morphemes; though they have partial phonetic-semantic relationship to other forms, they do not, in the words of Greenberg, "form a perfect square." *See also* MARGINAL SOUNDS (de la Garza).

phone substitution That feature of foreign accent whereby a given sound is regularly replaced by a native sound different in articulation, but not in phonemic definition (Spanish trilled /r/ for American /r/). *See also* PHONEMIC SUBSTITUTION.

phonetic 1. Pertaining to PHONETICS, or language sounds.

2. In Chinese writing, one of the symbols of a compound ideograph (the other is the RADICAL, *q.v.*), which gives a partial clue to the pronunciation of the spoken word represented by the ideograph. *Synonyms:* PHONETIC COMPLEMENT, PHONETIC INDICATOR.

phonetic alphabet 1. Any set of symbols designed to represent spoken language sounds.

2. The INTERNATIONAL PHONETIC ALPHABET (IPA), *q.v.*

phonetic alternation A phenomenon occurring when the difference between the alternants of one morpheme can be described in terms of PHONETIC MODIFICATION (*q.v.*) (de la Garza).

phonetic change Modifications of sounds in the course of the history and development of a language. *Synonym:* DRIFT.

phonetic complement In logographic or ideographic writing, a non-semantic element added to the logogram or pictogram to indicate the proper pronunciation and the significance of the sign in the context in which it appears. *Synonyms:* PHONETIC, PHONETIC INDICATOR.

phonetic indicator *See* PHONETIC, PHONETIC COMPLEMENT.

phonetic law The systematic formulation of the rules and principles which reflect sound shifts and other phonetic changes; "a 'phonetic law' is not an explanation, but something to be explained; it is nothing but a mere statement of facts, a formula of correspondence, which says nothing about the cause of change" (Jespersen); a formula derived from an observed uniformity in the development, under given conditions, of a sound or sound combination in a given area and during a given period of time (Webster III). *Synonyms:* LAUTGESETZ, SOUND LAW.

phonetic modification The taxeme or feature of grammatical arrangement which involves a change in the primary phonemes of a form. The modification may be obligatory or optional, and it may or may not involve a difference in connotation. Where modification is obligatory, each alternant may be said to occur in conditioned environment; if the alternants do not have approximately the same range, the one with wider range may be called the basic alternant (the use of *do + not* or *don't* is optional, but with difference in connotation; the use of *duke > duch + ess* to express "female of *duke*" is obligatory, and the two phonetic forms, *duke* and *duch-*, are alternants which occur under given conditions). *See also* PRIMARY PHONEME (de la Garza).

phonetics 1. The science, study, analysis and classification of speech sounds, including their production, transmission, and reception. *See also* ACOUSTIC (*also* ARTICULATORY, EXPERIMENTAL, GENEMMIC, GENETIC) PHONETICS.

2. American and European term for the general description of the event of speech structure as such. In France, phonetics is often interpreted to mean the descriptive or synchronic study of sound (de la Garza).

phonetic spelling *See* NOMIC SPELLING, PHONETIC WRITING.

phonetic symbols The symbols used in the INTERNATIONAL PHONETIC ALPHABET (IPA) (*q.v.*), or any other phonetic alphabet.

phonetic transcription 1. The representation of a phoneme, sound or utterance in a phonetic alphabet.

2. Rendering speech (anything pronounced) by the graphic method (writing). *See also* BROAD (*also* NARROW, PHONEMIC) TRANSCRIPTION.

phonetic variants 1. ALTERNANTS; ALLOMORPHS in COMPLEMENTARY DISTRIBUTION, each occurring in a specific environment. Morphophonemic and sandhi statements center about POSITIONAL VARIANTS of one functional morpheme (Bloomfield, Harris, Zipf).

2. NON-DISTINCTIVE variations in phonemic analysis, which occur within a margin, and can be subsumed under a single feature. They are facultative and nonfunctional, and may be classified as RANDOM VARIATIONS, variations due to STYLE (age, sex, size, weight, social occasion, social class), emotion, etc. *See also* CHARACTEROLOGY OF SPEECH, NON-DISTINCTIVE, NON-FUNCTIONAL, PARALINGUISTICS (de la Garza).

phonetic writing 1. The use of phonetic symbols to represent individual sounds or syllables, as opposed to IDEOGRAPHIC or LOGOGRAPHIC WRITING (*q.v.*).

2. A system of writing where each sign represents one spoken sound only, and each spoken sound is represented by one written sign only. *See also* IPA.

phoneti(ci)zation The representation of articulate sounds phonetically, through a PHONETIC TRANSCRIPTION (*q.v.*).

phoniatry The remedial science that attempts to correct speech defects (Entwistle).

phonics A method of teaching reading and pronunciation by learning the phonetic value of letters and groups of letters (the different value of *ight* in *freight* as opposed to its value in *night, light, might,* etc.) (Webster III).

phonogenetic phonetics *See* ACOUSTIC PHONETICS.

phonogram 1. A character or symbol representing a word, syllable or phoneme. *See also* IDEOGRAM.

2. A succession of orthographic letters occurring with the same phonetic value in many words (*-ight* of *light, fight, plight,* etc.; used to teach PHONICS, *q.v.*).

3. A compound character in Chinese writing, consisting of a RADICAL and a PHONETIC (*q.v.*).

4. A graph obtained by the aid of laboratory apparatus for the study of spoken phonemes.

phonological components Hall's term for DISTINCTIVE (*q.v.*) features.

Phonologie European term for PHONEMICS (*q.v.*).

phonology 1. A full description of the sounds of a language.

2. A study of the changes, modifications and transformations of speech sounds during the history and development of a language or dialect, considering each phoneme in the light of the part it plays in the structure of speech forms, and accepting it as a unit without consideration of its acoustic features (Dorfman). Phonology may be subdivided into two branches: HISTORICAL (the history and theory of sound changes), and DESCRIPTIVE (the sounds of the language and their permissible combinations at any given historical stage); descriptive phonology may then be subdivided into PHONETICS and PHONEMICS (*q.v.*).

3. (a) Cover term for the general description of the speech structure event as such, in both America and Europe. (b) In Europe, PHONEMIK is often used as the equivalent of PHONOLOGIE (*q.v.*). (c) In France PHONOLOGY has a historical meaning, and is used in the diachronic approach to the study of sound, while the descriptive or synchronic approach is referred to as PHONETICS (de la Garza).

phonosymbolism A term used for cases where the phonological laws of development are not followed by reason of a factor of symbolization or onomatopoeia (Tuscan *bubbola,* instead of *bobbola,* from Latin *upupula*) (Migliorini). *See also* ANALOGY, FOLK ETYMOLOGY.

phonotactics The study of the sequences of phonemes, intermediate between phonemics and morphemics (Hill). *See also* DISCOURSE ANALYSIS.

phylogeny (linguistic) *See* HISTORICAL LINGUISTICS; the study of the history of a language, as opposed to the study of the speech of one individual (Hockett). *Opposite:* LINGUISTIC ONTOGENY.

physical phonetics *See* ACOUSTIC PHONETICS.

physiological phonetics *See* ARTICULATORY PHONETICS.

physiophonetics The treatment of a phoneme as it is heard (Entwistle, Courtenay). *See also* PSYCHOPHONETICS.

pictogram A written symbol denoting a definite object, of which it is a complete or simplified picture. *See also* IDEOGRAM, LINEAR WRITING, LOGOGRAM.

pictographic writing Writing consisting of PICTOGRAMS (*q.v.*). *Opposite:* LINEAR WRITING.

pidgin A creolized or hybrid version of a language, usually characterized by simplified grammar and by a limited and often mixed vocabulary, and used chiefly for intergroup communications (Melanesian Pidgin English, Haitian French Creole); an auxiliary or contact language that has no speech community of its own, but arises from casual contacts among people having no common speech background (Hall; he differentiates between a pidgin and a creole or creolized language, which grows out of a pidgin, but becomes the first language of the speech community). *See also* CREOLE, CONTACT VERNACULAR, HYBRID (*also* MAKESHIFT, MINIMAL, RELATIONAL, VEHICULAR) LANGUAGE.

pitch 1. Highness or lowness of tone; frequency of vibration in the musical sound of the voice; difference

in the relative vibration frequency of the human voice
that contributes to the total meaning of ear-appre-
hended speech by being, as in Chinese, an integral part
of the word and essential in conveying its minimal
meaning, or by varying according to the intended minimal meaning of a word having different meanings
(Webster III). *See also* PAUSE (or SUSPENSION) PITCH.
2. (a) One of the inherent qualities of speech sounds;
every speech sound, during the production of which
the vocal bands vibrate, has a FUNDAMENTAL PITCH.
Pitch is often a very important factor in the functioning
of the linguistic signal, as no speech can occur without
variations of some sort (tonal, intonational, emotive)
in the pitch of its sounds. (b) Anatomical conditions
provide speakers with natural ranges of pitch which
they cannot exceed; women, having shorter vocal cords
which are of smaller mass than men's, have upper
PITCH REGISTERS, while men have lower ones. (c) The
actual physical rate of the vibration of the vocal bands
is likely to change as the articulation of any sound
progresses. Variations in pitch may be either up or
down, but they must be at a more or less stable mean
frequency. Pitch may also have direction, being either
progressively rising or progressively falling. Two successive sound waves of the same speech sound need
not have the same length. (d) Auditorily, the human
hearing mechanism tends to smooth out or fail to hear
minor changes from vibration to vibration if the general level of pitch remains constant; however, it is quick
to perceive any tendency to rise or fall. All that needs
to be considered for linguistic purposes is what can be
heard; thus, it is the RELATIVE PITCH of speech sounds
which is a linguistic means of differentiation between
meanings. (e) Acoustically, pitch is counted in cycles
per second (c.p.s.), which relates to how many times
the vocal bands open and close to produce sound
waves; it is higher and faster for women, for reasons

stated above. On the spectrogram, voice pitch is read as spacing between the harmonics (theoretically, the amount of space between zero and the first). "The frequency of the perceived pitch equals the greatest common divisor of all the frequencies actually present in the tone." Since vocal cord vibrations are regular, spaces between harmonics are also regular. (f) Independent of voice pitch (which represents activity at the larynx), and not to be confused with it is the QUALITY or TIMBRE of the particular sound, which is readable in the strength (darkness) in certain frequency regions (the others are filtered out, relative to articulatory movements in the buccal cavity, above the larynx), and the number and frequency of FORMANTS. Pitch (harmonics) and formant frequencies usually change with TIME, but they need not necessarily change together. Voiced and voiceless vowels change slightly, but they stay in the same general area. (g) NOISE, composed at least in part of RANDOM FREQUENCIES, cannot be so represented on the spectrogram. (h) ABSOLUTE PITCH, that is, the inclusion of physical and acoustic overtones or higher harmonics, is not very important in speech; these are non-pitch characteristics (oscillations). Psychologically and perceptionally, however, they cause a different perception of sound, and are the decisive component so far as MELODY is concerned. Acoustically, this is called the QUALITY of the tone, and each additional harmonic affects the profile of each cycle of the wave, and thus the quality of the resultant complex tone. (i) Of importance to the phoneticist are : (1) the RELATIVE PITCH of the initial FUNDAMENTAL TONE; (2) the DIRECTION of any characteristic changes in pitch (rising, falling, rising-falling, etc.); (3) the MODE of change (abrupt/slurred, etc.); (4) the DEGREE of change. It is of linguistic importance that pitch is an integral part of some meaningful units : the morpheme, speech measure or clause. Production of significant pitch characteristics or patterns in these speech forms is called INTONATION. MELODY usually marks higher units. *See also* FUNCTIONS OF PITCH, PITCH ACCENT, PITCH LEVELS, TONE LANGUAGE (de la Garza).

pitch accent   1. Prominence given to a syllable or word by a raised pitch, or a change of pitch (Webster III). *Synonyms:* CHROMATIC (*also* MUSICAL) ACCENT. *Opposites:* INTENSITY (*also* STRESS) ACCENT.

2. Where tonal movements (as distinguished from levels) are used as a distinctive feature, the pitch accent can be a simple monosyllabic tone, or a complex polysyllabic one (Swedish [andən], "the ghost," vs. [andən], "the duck"). The pitch difference here is associated with the stress pattern, and could conceivably be obscured by sentence intonation. Where it might be difficult to identify, the context could give the cue as to what is intended by the speaker. *See also* PITCH, STRESS, TONE LANGUAGE (de la Garza).

pitch functions   *See* FUNCTIONS OF PITCH.

pitch level   1. *See* TONE LANGUAGE.

2. One of the tones that distinguish meaning; in a transcription, distinctive tones may be numbered or indicated by horizontal or other lines at various levels (Walsh); the pitch levels for American English are described as four in number: low, mid, high, extra high (Hockett, Gleason).

pitch range   The possibility of spreading the pitch upward or downward, or narrowing it from above or below (Trager).

pitch registers   *See* PITCH.

plereme   1. Linguistically, a morpheme, or anything pertaining to grammar (Hockett).

2. A unit of expression that has content, as opposed to a CENEME (*q.v.*); the aspect of language concerned with grammar (i.e., the level of CONTENT, including

morphology, syntax as form, and semantics as substance) (Hjelmslev).

plosive A consonant that momentarily halts the flow of breath, and is produced by completely closing the nasal and oral air passages (IMPLOSION), resulting in a retention of air (HOLDING PERIOD, PAUSE OF SILENCE), then suddenly opening the closure and releasing the breath (EXPLOSION); this final phase may not invariably occur; it may be accompanied or not by vibration of the vocal cords (VOICED: /d/, /b/, /g/; VOICELESS: /t/, /p/, /k/). *Synonyms:* EXPLOSIVE, MUTE, OBSTRUCTIVE, OCCLUSIVE, OPENING SOUND, STOP. *See also* FRICATIVE, SPIRANT.

plural of approximation The plural of numerals referring to decades in the lives of individuals or in centuries ("he is in his *sixties,*" "the gay *nineties*") (Jespersen).

plurative A morpheme whose function it is to confer upon a word the force of a plural (Meillet and Cohen). *Opposite:* SINGULATIVE.

plus juncture *See* OPEN JUNCTURE.

pointer (word) Bodmer's term for a demonstrative. *Partial synonyms:* EMPTY WORD, FORM WORD, FUNCTION WORD, MARKER, PARTICLE.

point of articulation 1. The point where the articulators (*q.v.*) meet the immovable speech organs (*q.v.*).

2. The point of maximum constriction in the pharynx or mouth.

3. One of the three variables in the traditional phonetic description of speech sounds; used in describing how the buccal cavity is formed, i.e., what articulators normally come together to produce sound (normal articulators can be compensated for by certain adjustments of other parts; i.e., use of a different filter). *Synonym:* LOCALIZATION. *See also* AFFRICATE, FRICATIVE, LIQUID, MANNER OF ARTICULATION, NASAL, SEMI-VOWEL, STOP, VOICE, VOWEL (de la Garza).

polygenesis The theory that human language arose in

different areas of the world and among different groups of human beings independently of one another. *Opposite:* MONOGENESIS.

polyglot 1. As applied to a person, speaking several languages.

2. As applied to a text, containing versions of the same text in various languages. *Partial synonyms:* MULTILINGUAL, PLURILINGUAL. *Opposites:* MONOGLOT, UNILINGUAL.

polyonomy A large number of concrete, particular terms for an object (various separate words for falling snow, hard-packed snow, drifting snow, etc.), which reflect a certain view of the world and perpetuate it by passing it on to the oncoming generations (Kainz).

polyphony The representation by a single graphic sign of various sounds (English *s* in *sure, pleasure, sign, rose*). *See also* MONOPHONE.

polysemy 1. The use of the same word in two or more distinct meanings (*post*) (Ullmann).

2. Many meanings arising from the same original root, largely by a process of metaphor (Indo-European *reg gives rise to Sanskrit *rājah* and Latin *rēx,* but also to Anglo-Saxon *riht* and English *right*) (Gray); ultimately, such widely differentiated meanings as *rule, real, rich* arise in English from the original single root.

polysynthetic language A language where various words are combined (usually they are merged into the equivalent of a verb), with the resulting composite word representing an entire sentence, statement or idea; a language where the word often coincides with the sentence or phrase. *Synonyms:* HOLOPHRASTIC (*also* HOLOSYNTHETIC, INCAPSULATING, INCORPORATING) LANGUAGE.

polytonic language A language having several phonemic pitch levels, which serve to distinguish meanings of otherwise identical words (Chinese). *Synonym:* TONE LANGUAGE.

pooh-pooh theory The belief that language arose out

of ejaculations of surprise, pain, pleasure, etc. *Synonym:* INTERJECTIONAL THEORY.

popular etymology   *See* FOLK ETYMOLOGY.

popular word (or **form**)   A word or form developed in full accord with the phonological laws of its language (French *frêle,* as against *fragile*). *Opposite:* BOOK WORD, LEARNED WORD.

portmanteau morpheme   A simultaneous morph component; a morpheme represented by a single phoneme, and which represents two morphemes simultaneously (French {o}, *au,* which represents both *à* and *le,* as contrasted with the feminine *à la*) (de la Garza).

portmanteau word   A word coined by combining the first part of one word with the last part of another (*smog,* from *smoke* plus *fog; motel,* from *motor* plus *hotel*) (Lewis Carroll). *See also* BLEND, CONTAMINATION, CROSSING, TELESCOPED WORD.

position   The privilege of occurrence, or position, in a word of a phoneme with respect to its environment; with respect to a vowel, it often refers to whether the vowel is final in its syllable (FREE POSITION), or followed by a consonant in the same syllable (CHECKED POSITION); in the latter sense POSITION is sometimes used alone by European writers. *See also* FINAL (*also* INITIAL, MEDIAL, PROTECTED) POSITION.

positional variant   An allophonic variant due to distribution, or environment, or context (the phoneme /k/ has a front articulation in *key,* a back articulation in *cool*). *Synonyms:* ALLOPHONE, COMPLEMENTARY DISTRIBUTION, COMBINATORY (*also* CONDITIONAL, CONTEXTUAL) VARIANT.

position of articulation   *See* ARTICULATORY PHONETICS.

post-dental   1. A sound articulated with the tip of the tongue against the upper gum ridges. *Synonyms:* ALVEOLAR, GINGIVAL.

2. A sound articulated with the tip of the tongue against the back of the upper teeth. *Synonym:* DENTAL.

post-dorsal   Using the back part of the dorsum of the tongue to establish contact with an immovable speech organ.

post-palatal   Marouzeau's term for a sound articulated : (a) against the rear third or half of the hard palate; (b) against the rear half of the palate as a whole; (c) against the soft palate or velum. *Partial synonyms:* GUTTURAL, PALATAL, VELAR.

postposition   A particle or word placed after another word to indicate its grammatical or syntactical relationship to other words, and having the same function as a preposition (-*ward* in *skyward; no* in Japanese *hito no,* "man of," "of the man"; *ban* in Hungarian *Magyarországban,* "Hungarian land in," "in Hungary").

post-tonic   After the main accent.

post-tonic syllable   The syllable that follows the accented syllable.

post-velar   A consonant produced with the tongue farther back than the velar position, and the articulation against the rear half of the velum, or soft palate (Arabic *q*). *Partial synonym:* UVULAR.

potentialities, semantic   *See* SEMANTIC POTENTIALITIES.

pre-adjective   An adjective preceding the noun it modifies (Sweet).

pre-adjunct order   Putting the adjunct or modifying word before its head-word in forming compounds (Greek *hippo-damos,* "horse-taming") (Sweet).

pre-dental   A consonant produced with the front part of the tongue held near or touching the upper teeth (French *t, d*). *Synonyms:* DENTAL, POST-DENTAL 2.

predicate attribute   *See* CONNECTIVE CONSTRUCTION (Hockett).

predicative construction   An exocentric construction consisting of a topic (or subject) and a comment (or predicate) ("He — is a big man") (Hockett).

predicative syntagm   *See* SYNTAGM.

pre-dorsal A consonant articulated by using the front part of the dorsum (Martinet). *Opposite:* POST-DORSAL.

prefix An affix or formative consisting of a letter, syllable or syllables, placed before and fused with a word, to form with it a single unit and change its meaning; a sound or sequence of sounds occurring as a bound morpheme attached to the beginning of a word, base or phrase, to produce a derivative word or inflectional form (Webster III). *See also* AFFIX, INFIX, SUFFIX.

prefixal morpheme A morpheme which, with its allomorphs, serves as a prefix (*in-,* meaning "not," in *inactive;* the morphophonemic allomorphs of *in-* are the *im-* of *impossible,* used before a labial; the *il-* of *illiterate,* used before *l;* the *ir-* of *irregular,* used before *r;* etc.). *See also* ALLOMORPH, PREFIX.

pregnant construction The use of a case indicating not merely completion of the action indicated by the verb, but permanence of the result (Sanskrit *grāmayā* [dative] *gacchati,* "he goes toward the village"; *grāmam* [accusative] *gacchati,* "he goes to [and reaches] the village"; *grāme* [locative] *gacchati,* "he goes to the village," with the implication that he reaches it and stays there) (Gray).

pre-grammar 1. The study of the unorganized language of children. *See also* ONTOGENY.

2. Research into the state of the language in its prehistoric stages, and of the grammatical categories which cannot be accounted for by logical analysis (what psychological process led to classifying German *Weib* and *Kind* as neuters?) (Entwistle).

prelinguistics 1. The physiology of speech (Lloyd).

2. Language sounds considered as noise (Trager and Hill).

3. According to Trager, the physical and biological events (acoustic and articulatory phonetics) organized as the basis for MICROLINGUISTICS (*q.v.*), in the larger

system of MACROLINGUISTICS (*q.v.*). *See also* META-
LINGUISTICS, PARALINGUISTICS.

pre-palatal   1. A consonant articulated with the dorsum
against or close to the velum (Martinet).
2. A consonant articulated against the front third or
half of the hard palate or the front third of the palate
as a whole (Webster III).

pre-pausal juncture   The type of juncture that occurs
when the stream of breath ceases before a pause
(French *il est tout vert* vs. *il est ouvert*) (Hall).

prescriptive   Indicating what should be said, which may
or may not be descriptive of what is actually said; the
linguist describes; the language teacher, basing himself
on this description, prescribes (Walsh). *Synonym:*
NORMATIVE. *Opposite:* DESCRIPTIVE.

prescriptive grammar   The presentation of a language's
grammar as a set of rules which must be obeyed by all
who wish to be considered as speakers of the standard
language. *Synonyms:* NORMATIVE GRAMMAR, STATICS.
Opposite: DESCRIPTIVE GRAMMAR.

presentational affix   A word capable of being used as a
prefix, or as a suffix, or as a separate word with a distinct and independent meaning of its own (*wise* in *wise
guy, wiseacre;* in *lengthwise;* in *wise man,* in *wondrous
wise*).

presentative   In English, the infinitive used without *to*
("He did nothing but sit") (Joos).

presentive word   A word that directly conveys an idea,
concept, picture or notion of an object to the mind of
the listener.

Presslaute   *See* PHARYNGEAL.

Presstimme   *See* PHARYNGEAL.

pressures, paradigmatic and syntagmatic   The conflicting
tendencies of a linguistic unit to assimilate itself to its
context in the speech chain (syntagmatic), and to differentiate itself from its neighbors in the system (paradigmatic) (/ata/ turns into /ada/, with continuous

vibration of the vocal cords [assimilation of voicing]; but if /ada/ already exists in the system, there is a resistance to the above change which would be absent if /ada/ were not in existence) (Martinet). *See also* HOLES IN THE PATTERN.

pressure stop A stop attended by an upward or forward movement of the speech organ at the point of inner closure, so that when the outer closure is broken there is a small expulsion of air from the mouth (Bloch and Trager). *Opposite:* SUCTION STOP. *See also* EGRESSIVE.

prestige center A locality from which innovations radiate to outlying areas because its inhabitants have prestige, and others wish to imitate them (Rome for the Roman Empire; Paris for medieval and modern France). *Synonyms:* FOCAL AREA, RADIATING CENTER. *See also* GRADED (*also* RELIC, TRANSITION) AREA.

prestige language (or **dialect**) The language, dialect or class speech viewed culturally as being standard and used by the "best" speakers (British U, as against non-U; cultivated Parisian in France; upper-class Florentine in Italy). Linguistically, it is not more systematic or regular than any other dialect.

pretonic Before the main accent.

pretonic syllable The syllable that precedes the stressed syllable.

preverb 1. A verbal prefix, often identical with a preposition, and interchangeable in use with it (Latin *ob* in *ob vos sacro,* later *obsecro vos,* "I beseech you") (Gray).

2. A prefix or particle that occurs before a verb base (*be* in *become*) (Webster III).

primary analogy The occasional influence of analogous forms in the borrowing language on the shape of the borrowed element (English *factory* becomes *factoría* in the Spanish of New York Puerto Ricans because of the existence of *zapatería, panadería,* etc., in Spanish).

primary compound *See* BASE COMPOUND.

primary language The indigenous tongue of a region, spoken with minor variations as a mother tongue by all or most of the inhabitants, who may also possess a secondary widespread tongue (French for the inhabitants of the Province of Quebec, some of whom also speak English).

primary phoneme 1. A simple, non-compound phoneme.

2. A speech feature or element any change in which has a direct bearing on the meaning of a word or utterance (Dorfman). *See also* PHONETIC MODIFICATION.

primary stress The main stress in the pronunciation of a word. *See also* ACCENT, STRESS.

primary vowels A set of eight vowels used by IPA (*q.v.*), where lip and tongue action are in accord with each other (the smaller the volume of the oral resonator, and the larger the opening, the higher the frequency or pitch). Thus, unrounded [i, e, ε, a, ɑ] are produced with small oral resonators and large openings, while rounded back [ɔ, o, u] are produced with relatively large oral resonator and small opening. Therefore, in listed order, there is gradual tongue lowering and retraction, and the frequency scale goes from highest to lowest:

```
        2nd F
        (oral cavity)    –
                            –
                         –
                      –
                   –
                –
Fundamental F            –
(pharyngeal cavity) – – – – – – – –
                    i  e  ε  a  ɑ  ɔ  o  u
```

See also SECONDARY VOWELS (de la Garza).

primary (or **prime**) **word** 1. A word not derived from another.

2. A substantive (Jespersen).

primitive *See* PROTO-, UR-.

Primitive Romance *See* VULGAR LATIN.

privative A generic term for prefixes, suffixes and other elements of word formation indicating the lack or absence of something (*non-, un-, -less*).

privative opposition The type of contrast that occurs when one member of a contrastive pair is characterized by the presence, the other by the absence, of a given feature (nasalization vs. lack of nasalization, voiced vs. unvoiced articulation; [d] = [t] + voice) (Trubetskoi).

privilege of occurrence Said to be possessed by words and groups of words (form-classes or constituent classes) which have the possibility of occurring in a given construction pattern or environment and of being substituted for one another ("the man who lives there," "the dweller," "he," have the same privilege of occurrence in a construction where they would be immediately followed by "wants to see you") (Hockett).

pro-adjective A word used instead of an adjective ("the black *one*") (*sic*) (Hall).

process The actual text at our disposal, having a "both . . . and" function (LOGICAL CONJUNCTION) (in the word *set*, there is COEXISTENCE among the phonemes *s, e* and *t*, since all three actually occur in the text) (Hjelmslev).

process verb In English, a verb used in the progressive form ("The judge is hearing the case now") (Joos). *See also* STATUS VERB.

proclitic A word or particle without sentence stress which is accentually dependent on the immediately following stressed word, and pronounced with it as one phonetic unit (Webster III); a non-syllabic word pronounced as part of the following word (the abbreviated form of *it* in *'tis;* Russian *v* in *v Moskve*). *Opposite:* ENCLITIC.

productive *See* PRODUCTIVITY.

productive prefix (or **suffix**) A prefix or suffix that can be and still is used to form new derivatives (*re-*, *-ish*) (Jespersen). *See also* PRODUCTIVITY.

productivity 1. The relative freedom with which the speakers of a language introduce new forms into the language, according to the example (analogy) of an already existing form; the form used as an example is the PRODUCTIVE form (*-ish* of *yellowish* can be applied to *five-thirty* and produce *five-thirtyish*); *-acious* of *audacious, pugnacious* goes on to *curvacious, predacious* (also *curvaceous, predaceous*); *-tel* of *hotel,* after creating *motel, boatel,* goes on to the Japanese-English hybrid *ryotel,* consisting of Japanese *ryokan,* "inn," blended with *-tel.*
2. A grammatical pattern can be productive syntactically (this is the most common), inflectionally, and derivationally (here new forms usually have idiomatic or symbolic value) (the paradigmatic class {z} /-z ~ -iz ~ -s/, used as a "plural for nouns," or a "third person singular for verbs," is a productive class in English, being applied to new nouns and verbs as they are introduced into the language). *See also* EXPANSION. *Opposites:* OBSOLESCENT, UNPRODUCTIVE (de la Garza).

progressive assimilation Assimilation (*q.v.*) of a phoneme which follows the assimilatory phoneme; this may be a regular or a sporadic process in a given language. *Synonym:* LAG. *See also* ACCOMMODATION 2.

progressive dissimilation A sporadic sound change which involves the dissimilation (*q.v.*) of a phoneme under the influence of a preceding dissimilatory phoneme.

pronunciation borrowing A speaker's imitation of someone else's pronunciation of a word which is already familiar to the borrower (mutually intelligible); the motive for it is usually prestige (a Midwesterner who goes East and pronounces his usual /mérij/, /hérij/ as /mǽrij/, /hǽrij/). *Opposite:* GRAMMATICAL BORROWING (de la Garza).

proparoxytone A word bearing its main accent on the syllable immediately preceding the penult (i.e., on the third from the last syllable: *nítrogen*). *See also* OXYTONE, PAROXYTONE.

proper compound A compound in which the members are so intimately fused that only the last member is inflected (*drum major*). *Opposite:* IMPROPER COMPOUND.

proper name The name of a specific person or place; usually capitalized in English. *Synonym:* NAME WORD. *See also* ONOMASTICS.

pro-phrase *See* CONJUNCTIVE (Hall).

proportional analogy (or **extension**) That form of analogy which follows the pattern x:y :: z:? (when in Italian development *vi* or *ve* came to mean both "you" and "there," *ci* and *ce,* which originally meant only "here," got to acquire also the meaning of "us," replacing the older forms *ni, ne*) (Sturtevant).

proportional opposition The form of contrast occurring when the same contrastive feature in a given pair occurs also in other pairs (voice vs. lack of voice in *b-p, d-t, k-g*) (Trubetskoi). *Opposite:* ISOLATED OPPOSITION.

pro-predicate complement A word used to replace an entire clause (Spanish no *lo* creo) (Hall).

pro-presentative The quality of language whereby an utterance conveys meaning without an actual presentation of an object, quality or event; or by which a REFEREND (*q.v.*) may call up another referend or other referends (Whatmough).

prop word A word that replaces a substantive; a noun or pronoun of indefinite meaning which takes on the qualifications of an adjective, giving the latter a virtual noun construction ("two apples, a red *one* and a green

one; books, manuscripts, and other literary *things"*)
(Webster III). *Synonym:* ANAPHORIC WORD.

prosiopesis *See* APHESIS.

prosodeme A prosodic (or suprasegmental, or secondary, or non-linear) phoneme (quantity, loudness, tone,
pitch, etc.).

prosodic features 1. Features which include accent,
pitch, cadence, and pauses; they do not change the
meaning of an utterance, but convey additional, con-
comitant information through their conventional acceptance by the speaking group (Hughes; he and
others, Webster III among them, use PROSODIC as synonymous with SUPRASEGMENTAL; other linguists
reject this equivalence, and some even fail to use the
term PROSODIC).
2. Etymologically, "what is added to the sound";
phones of stress, pitch, duration, juncture and syllabicity, all of which reflect the activity that takes place
below the glottis, thus dealing with the QUANTITY of
the sounds as functions of power (intensity) and number of vibrations (frequency) in a given relative
amount of time. Thus, they are *relative* qualities, or
attributes of sound. Such phones are defined according
to their form, and can be analyzed as segmental or
suprasegmental, depending on their function. *Opposite:* TIMBRE. *See also* SEGMENTAL, SUPRASEGMENTAL
(de la Garza).

prosodic sign *See* SIGN, PROSODIC.

prosody A general term for suprasegmental phonemic
phenomena.

prosthesis, prosthetic *See* PROTHESIS, PROTHETIC.

protected consonant A consonant preceded by another
consonant which prevents changes that would otherwise take place (*t* in Latin *montem, partem,* is protected
by the preceding *n* or *r,* and does not voice as it would
in intervocalic position).

prothesis The prefixing of an inorganic vowel or syllable to a word, for easier pronunciation or for other reasons (Latin *spiritum* > Vulgar Latin *ispiritum* > Italian (*i*)*spirito,* Spanish *espíritu,* French *esprit*). *Synonym:* PROSTHESIS.

prothetic vowel The vowel, usually *i,* prefixed to impure *s* (*s* plus consonant) in Vulgar Latin, remaining as a movable *i* in Italian, where it is used only after words ending in consonant, turning to *e* in Spanish and Old French, with subsequent widespread loss of the originally initial *s* in modern French (*statum* > *istato* or *stato, estado, estet, été*). *Synonym:* PROSTHETIC VOWEL.

proto- Combining form designating the earliest known, or the artificially reconstructed original, form of a language or word (Proto-Germanic, Proto-Indo-European). *Synonyms:* PRIMITIVE, UR-.

pro-verb A word used to replace a verb ("He doesn't go there, but I *do*") (Hall).

pseudo-semantic development The acquisition by a word of a new meaning, not by spontaneous development, out of an earlier meaning, but by influence of some other term in the same ASSOCIATIVE FIELD (*q.v.*) (*boon,* originally "petition," "request" in Old Norse, acquires the meaning of "blessing," "advantage" from semantic crossing with a homonymous *boon* ["boon companion"] that comes from Old French *bon*) (Orr).

pseudo-subjunctive A form of verbal hyper-correction ("he asked if supper were ready") (W. M. Ryan).

psycholinguistics The study of linguistics as connected with human behavior; of verbal behavior that attempts to integrate the linguist's view of language as a structured system of signs and the psychologist's view of language as learned behavior (Walsh); the study of linguistic behavior as conditioning and conditioned by psychological factors, including the speaker's and hearer's culturally determined categories of expression and comprehension (Webster III).

psychological phonetics   *See* ACOUSTIC PHONETICS.

psychophonetics   The treatment of a phoneme as the image aimed at in the speaker's mind (Courtenay, Entwistle). *See also* PHYSIOPHONETICS.

pure marker   A MARKER (*q.v.*) which signals a relationship between constituents without itself being one. *Opposite:* IMPURE MARKER.

pure-relational element   A language form having only a grammatical function (*and, but*) (Sapir).

Q

Q Celtic   *See* P AND Q CELTIC.

quadruplets   Four words of the same language any one of which is a doublet with any of the other three (*gentle, genteel, Gentile, jaunty*). *See also* DOUBLET, TRIPLET.

qualifier   A word or word group qualifying, limiting or modifying the meaning of another word. *See also* VOCAL (or VOICE) QUALIFIER.

qualitative accent   Accent based on stress and/or pitch.

qualitative gradation   *See* ABLAUT. *Synonym:* ABTÖNUNG.

quality   1. The identifying characteristic of a vowel sound, determined chiefly by the resonance of the vocal chambers in uttering it (Webster III).

2. *See* PITCH, TIMBRE.

quantifiable noun   *See* MASS NOUN.

quantifier   A numeral or other word denoting quantity when used to modify another word (*two, thirty, much, many*).

quantitative accent   Accent based on duration (long or

short vowels or syllables). *See also* DURATION, INTENSITY, STRESS.

quantitative gradation Lengthening, shortening, or suppression of vowels. *Synonym:* ABSTUFUNG. *See also* ABLAUT.

quantity 1. Duration or length; the relative amount of time during which the vocal organs stay in the position required for the articulation of a sound.

2. A term that refers to the activity which takes place below the glottis in sound production : pitch, stress, duration, juncture and syllabicity, all functions of power, and number of vibrations, in a given relative amount of time. The FREQUENCY, INTENSITY, and DURATION of a speech sound. *Synonyms:* PROSODIC FEATURES, VOWEL QUANTITY. *Opposites:* TIMBRE, VOWEL QUALITY (de la Garza).

quantity mark A diacritic placed over a vowel or diphthong to indicate that it is to be pronounced long or short ($\bar{a}$, $\breve{a}$). *See also* BREVE, MACRON.

quasi-auxiliary In English, a verb that may be followed by an infinitive (*begin, ask, appear*) (Joos).

questione della lingua A discussion originated by Dante as to the true nature and origin of the Italian literary language (whether it is based on Florentine Tuscan pure and simple, or represents a partial compromise or merger of various dialectal forms of northern, southern and central Italy).

R

radiating center *See* FOCAL AREA, PRESTIGE CENTER.

radiation of synonyms A tendency, when a word is given a transferred sense, for its synonyms to develop along parallel lines (Ullmann).

radical 1. That part of a derived word which is phonetically and semantically the vehicle of the basic meaning; one or more sounds or syllables, common to all words relating to or signifying the same idea or concept, and thus capable of being regarded as the semantic vehicle of the idea or concept (Webster III); the inflectional theme or root (Saussure). *Partial synonyms :* BASE, ROOT, STEM.

2. In Chinese writing, any one of 214 elementary ideographs forming categories of sense and combined with phonetics to form phonograms whose meaning they suggest (Walsh). *Partial synonyms :* DETERMINATIVE, KEY, SEMANTIC INDICATOR.

radical flection A type of inflection where the endings are attached directly to the root or root base of a word.

radical language *See* ISOLATING (*also* AMORPHOUS, ATOMIC, ANALYTICAL, FORMLESS) LANGUAGE.

random variations Speech phenomena (e.g., a BURST, *q.v.*) which are articulated at random. Such variations are PARALINGUISTIC (*q.v.*). *See also* CHARACTEROLOGY OF SPEECH, PHONETIC VARIANTS, STYLISTICS (de la Garza).

range Combined environments; the class of all the environments in which the member morphs of a morpheme occur or are distinctive (de la Garza).

rank The standing of words in their mutual relations as qualified and qualifying terms (Webster III). *See also* JUNCTION, NEXUS.

realization The production of an actual sound objectivizing the speaker's concept, and accepted by his hearer as his own realization (Hughes). *Synonym:* ACTUALIZATION.

received pronunciation The term applied to the pronunciation heard or "received" in the more educated circles of Britain; more or less interchangeable with the King's (or Queen's) English.

recessive accent 1. The tendency to place strong stress on the initial syllable, with possible deletion of a secondary accent (British pronunciation of *dictionary* as ['dikʃənri]) (Bronstein).

2. Historically, the accent on the initial syllable of words of Germanic origin; or, as in Latin and Greek, as far back as the accentual habits of the language permit.

reciprocal assimilation The assimilation of two phonemes under each other's influence (Latin *rapidum* to Italian *ratto,* with unvoiced feature from *p,* dental feature from *d*). *See also* ACCOMMODATION 1, ASSIMILATION.

recomposition 1. Historically, the process whereby a root and a prefix, which have already undergone composition with appropriate phonological changes (Latin *re* and *claudo* to *recludo*) are later put together again in their original forms (*reclaudo*) (Marouzeau).

2. The formation of compounds of the type of *television, telecast,* where *tele-,* behaving like an affix, combines freely with monemes and syntagms that exist outside the combination in question, and new syntagms are formed from elements which are extracted by analysis (Martinet).

reconstruction Determining the original, unrecorded state of a language, or of a form of an unrecorded parent language, or of an unrecorded form of a recorded language, by means of a comparison of recorded descended languages or forms. *See also* INTERNAL RECONSTRUCTION.

recutting The reshaping of morphemes on the basis of a mistaken interpretation of morphemic boundaries (French *argent* gives rise to *argentier* at a time when final *-t* is pronounced; later, when it becomes silent, the suffix is taken to be *-tier* instead of the historically correct *-ier* from Latin *-arium;* this "incorrect" ending is then added to *bijou* to form *bijoutier*) (Hockett). *Synonym :* MORPHOLOGICAL EXTENSION 2. *See also* BACK FORMATION.

reduced grade *See* ABTÖNUNG, ABSTUFUNG.

reduced sentence A construction in which the elements of a sentence are put into a form which does not constitute an independent sentence, but can be enclosed as an endocentric construction in another sentence ("I want to go," as against "I want that I should go" of certain languages; *"ein durch die Stadt fliessender Fluss"* "a through-the-city-flowing river," as against "a river that flows through the city") (Hughes).

reduced vowel *See* MURMURED VOWEL.

reduction 1. Phonetically, the process whereby a full form is cut down to a shorter or reduced form (*flu* from *influenza;* French *m'sieu* from *monsieur;* Italian *ser* from *messere*). *Synonym :* SHORTENING. *See also* ALLEGRO FORM, CLIPPED WORD, STUMP WORD.
2. Historically, the process whereby a vocabulary item loses part of its original meaning, but continues in use (*house* loses some of its connotations in the face of the encroachments of *home,* but continues in use) (Lehmann).

redundancy 1. That part of the communication which can be eliminated without the loss of essential information (Webster III).
2. The availability of greater resources than are needed for conveying a message (Hall).

3. Phonetically, the absence of certain allophones in certain environments, permitting them to occur in abnormal speech ("I'll sp-hit in your eye!") (Hall).

4. Phonemic combinations that are possible but not utilized in a given language (*blid, drit,* which conform to the English phonemic pattern, but do not appear as words in our present vocabulary, remaining, however, available for possible future use) (Hall).

reduplication 1. Descriptively, a morphological process whereby there is a repetition of a radical element or part of it, occurring usually at the beginning of a word, occasionally within the word.

2. Historically, reduplication has often been grammatically functional in Indo-European languages in the formation of certain tenses (Greek *pempō,* perfect tense *pepompha,* with reduplicative prefix).

reduplicative morpheme The element which is repeated in the morphological process of REDUPLICATION (*q.v.*) (initial *p* of *pempō,* reduplicated in the perfect *pepompha*).

reference The semantic meaning of a word or expression; the mental content thought of by the speaker when using a word or expression as a semantic symbol, and/or called forth in the mind of the hearer.

referend 1. The vehicle or instrument of an act of reference (Dorfman).

2. That which is symbolized or referred to by a verbal symbol (the referend of *rain* is the moisture of the atmosphere, condensed and falling in visible drops) (Whatmough).

referent The object in real life symbolized by the linguistic sign or word. *Synonym:* REFEREND 2.

referential meaning The general (lexical, semantic) meaning of a word. *See also* DIFFERENTIAL MEANING.

referred speech *See* DISPLACED SPEECH, NON-IMMEDIATE SITUATION.

reflex The descendant of an older form (Italian *uomo* is the reflex of Latin *homo*). *Opposite:* ETYMON.

reflexive middle *See* DYNAMIC MIDDLE.

regional language A language that imposes itself as a SECONDARY TONGUE (*q.v.*) over an area to all or part of which it is not indigenous; it differs from a COLONIZING LANGUAGE to the extent that it does not or need not involve absolute political control (Russian in such satellite nations as Poland, Czechoslovakia, Rumania, Bulgaria; English in the Caribbean area). *Synonym:* AREA LANGUAGE. *See also* SPHERE OF INFLUENCE.

re(tro)gressive assimilation *See* ANTICIPATION, ASSIMILATION, INFECTION.

re(tro)gressive dissimilation *See* DISSIMILATION.

re(tro)gressive formation *See* BACK FORMATION, INVERSE DERIVATION, RÜCKBILDUNG.

regular alternation The type of alternation which occurs most frequently under the same conditions (French feminine adjectives ending in /-øz/, which have a regular masculine alternant in /-ø/ (*heureuse ~ heureux*), and a rarer masculine alternant in /-œr/ (*menteuse ~ menteur*), which could be described as irregular). Most instances of AUTOMATIC ALTERNATION (*q.v.*) are regular, as are also some cases of NON-AUTOMATIC ALTERNATION (*q.v.*), such as the example above. Regular alternation may be PHONETIC, or AUTOMATIC, or GRAMMATICAL (*q.v.*). *See also* IRREGULAR ALTERNATION (de la Garza).

regularist A believer in the universal validity of SOUND LAWS (*q.v.*). *Synonym:* NEOGRAMMARIAN.

regular sound change 1. In historical linguistics, sound change which occurs under all conditions; i.e., practically without exception. It usually involves the explanation of a CONDITIONED SOUND CHANGE (*q.v.*), which affected an original change; but regular sound change may be CONDITIONED or UNCONDITIONED. *Opposite:* SPORADIC SOUND CHANGE. *See also* NEOGRAMMARIANS.

2. For descriptive linguistic terminology, see PRODUC-
TIVE (de la Garza).

relational word A word serving to express grammatical
or syntactical relationship between NAMING WORDS
(*q.v.*). *See also* EMPTY WORD, FUNCTIONAL FORM,
FUNCTOR.

relation(al) language A tongue for regional communi-
cations among peoples of different speech (Meillet and
Cohen). *See also* CONTACT VERNACULAR, LINGUA
FRANCA, TRADE LANGUAGE, VEHICULAR LANGUAGE.

relative pitch *See* PITCH.

release 1. The movement of the speech organs from a
position of articulation to a state of rest (Dorfman);
the act or manner of ending a sound; the movement of
the speech organs in the quitting position for a spoken
sound (Webster III). *Partial synonyms:* ABGLITT, AB-
SATZ, AUSLAUT, DETENTE, OFF-GLIDE 1.
2. The breaking of the outer closure of a stop (Bloch
and Trager); letting the air out when the HOLD is broken
(Hall).
3. The third, or final, phase of a STOP (*q.v.*) (de la
Garza).

relevant Having a function in a given system. *Partial
synonyms:* DISTINCTIVE, PHONEMIC, SIGNIFICANT.

relic area A region retaining older linguistic forms which
have been lost or have undergone greater change in
other regions (the Ozarks area, where some Elizabe-
than forms not used elsewhere survive). *See also* FOCAL
(*also* GRADED, TRANSITIONAL) AREA.

relic form A form showing or suggesting obsolete linguistic features of the language under consideration
(Ozarkian *nary* for *no* or *nothing*).

religious factor *See* LITURGICAL COEFFICIENT.

repertory *See* CLOSED (*also* OPEN) REPERTORY.

repetitive compound A compound with identical members (*choo-choo, bye-bye, goody-goody*) (Bloomfield).
See also REDUPLICATION.

replacement 1. Historically, a CORRESPONDENCE (*q.v.*) between two stages of the same language (where Latin has -*ct*-, Italian has -*tt*-) (Hoenigswald). *See also* AF-FINITY 2.

2. Descriptively, a differentiation of phonemes in the word-stems of two or more grammatically distinct forms (*men* vs. *man, geese* vs. *goose,* showing a replacive plural morpheme instead of the productive -*s* plural suffix). *See also* BASE FORM, INTERNAL MODI-FICATION, SUPPLETION, SUPPLETIVE, SYMBOLISM.

3. Geolinguistically, the process by which a LANGUAGE OF COLONIZATION turns not only into the official, but also into the national and indigenous language of an area (English in the United States and Canada; Spanish in Mexico and Peru).

replacive 1. In the morphemic process of INTERNAL MODIFICATION, that morpheme which replaces another within the word in order to express grammatical relationship; it becomes fused with that word (in English, the singular *oo* of *goose* is replaced by the *ee* of *geese* in the plural; this *ee* could be described as a replacive morpheme) (de la Garza).

2. Historically, *see* ABLAUT, (QUALITATIVE) VOWEL GRADATION.

replica The shape of a loan word as pronounced in the borrowing language (Puerto Rican *pikol* for *pickle,* or *marqueta* for *market*).

representational That aspect of language which characterizes the subject of discourse, as against APPELLATIVE (characterizing the hearer) and EXPRESSIVE (characterizing the speaker) (Trubetskoi).

reshaping A sporadic change whereby a form of unusual shape is reinterpreted as though it consisted of a sequence of more familiar morphemes represented by more familiar shapes, usually because the speaker is not sufficiently familiar with the form he wants to use. This reinterpretation involves an actual change of phonemic shape, and the form intended is *not* a learned one (were it not for reshaping, such forms as *crayfish* or *crawfish, mushroom,* and *female,* would appear as /krévəs/, /múwsəràn/, /féməl/). *See also* BACK FORMATION, MALAPROPISM, METANALYSIS (de la Garza).

residual phoneme (or **residue**) The phoneme that remains after the merger of one of its allophones with another phoneme (in Latin, -*s*- between vowels turns into -*r*- and merges with *r;* but *s* is left as a residue in other positions, such as the initial and final) (Hoenigswald).

residue forms Forms which do not accord with any phonetic law that can be postulated (Latin *miser, caesaries,* which escape the law that intervocalic *s* becomes *r,* and do not seem due to borrowing or analogy) (Sturtevant); there is, however, the possibility of a dissimilatory influence exerted by the *r* in the following syllable in both the examples cited). *See also* DISCREPANT CORRESPONDENCE, LAUTGESETZ, NEOGRAMMARIANS, SOUND LAW, SPORADIC SOUND CHANGE.

resolution of medial groups Analysis of the interludes into recurrent onsets and codas (Spanish -*ntr*- is resolvable, since it can be analyzed as a combination of the recurrent coda -*n*- plus the onset *tr*-; but -*bstr*- of *obstrucción* is not resolvable, since -*bs*- is not a recurrent coda) (Hockett).

resonance The effect produced by the vibration of the vocal cords in pronouncing voiced consonants; it may also involve the joining of the oral and nasal cavities, resulting in a nasal resonance.

resonant A vowel or semi-vowel or consonant (liquids and nasals) produced by shaping but not obstructing the sound, using the mouth and throat as resonance chambers (Walsh); the sole acoustic effect is the product of the vibration of the vocal cords and its resonance (vowels, [m], [n], [ŋ], [l], [r], [j], [w]). *Oppo-*

site: OBSTRUENT (*including* STOPS, FRICATIVES, AFFRICATES). *See also* VIBRANT.

restricted stress Stress not bound to one particular position in the word, nor free to occur in any position (the stress of Spanish or Italian). *See also* BOUND (*also* FREE) STRESS.

retracted Produced with the tongue drawn back from a given position. *Partial synonyms:* SPREAD, UNROUNDED, VELARIZED.

retroflex A sound produced with the tongue tip curled up and back until its undersurface touches the hard palate (Russian ш, ж, щ). *Synonyms:* CACUMINAL, CEREBRAL, DOMAL, INVERTED.

retroflexion Secondary feature whereby the tongue tip is curled up, but does not participate actively in the articulation of a sound; it is only used additionally. *See also* SECONDARY FEATURES (de la Garza).

retrogressive *See* REGRESSIVE.

reverse spelling 1. *See* INVERSE SPELLING.

2. Spelling that is unphonetic and unetymological, imitating the same spelling in other words, where it is etymological but no longer phonetic (*limb* from *lim,* on the analogy of *lamb; delight* from *delit,* on the analogy of *light*).

rhotacism 1. The use of the phoneme *r* instead of another, usually *l,* in certain positions (Roman dialect *er cortello* for *il coltello,* Portuguese *branco* < *blank*). *Opposite:* LAMBDACISM.

2. The shift from intervocalic voiced *s* ([z]) to [r], characteristic of both Latin and most of the Germanic languages (*generis* from *genesis; forlorn* from *lose*).

rhotacization Saussure's term for RHOTACISM.

rhyme The use of an identical sound or syllable at the end of adjacent words or of words placed at definite intervals, as in lines of poetry. *See also* ASSONANCE, CONSONANCE.

rhyme word 1. A word that has undergone a semantic shift because it is rhymed with other words of related connotations.

2. A word that has undergone a change in form to rhyme with words of related meaning (Latin *frīgidus* > *frĭgidus* to rhyme with *rĭgidus*).

rhythm A harmonical succession of sounds, consisting in regular periodicity in a series of phonemes, constituting or contributing to measured movement or musical flow of language. It may depend on syllabic quantity, as in Latin and Greek, or on stress, as in English. *See also* SENTENCE RHYTHM.

Riksmål A form of Norwegian based on evolution from the literary form of Danish, and used until recently. *See also* LANDSMÅL, NEW NORWEGIAN, NYNORSK.

rill spirant The sibilants /s/ and /z/, in the production of which the air issues through a tiny median opening (Hockett). *Opposite:* SLIT SPIRANT.

rising diphthong A diphthong in which the non-syllabic element precedes the syllabic, and the final vowel element is more prominent than the preceding (French [nɥi], *nuit*). *Opposite:* FALLING DIPHTHONG. *See also* GLIDE.

rolled consonant A consonant produced by a rapid tapping (many flaps) of the front of the tongue against the alveoli (Spanish *r*), or of the uvula against the back part of the tongue (Parisian *r*).

Romance languages The modern descendants of Latin (French, Spanish, Italian, Portuguese, Rumanian, which are national tongues, with the frequent addition of Provençal, Catalan, Rheto-Rumansh, Sardinian, Dalmatian).

Romanization The transliteration of another system of writing into the Roman alphabet; the representation or TRANSLITERATION (*q.v.*) in Roman alphabet characters of the sounds of a language whose native script is of the logographic or syllabic variety (Chinese, Japanese, Amharic, etc.).

root 1. A meaningful morpheme recurring with affixes or replacives in grammatically different forms (*hold* is the root of *holds, held, beholden, withholding,* etc.); an ultimate constituent element common to all cognate words, which remains after the removal of all flectional endings, formatives, etc.; it is usually present in all members of a group of words relating to the same idea, and can thus be considered as the ultimate semantic vehicle of a given idea or concept in a given language. *Partial synonyms:* BASE, KERNEL, NUCLEUS, RADICAL, STEM, THEME.
2. In the Semitic languages, a series of consonants, usually three in number, acting as a disconnected morpheme, and recurring with internal vowels (affixes) in a set of related words (KTB, which enters into all words having to do with writing).
3. The minimal, irreducible BASE (*q.v.*).

root base The root or radical of a word; in flectional languages, flectional endings are appended to this form. *Synonym:* BASE OF INFLECTION.

root inflection The modification of the meanings of words by internal vowel changes (ABLAUT, GRADATION, MUTATION, *q.v.*) without the use of prefixes or suffixes (Dorfman).

rounded vowel A vowel produced with rounded lips (r*u*le).

rounding Pronouncing a sound with the lips rounded or forming a semicircle. *Synonym:* LABIALIZATION. *Opposites:* DELABIALIZATION, UNROUNDING. *See also* SECONDARY FEATURE.

Rückbildung *See* BACK (*also* REGRESSIVE) FORMATION, INVERSE DERIVATION.

Rück-umlaut The absence of umlaut of the stem vowel as the result of the loss of *i* in the following syllable before the umlaut period (Webster III).

S

sabir A term concocted by Molière, but based on LINGUA
FRANCA (*q.v.*). *Synonyms:* CONTACT VERNACULAR,
VEHICULAR LANGUAGE.

sandhi 1. A term used to describe changes in the sounds
of adjacent words; SANDHI VARIATION is the creation of
a third form from the juxtaposition of two other forms;
the rhythm and intonation of sandhi will occur only at
normal speed of speech, and will be distorted or ob-
literated by any slowing-up process; sandhi may be IN-
TERNAL (*Sutton* from *Southtown*) or EXTERNAL ("I'll
meech you" for "I'll meet you"); some common forms
of sandhi are French LIAISON (*les amis*) and ELISION
(*l'ami*); Spanish SYNALEPHA (*la amiga*); it is conditioned by the context ("the cow" vs. "the old cow";
"he'll go" vs. "he will if he can"). *Synonym:* SYNTAC-
TIC PHONOLOGY. *See also* EXTERNAL (*also* INTERNAL)
SANDHI, LENITION, MUTATION, OPTIONAL EXTERNAL
SANDHI, SANDHI ALTERNANTS, SANDHI FORM.

2. A putting together; features of modulation and of
phonetic modification in syntactic constructions; occurs
in included positions (de la Garza).

sandhi alternants Forms that are sometimes mandatory,
sometimes optional, in replacement of other forms under given syntactic conditions ("it's," "he's," "I'm,"
"I'll," but not "that's the kind of person I'm").

sandhi form The form of a word or word group used
in INCLUDED POSITION (*q.v.*), as linked up with other

elements in an utterance (Dorfman). *Opposite:* ABSO-
LUTE FORM.

satellite *See* PEAK SATELLITE.

satellite language The language of a country which, without being a colonial possession, is under the strong
political influence of another country, and whose language is subject to pressure from the dominant language and borrows willingly and freely from it (Rumanian, Bulgarian, Czech, with respect to Russian;
Caribbean Spanish and Etiemble's *Franglais* with respect to English).

satem languages Those Indo-European languages in
which some of the original velar stops turned to palatals or alveolar fricatives (Balto-Slavic, Indo-Iranian,
Armenian, Albanian, occasionally Greek). *See also*
CENTUM LANGUAGES.

schwa *See* SHWA.

science of language *See* LINGUISTICS.

second articulation The division of a moneme (*q.v.*)
into phonemic units (*tête,* a conceptual unit, articulated
as /tet/) (Martinet).

secondary articulation Such added features to ordinary
articulation as aspiration, nasalization, pharyngealization, etc. *Synonym:* CO-ARTICULATION. *See also* SEC-
ONDARY FEATURES.

secondary compound 1. A compound consisting of a
simple word and a compound word, or of two compound words. *See also* BASE COMPOUND, COMPOUND
WORD (Dorfman).
2. *See* STEM COMPOUND.

secondary derivative A word derived from another word
which is itself a derivative (*mannishly* from *mannish*
from *man*) (Dorfman).

secondary features Secondary articulations which can
be conceived as modifications imposed on a basic
speech sound which is defined in terms of activity at
the larynx, point of articulation, and manner of articu-

lation. *See* ASPIRATION (VS. NON-ASPIRATION), FAUCALI-
ZATION, GLOTTALIZATION, INGRESSIVE (VS. EGRESSIVE),
INJECTIVE (VS. EJECTIVE), LABIALIZATION (*also*
ROUNDING), LABIOPALATALIZATION, NASALIZATION, PAL-
ATALIZATION, PHARYNGEALIZATION, RETROFLEXION,
TENSE (VS. LAX), VOICED (VS. UNVOICED, VOICELESS)
(de la Garza).

secondary language 1. The written language, as opposed
to the spoken tongue.

2. A CULTURAL LANGUAGE (*q.v.*).

3. A non-indigenous language that serves a speech community as a major means of communication (English
in India, French in the Congo, Russian in various Soviet Republics). *Partial synonyms:* AREA (*also* COLO-
NIAL) LANGUAGE.

secondary phoneme 1. According to Bloomfield, phonemes which do not appear in any morpheme, but only
in grammatical arrangements of morphemes (de la
Garza).

2. Any variation in the utterance of a sound or word
(a difference of tone, pitch, stress, duration, etc.) that
serves to express or imply different shades of meaning;
a speech feature that is a secondary phoneme in one
language (pitch or tone in English) is often a PRIMARY
PHONEME in another language (pitch or tone in Chinese). *See also* NON-LINEAR PHONEME, PROSODEME,
SUPRASEGMENTAL PHONEME.

secondary stress A stress weaker than the PRIMARY
STRESS (*q.v.*), falling on a different syllable of the word
(American *interèsting,* as opposed to British *ínt'resting,*
has secondary accent on the penult). *See also* ACCENT,
STRESS.

secondary vowel A vowel in the production of which
the volume and orifice of the oral resonator counteract
each other; i.e., small volume plus small orifice (as in
[y, o, œ, ɐ, ɒ]); large volume plus large orifice (as

in [ʌ, ɤ, ɯ]). *Opposite:* PRIMARY VOWEL (de la Garza).

secondary word 1. Jespersen's term for ADJUNCT WORD (*q.v.*).

2. A word whose immediate constituents are free forms (*catfish;* i.e., compound words); or free and bound forms (*boyish, fisher;* i.e., derived secondary words).

secretion A phenomenon whereby an integral portion of a word or form acquires a new grammatical significance, is then felt to be something added to the word, and is applied to other forms of a similar nature (in *mine, thine,* the *n*-element is in origin an integral part, but since these forms in later development lose the *n* in certain positions, becoming *my, thy,* while the older forms are retained in their pronoun function, the *n* is taken to be a pronominal suffix and is extended to such forms as *ourn, yourn, his'n, her'n*) (Jespersen).

segment (of speech) A sound or lack of sound having indefinite borders, but with a center produced by a crest or trough of stricture during the even motion of an initiator (Pike); a minimal portion of speech consisting of a spoken language item known as a vowel or consonant.

segmental 1. Pertaining to features which clearly follow one another in the stream of speech (Hockett).

2. A sound (or lack of sound) having indefinite borders, but having a center that is produced by a crest or trough of stricture during the even motion or pressure of an articulator (Pike). *Opposite:* SUPRASEGMENTAL.

segmental phonemes Phonemes arranged in sequence in the spoken chain; vowels and consonants, as contrasted with suprasegmental phonemes, such as intonation, pitch, and juncture; one of the phonemes of a language that can be assigned to a relative sequential order of minimal segments (Webster III); for American English, most phoneticians admit 11 vocoids, 25 contoids, including 3 semi-vowels, and 8 diphthongs. *Synonym:*

LINEAR PHONEME. *Opposites:* NON-LINEAR (*also* SU-PRASEGMENTAL) PHONEME.

segmental phonemics The study of SEGMENTAL PHO-NEMES (*q.v.*). *Synonyms:* PHONOLOGIE, PHONEMATICS, PHONEMICS.

segmentation The division of a linguistic corpus or ut-terance or word into portions, each of which represents a single phoneme or morpheme.

semanteme The ultimate, smallest, irreducible element or unit of meaning, such as a base or root containing or representing the general meaning of a word or group of derivatives (*travaill-* of *travaillons*) (Dorfman); a symbol expressing a purely lexical idea, simple or com-plex, root or inflected form or compound word (Bally); a word (*dog*) or a base (Latin *can-* of *canis*) express-ing a definite image or idea, and distinguished from a morpheme (Webster III). *See also* CONTENT WORD, FORMANT, FULL (*also* LEXICAL, VOCABULARY) WORD.

semantic amalgam *See* AMALGAM.

semantic change Change in the meaning of words.

semantic complement *See* DETERMINATIVE, IDEOGRAPHIC WRITING.

semantic contagion The transfer of a semantic connota-tion or characteristic of a word or spoken element to another word, usually associated with the former. *See also* ANALOGY.

semantic extension 1. *See* ANALOGY.

2. A modification or amplification of the meaning of a word or expression on the basis of analogy (*q.v.*) with an existing and generally used pattern.

semantic indicator *See* DETERMINATIVE.

semantic meaning *See* LEXICAL (*also* REFERENTIAL) MEANING.

semantic potentialities (*virtualités*) All the possible meanings of a sign, realized only separately and indi-vidually in a context (the various meanings of *house* in "he is in the house," "the House of Hapsburg," "he represents a business house," etc.) (Martinet). *See also* CONNOTATION, DENOTATION.

semantic rejuvenation The bringing back of an old and no longer used meaning (Joyce's use of *propose* in the sense of "to place before," or of *supplant* in the sense of "to plant under") (Schlauch).

semantics The study of meaning in language, including the relations between language, thought and behavior; a science dealing with the relations between REFERENTS and REFERENDS (*q.v.;* linguistic symbols, words, expressions, phrases, and the objects or concepts to which they refer), and with the historical changes in the meanings of words; the study and classification of changes in the meanings of words and forms, including specialization, expansion, generalization, enhancement and pejoration of meaning, the ramifications of simile and metaphor, the relations between linguistic signs and what they refer to as well as between one another, and human behavior, conscious or unconscious, in reaction to language signs. *Partial synonyms:* SEMANTOLOGY, SEMASIOLOGY, SEMIOTICS, SIGNIFICS. *See also* CONNOTATION, DENOTATION.

semantic shift *See* SEMANTIC CHANGE.

semantic triangle The combination of the symbol, the referent, and the thought or reference (Ogden and Richards).

semasiography All pictorial, ideographic, and logographic systems of writing (Gelb).

semasiology *See* SEMANTICS.

sematology *See* SEMANTICS.

seme An element of meaning (Hall).

semeiology *See* SEMIOLOGY.

sememe Any element of semantic significance of a given word; the meaning of a morpheme. *See also* LEXEME.

semi-consonant *See* GLIDE, SEMI-VOWEL.

semi-contoid 1. *See* SEMI-CONSONANT.

2. A glide that involves audible friction (Hall).

semi-learned A word or form whose popular development (development in accordance with the phonological laws of the language) has become arrested, usually because the word at one point of history becomes the exclusive property of the more learned classes (French *esprit* from Latin *spiritum* if fully popular should have gone on to *éprit* or *épri;* if fully learned it should have been *spirite;* its form indicates that it had fully popular development until the fourteenth century or thereabouts, then became arrested). *See also* LEARNED WORD, POPULAR WORD.

semiology The science and study of signs in general, of which linguistics is only one subdivision (Saussure).

semiotics The general philosophical theory of signs and symbols, dealing especially with their function in both artificial and natural languages, and including syntactics, semantics and pragmatics (Webster III); the analysis of language with regard to use (from the pragmatic standpoint); to meaning of the linguistic signs (from the semantic standpoint); and to the relations between signs without reference to their meaning (from the syntactic point of view) (Kraft). The science which formulates the theoretical bases of total sensory communication in human cultures (M. Mead).

semi-plosive Dorfman's term for AFFRICATE.

semi-syntactic compound A compound word where the relationship of the members conforms in general with the syntactic rules of the sentence, save for slight deviations. *See also* COMPOSITION.

semi-vocoid 1. *See* SEMI-VOWEL.
2. A glide that does not involve audible friction (Hall).

semi-vowel 1. A sound intermediate between a vowel and a consonant, partaking of the nature of both; a vocoid accompanying another vowel, but not having or constituting a peak of sonority; one of the glides ([j], [w], sometimes [r]). *Synonyms:* GLIDE, SEMI-CONSONANT; a distinction is made by some phoneticians, who reserve SEMI-VOWEL for the off-glide *y* or *w* of *boy, bow,* and use SEMI-CONSONANT for the on-glide of *yes, war.*

2. A voiced sound generally produced without noise, and articulated fast (not sustained). Its articulation corresponds to that of the closed vowels; but it is shorter, and characterized by constant movement or transition, rising or falling from one point to the other, with swift frequency change. The semi-vowels may be extended to include the voiceless [h] sound produced at the larynx. The IPA uses the same type of symbols as for fricatives to designate semi-vowels. *See also* CLOSED VOWEL, FALLING DIPHTHONG, NOISE, RISING DIPHTHONG, TRANSITION (de la Garza).

sentence 1. A number of words grammatically and syntactically arranged to constitute a grammatically complete unit of meaning, and phonemically distinguished by various patterns of stress, pitch, and pauses.

2. In any given utterance, an expression which is not in construction with any other part of the utterance (Bloch and Trager).

sentence pattern The arrangement normally used in a language (Roberts suggests the following seven patterns as regularly occurring in American English speech: "He speaks"; "He is ill"; "He eats bread"; "He is my brother"; "He gave me a book"; "He called me a fool"; "There are books here").

sentence phonetics The study of phonetic changes taking place in form according to the function of the word in the sentence. *See also* MORPHOPHONEMICS, SANDHI, TAXEME.

sentence rhythm Recurring stress on certain syllables; may be symmetrical (as in Spanish), or asymmetrical (as in English). *See also* SENTENCE STRESS.

sentence stress Stress within the sentence as a whole, often expressing emphasis on certain constituents of the sentence, shades of meaning, etc.; the manner in which stresses are distributed on the syllables of words arranged into sentences (Webster III). *Synonyms:* GRAMMATICAL STRESS, INTONATION, MORPHOPHONEMIC STRESS.

sentence word A single word expressing a complete thought, and used as a complete grammatical unit ("Go!").

separable prefix A prefix which can also be used as a free form (German *aufstehen, "Stehen Sie auf!";* English *outcome, to come out*).

separable suffix A suffix which can also be used as a free form (*childlike, like a child*).

sequence sentence (or **utterance**) An utterance which must be linked up with something previously mentioned; it may be a complete answer, even if not a complete sentence, in response to a situation sentence ("Will you be sure to do it?", "I will.") (Fries). *Opposite:* SITUATION UTTERANCE. *See also* INCLUDED SENTENCE.

sequential expansion The addition of new elements after what is already present ("It's good"; "It's good enough") (Hall).

series 1. The horizontal listing of a row of phonemes on the basis of a relevant common feature (voiceless series: [p], [t], [k]; voiced series: [b], [d], [g]) (Martinet). *Opposite:* ORDER.

2. A set of vowels connected by ablaut (*q.v.*), historically; or by internal modification, descriptively (*ring, rang, rung*).

sermo familiaris An expression used in the writings of some Latin authors to indicate clear-cut social or local levels of speech in ancient Rome and the Roman Empire. *Partial synonyms:* SERMO COTIDIANUS (seemingly used by the more cultured classes in everyday speech); SERMO PLEBEIUS (used by the lower classes); SERMO RUSTICUS (used outside the city of Rome, and possibly tinged with Oscan, Faliscan, and other influences).

set, structural *See* STRUCTURAL SET.

shape, phonemic Hockett's term for ALLOMORPH. *See also* CANONICAL FORM, GRAPHIC SHAPE.

shape change A phenomenon occurring when a shape (canonical form) possible in the language, but heretofore "uninhabited" by any form, is brought into use, with a resulting change in economy in the language. This may happen when loan words become part of a language's lexicon. *See also* CANONICAL FORM, LEXICON, LOAN WORD, MORPHOPHONEMIC ECONOMY (de la Garza).

sharp transition *See* OPEN JUNCTURE.

shibboleth A linguistic device to tell the nationality or linguistic affiliation of the speaker (the inability to pronounce a phoneme in a certain manner); a sound or word containing a sound whose proper articulation is difficult for a non-native, and whose mispronunciation is regarded as reliable indication that the speaker is not native (Webster III).

shifter A word that changes its meaning, taking its color from the context ("a president is *young* at forty, but a prizefighter at forty is not so young"), or from the situation or speaker (*I, me*) (Sturtevant).

shifting stress A change in the stress pattern of a word due to dialectal or individual preference (*ínfluence, inflúence*), contrast (*bíologic, geológic; óffense and défense*), or to change the meaning (*présent, presént*) (Bronstein). *See also* SHIFT OF ACCENT.

shift of accent 1. Historically, the displacement of the main stress in a word from one syllable to another (Latin *fuĕrunt* > Vulgar Latin *fúerunt* > Italian *fúrono*, French *fúrent;* but Spanish *fuéron* shows the original stress).

2. Descriptively, in a paradigm, the displacement of the main stress from root to ending, or vice versa, in accordance with the accentual pattern of the language (Polish *dóbry*, but genitive *dobrégo*, as in Polish the

stress is always on the penult). *See also* SHIFTING AC-
CENT.

shift signs Marks appended to the vowel signs of the
phonetic alphabet to show differences in the articulation of the corresponding vowel signs.

shortening 1. In connection with a phoneme, reduction
of the time required to utter it.

2. In connection with a word, omission of part of it in
speech or writing. *See also* CLIPPED WORD, COMPENSA-
TORY SHORTENING, REDUCTION, STUMP WORD.

shwa The colorless, indistinct, neutral vowel sound represented by the symbol [ə]; the unstressed, mid-cen-
tral vowel sound of the two *a*'s in *A*merica (und*e*r,
neighb*o*r, German g*e*nug, bitt*e,* French j*e,* l*e*ver). *Alternative spellings:* schwa, shva.

sibilant A fricative consonant in the production of which
the tongue comes into contact with the hard palate
(*s*oft, *z*one, *sh*ore, a*z*ure, *ch*urch, *j*eer); the term is
often restricted to *s* and *z* alone, with the other sounds
described as two sounds (palatal stop + palatal fricative), or one sound (affricate).

sigmatic A formation characterized by the presence of
s, as in the Indo-European aorist (Latin *scripsi* =
scrib-*s*-i; Greek *epempsa* = e-pemp-*s*-a).

sign 1. The word considered as the symbol of the SIG-
NIFIED (*q.v.*).

2. A lexical unit consisting of the SIGNIFIER and the
SIGNIFIED (Saussure); the smallest unit of language
having meaning; a SOLIDARITY (*q.v.*) between an expression form and a content form, manifested by an
expression substance and a content substance (Hjelmslev). *See also* FIGURA.

sign, linguistic The combination of both concept and
sound-image, or of SIGNIFIER and SIGNIFIED (Saussure); any utterance or part of an utterance that
makes sense; it includes the SIGNIFICATUM (meaning

or value: "bed"), and the SIGNIFICANS (phonetic manifestation: /bed/) (Martinet).

sign, prosodic Grammatically, a secondary or supra-segmental unit such as a rise of pitch in the question "It's raining?", as against the statement "It's raining"; here the rise of pitch is the SIGNIFIER or SIGNIFICANS, and the question content is the SIGNIFIED or SIGNIFI-CATUM (Martinet). Do not confuse with PROSODIC FEATURE. *See also* MODULATION, SECONDARY PHONEME.

signal A spoken sound, form, or combination of sounds or forms that communicates meaning or a difference of meaning (Webster III). *See also* MARKER.

signal syndrome A complex of signal material which has meaning at any given instant in the course of interaction among human beings in a given culture (Hayes).

significans Martinet's term for SIGNIFIER or SIGNIFICANT (*q.v.*).

significant 1. A complex of sounds, characteristic and essential to the determination of a larger element of language, whereby the speaker gives expression to the SIGNIFIED (*q.v.*).

2. *See* DISTINCTIVE, PHONEMIC.

significatum Martinet's term for SIGNIFIED (*q.v.*).

significs The science of meaning; the scientific analysis of significance. *Synonyms:* SEMANTICS, SEMIOTICS.

signified The concept or object which is phonetically symbolized by the spoken word (Saussure). *Synonym:* SIGNIFICATUM.

signifier The sound-image or linguistic symbol which stands for an object or concept in the common mind of the speaking community (Saussure). *Synonyms:* SIGNIFICANS, SIGNIFICANT 1.

sign-token The physical fact of a sign-type used on a particular occasion in speech, writing, gesture, etc. (Crystal). *Synonym:* PAROLE. *See also* SIGN-TYPE.

sign-type A universal; the existence of a sign apart from its use on any given occasion (Crystal). *Synonym:* LANGUE. *See also* SIGN-TOKEN.

simplex word A free form without affixes or other components (*single, build, wall*) (Webster III). *See also* COMPLEX WORD, COMPOUND WORD.

simplification 1. Historically, the reduction of a language's structure from a synthetic to an analytical state. 2. The reduction of a double, or geminated, to a single consonant (Latin *abbatem* to Spanish *abad;* Latin *communem* to Italian *comune*). *Opposite:* GEMINATION.

sing-song theory The belief that language arose out of primitive chants which at first were inarticulate.

singulative A morpheme having for its function to give a word the force of a singular, usually by way of opposition to a collective (*rice, rice-grain*) (Meillet and Cohen). *Opposite:* PLURATIVE.

sistant An intermediate stretch in a chain of speech during which the emission of the sound continues while the organs remain motionless (Saussure). *See also* HOLD.

situational dialect A form of speech independent of region and cutting across categorizations based on degree of formality or degree of deviation from some standard (Hayes).

situation utterance An utterance which may begin the conversation without depending on previous information for intelligibility; a complete sentence (Fries). *Opposite:* SEQUENCE UTTERANCE.

slang 1. Language peculiar to a group. *Synonyms:* ARGOT, JARGON.

2. Non-standard vocabulary characterized by extreme informality, whose currency is not limited to a region, composed of coinages or arbitrarily changed words, clipped forms, extravagant, forced, or facetious figures of speech, verbal novelties, and subject to rapid decline into disuse (Webster III); a type of language

in common use, produced by popular adaptation and extension of meaning of existing words and the coinage of new words without regard for scholastic standards and the principles of the linguistic formation of words, and peculiar to certain classes and social or age groups. *Partial synonyms:* COLLOQUIALISMS, SUBSTANDARD LANGUAGE, VULGARISMS.

slender consonant A consonant immediately preceding or following a SLENDER VOWEL (*q.v.*) in the same word; a consonant having an allophone that characterizes it when it is pronounced with a front vowel (Webster III).

slender vowel *See* FRONT VOWEL. *Synonyms:* BRIGHT (*also* PALATAL) VOWEL.

slit fricative A fricative pronounced with the tongue opening relatively wide horizontally and shallow vertically, while the tongue is relatively flat (*th*) (Gleason). *Synonym:* SLIT SPIRANT. *Opposite:* FISSURE, GROOVE FRICATIVE.

slit spirant A sound produced with a relatively flat opening between the tongue and the roof of the mouth; the sounds of [θ] and [ð], where the air issues through a transverse slit (Hockett). *Synonym:* SLIT FRICATIVE. *Opposites:* GROOVE (*also* RILL) SPIRANT.

slot The position that a word or phrase occupies in a frame or pattern (Walsh); the significant positions which elements occupy with respect to each other, such as the subject normally preceding the predicate, or the determiner preceding the head ("The trains — aren't running on time") (Hall).

slur The intermingling between each sound and the next (Hall). *See also* SMEAR.

smear The blending of sounds in our perception, with the SLUR modifying them so as to warn us of the next sound, or blending with the immediately preceding sound (Hall).

social stratification Those differences in the language of a single locality which are due to the social or educational level of the speakers. *See also* CLASS LANGUAGE, JARGON, SUBSET.

sociative morpheme 1. A compound form which is a primary derived word, and which consists of two dependent or bound morphemes (*propel, proceed, expel, exceed*). *See also* BOUND MORPHEME.

2. A compound form consisting of a unique morpheme (*q.v.*), which can only occur here (as a bound form), plus a free form that can recur independently (*cran* + *berry* in *cranberry*). *See also* FREE FORM, UNIQUE MORPHEME.

3. A compound form consisting of a stem (*q.v.*) plus a free form (*therm-o* + *meter* in *thermometer*). *See also* FREE FORM, STEM (de la Garza).

soft consonant *See* MEDIAL (*also* MIDDLE, VOICED) CONSONANT.

solidarity The combination of expression and content, which is the necessary pre-condition for language; both content and expression are FUNCTIVES in a single FUNCTION (Hjelmslev).

solid compound A compound consisting of two components written as one word and having a meaning often different from that of the individual components (*railroad*). *Synonym :* FUSED COMPOUND.

sonant 1. A voiced consonant. *Opposite :* SURD. *See also* MEDIAL CONSONANT, RESONANT, SONORANT.

2. A SYLLABIC (*q.v.*).

3. A SEMI-VOWEL (*q.v.*).

sonorant A term used to include both nasals and liquids, both characterized by sonority (Hockett). *See also* LIQUID, NASAL.

sonority Impressionistic term relating to the quality of speech sounds, which is determined primarily by the size of the resonance chamber through which the air stream flows (Bloch and Trager).

sonorization Historically, the VOICING (*q.v.*) of intervocalic consonants.

sonorousness The amount of sound involved in the perception of a speech element.

sotto voce *See* MURMURED VOWEL. *See also* HALF VOICE.

sound change Historically, any changes in a speech sound or phoneme, whether due to its internal character (AUTOMATIC, AUTONOMOUS, FUNCTIONAL, SPONTANEOUS, UNCONDITIONED SOUND CHANGE), or to the influence of another adjacent or nearby phonetic element (CONDITIONED SOUND CHANGE).

sound law *See* LAUTGESETZ, NEOGRAMMARIANS, PHONETIC LAW, RESIDUE FORMS.

sound shift Historically, a change in phonemic pattern occurring automatically and regularly in the development of a language. *See also* CONSONANT SHIFT, GERMANIC SOUND SHIFT, GRIMM'S LAW, REGULAR SOUND CHANGE, VOWEL SHIFT, UNCONDITIONED CHANGE.

sound spectrograph An electronic instrument used in acoustic phonetics, designed to record the frequencies of speech sounds as measured in cycles per second, and the amplitude at any given frequency, as functions of time. *See also* SPECTROGRAPH (de la Garza).

sound symbolism A phenomenon occurring when the sound-meaning relationship of a word is not totally arbitrary; i.e., when the probabilities are not equal; some sound-meaning combinations have more chance of coming about; this is known to occur for particular terms (nursery words such as *mama* and *papa,* where the forms are *not* accidental, insofar as they fit into the system of the languages that use them, yet *are* accidental insofar as approximately 60 per cent of the world's languages have nasal sounds in the word for "mother," while only 20 per cent have non-nasal sounds, and 60 per cent have stop sounds in the word for "father," while only 20 per cent have nasals). Such sound-meaning convergence is a non-historical, accidental process (de la Garza).

sound type One of the types or classes into which the sounds of a language may be divided (consonants, sonants or semi-vowels, vowels, with further subdivision into stops, continuants, aspirates, voiced, unvoiced, etc.).

source language 1. The natural language of the learner. *Opposite :* TARGET LANGUAGE.

2. The language being translated into another language.

3. The language from which another language borrows (Walsh).

4. The language on which a PIDGIN (*q.v.*) is primarily based, as opposed to the local, indigenous language (Hall).

space-direction sequence The arrangement given to written symbols to represent the time-sequence of speech (writing in the Roman, Greek or Cyrillic alphabets, which is horizontal and left-to-right; in Arabic and Hebrew, which is horizontal and right-to-left; in Chinese, which is normally vertical and top-to-bottom, with the columns going from right to left) (Fries).

spatial linguistics The study of synchronic forms, such as are found in linguistic atlases, with a view to determining from them what happened in the past (Entwistle).

specialization of meaning Semantic change whereby a word formerly endowed with a broader range of meaning, or a variety of meanings, is restricted to a single meaning-function (French *rente,* "income" in general, to English *rent,* "income from the leasing of land or buildings").

specialized meaning A very narrow or specific meaning (*cloth,* plural *cloths,* but irregular plural *clothes,* used in the sense of "garments").

specific grammatical category An element in a system or classification (the English plural, the Spanish feminine, the Latin accusative) (Hockett). *Opposite :* GENERIC GRAMMATICAL CATEGORY.

spectrogram The record of a SPECTROGRAPH (*q.v.*).

spectrograph An instrument which permits the seeing and recording of frequencies of harmonics, relative amplitude of sound waves, and the duration of sound. *Synonym:* SOUND SPECTROGRAPH.

speech 1. The verbal expression of thought.
2. The faculty of uttering articulate sounds.
3. *See* PAROLE (Saussure).

speech form *See* LINGUISTIC FORM.

speech island A relatively small speech community surrounded by a larger area occupied by people speaking a different language or dialect (Gallo-Italian towns such as Nicosia in Sicily). *Synonym:* LINGUISTIC ISLAND. *See also* LANGUAGE BOUNDARY.

speech lapse A slight deviation from what is right or proper in speech, through lack of care or negligence; a gradual slipping, gliding, or passing away from the norm; an imperceptible movement; a "slip of the tongue" (de la Garza).

speech organs Any of the organs, whether movable (tongue, lips, etc.) or immovable (teeth, palate, etc.), which play a part in the production of articulate speech. *See also* ARTICULATORY PHONETICS, CAVITIES OF SPEECH ORGANS, IMMOVABLE (*also* MOVABLE) SPEECH ORGANS.

speech segment *See* SEGMENT.

speech stretcher A machine used in ACOUSTIC (*also* EXPERIMENTAL or LABORATORY) PHONETICS, which permits the playing back of speech samples at different rates of speed, but without change of pitch; its purpose is to analyze the effects of DAMPING (*q.v.*); it operates from a record, without altering normal acoustic effects (de la Garza).

spelling The conventional representation in writing of the spoken word, applicable only to alphabetic forms of writing. *See also* NOMIC SPELLING, ORTHOGRAPHY.

spelling pronunciation A pronunciation based on the written form of the word, despite the existence of a commonly used divergent spoken form (*towards* pronounced in two syllables as *to-wards,* or *boat-swain* instead of *bosun*). *Partial synonyms:* HYPER-CORRECTION, HYPER-URBANISM, OVER-CORRECTION.

sphere of influence Geolinguistically, a territorial area within which a language is widespread though not native (Russian in eastern Europe, English and French in western Europe). *See also* AREA (*also* PRESTIGE, SECONDARY, SUPERIMPOSED) LANGUAGE.

spirant A consonant sound produced by restricting but not interrupting the flow of breath; a sound produced with some constriction, but also some degree of aperture at the point of articulation ([f], [v], [s], [z], [š], etc.), and air blown against this narrow strip. *Partial synonyms:* CONSTRICTIVE, CONTINUANT, FRICATIVE, GROOVE (*also* RILL) SPIRANT, SLIT SPIRANT, STATIC CONSONANT; Martinet restricts SPIRANT to cases where the friction is not clearly perceived, and FRICATIVE to cases where the friction is clearly perceived. *See also* OBSTRUENT, OCCLUSIVE, STOP.

split Phonemically, the bifurcation or division of what is originally a single phoneme into two (Middle English short *u,* pronounced as in *put,* bifurcates into the original /ʊ/ and the /ʌ/ of *run;* Latin *c,* always /k/, bifurcates into Italian /k/ before *a, o, u* or consonants and /č/ before *e, i*) (Lehmann). *See also* SPLITTING.

splitting The process whereby a single phoneme develops two or more allophones (if a language had originally precisely the same sound for initial and final *t,* and later developed the difference at present observable in American English, the phoneme would be said to have split into allophones) (Hockett). *See also* SPLIT.

spoken chain The flow of speech in a given situation.

spontaneous phonology The study of UNCONDITIONED (*q.v.*) sound changes. *Opposite:* CONDITIONED PHONOLOGY.

spontaneous sound change A change assumed to have

been caused by the character of the sound itself, independently of any influence from its phonetic environment. *Synonyms:* AUTONOMOUS (*also* UNCONDITIONED) SOUND CHANGE. *Opposites:* COMBINATORY (*also* CONDITIONED, DEPENDENT, FUNCTIONAL 2, HETERONOMOUS) SOUND CHANGE. *See also* PARADIGMATIC CHANGE (resulting from pressures in the phonemic system); SYNTAGMATIC CHANGE (resulting from pressures in the flow of speech) (Martinet).

spoonerism An interchange of sounds or syllables, deliberate or accidental, often designed for comic effect ("I fool so feelish" for "I feel so foolish"; "ossifer" for "officer"). *See also* MALAPROPISM, SHAPE CHANGE.

sporadic alternation The substitution (unpredictably and at random) of one phoneme for another due to hurried or sloppy speech ("That glock's an hour fast"; French /RiguRøz/ ~ /RiguRœz/) (Hockett).

sporadic change 1. *See* SPORADIC SOUND CHANGE.
2. *See also* ADDING (*also* DOUBLING), BACK FORMATION, BLENDING, CONTAMINATION, FOLK ETYMOLOGY, MALAPROPISM, METANALYSIS, RECUTTING, RESHAPING, STUMP WORD 2 (or CREATIVITY BY SHORTENING) (de la Garza).

sporadic sound change A phenomenon that takes place irregularly, but not under totally unspecified conditions. It usually deals with one type of particular sound (or sounds) when found in certain environments. According to Sturtevant, nasals, liquids and sibilants tend especially to be involved ([l] and [r] in Latin tend to interchange, so that *peregrinum* becomes Italian *pellegrino* and French *pèlerin*). The Neogrammarians explained such changes as RESIDUE (*q.v.*), and described them as (a) being conditioned and regular; (b) having occurred by chance, or being due to SYMBOLISM (*q.v.*); or (c) being due to meaning factors. For other types of sporadic sound change, *see* ANTICI-

PATION, DISSIMILATION, DISTANT ASSIMILATION, HAP-
LOLOGY, METATHESIS, SPEECH LAPSE (de la Garza).

spread vowel A vowel in which the lips are spread out,
not rounded (met). *Partial synonyms:* RETRACTED,
UNROUNDED. *Partial opposite:* ROUNDED.

Stammbaumtheorie *See* FAMILY TREE THEORY.

standardization The process of leveling out local and
class differences in language; this may be consciously
brought about by government policy reflected in education, or take place spontaneously and unconsciously as
the result of improvements in travel and communications (TV, radio, spoken films, etc.). *Synonym:* DEDI-
ALECTALIZATION. *Opposite:* DIALECTALIZATION. *See
also* CENTRIPETAL FORCES.

standard language That dialect of a language which has
gained literary and cultural supremacy over the other
dialects and is accepted by the speakers as the most
proper and socially desirable form of the language
(Parisian French, Kuo-yü in China). *See also* LITER-
ARY (*also* NATIONAL) LANGUAGE.

starred form A word or form to which an asterisk has
been prefixed to show that it is hypothetical or unattested, and reconstructed on the basis of known data
and linguistic laws (Indo-European **swesor,* the hypothetical ancestor of *sister* and kindred forms). *Opposite:* ATTESTED FORM.

static consonant *See* CONTINUANT. *Partial synonyms:*
CONSTRICTIVE, FRICATIVE, SPIRANT. *Opposites:* KI-
NETIC CONSONANT, OCCLUSIVE, PLOSIVE, STOP.

static linguistics Saussure's term for SYNCHRONIC LIN-
GUISTICS.

statics Jespersen's term for a descriptive grammar which
considers grammatical phenomena as isolated, and
grammatical rules as arbitrary regulations. *See also*
NORMATIVE (*also* PRESCRIPTIVE) GRAMMAR.

statistics 1. A systematic collection and tabulation of
meaningful, related facts and data.

STRESS

2. A systematic study and interpretation of such collection and tabulation.

status verb A verb that is not used in the progressive form ("I hear it now") (Joos). *See also* PROCESS VERB.

stem The ROOT (*q.v.*) of the word plus a THEMATIC MORPHEME (*q.v.*), or stem formative morpheme. *See also* BASE, KERNEL, RADICAL 1, ROOT, THEME.

stem base *See* BASE OF INFLECTION.

stem compound A compound in which at least one of the components appears in stem form (*hippo-potamus, baby-sit*). *Synonym:* SECONDARY COMPOUND.

stem formative morpheme Gleason's term for THEMATIC MORPHEME (*q.v.*).

stock A large group of related language families (Indo-European) (Hall).

stød A glottal modification in Danish at the end of a vowel or consonant sound. *See also* GLOTTAL CATCH (*also* STOP).

stop 1. A consonant that momentarily halts the flow of breath (voiced [b], [d], [g]; voiceless [p], [t], [k]). 2. A sound which has a complete blockage at one point, and which is flanked on at least one side, or on two, by a sudden transition (*q.v.*). There are normally three phases : the catch or implosion, the hold or occlusion, and the release or explosion; but the implosion or explosion can be absent. Different stops may be accompanied by various SECONDARY FEATURES (*q.v.*). *Synonyms:* CLUSIL, EXPLOSIVE, OBSTRUCTIVE, OBSTRUENT, OCCLUSIVE, OPENING SOUND, PLOSIVE. *See also* KINETIC CONSONANT, PRESSURE STOP, SUCTION (de la Garza).

stratification of language *See* CLASS LANGUAGE, SOCIAL STRATIFICATION.

stress 1. Intensity of utterance; special emphasis on a sound or sound group, the result of greater amplitude of the sound waves, producing relative loudness. *See also* ACCENT, PHONEMIC PHRASE.

2. Refers collectively to those phenomena of speech which are correlated with our sensations of muscle movement in the production of speech articulations. Stress is reflected in the quantum of muscular energy which goes into each articulatory movement (note that if the sound is to be recognized, energy must be expended with a considerable range, between two limits). Stress is thus a VARIABLE in speech (*see* ARTICULATORY PHONETICS). Energy expended by the speaker is recorded in his nervous system by KINESTHETIC sensations or FEEDBACK (*q.v.*). The minimum unit of stress is the SYLLABLE; the most prominent energy component of the syllable movement is the BREATH PULSE, which defines it. Since every syllable has stress, it is customary to consider stress as a relative quality of TIMBRE : thus, the speech sound is evaluated in terms of energy attached to timbre. Stress is also reflected in the amount of sound (INTENSITY, LOUDNESS) a given speech articulation makes. Since a relative measure of acoustic energy is inherent to each sound, acoustic measurements of speech energy are useful indicators of stress only when the energy of a given sound is compared with the energy of the same sound spoken under different circumstances. The syllable could also be whispered, yet strongly stressed (*see* ACOUSTIC PHONETICS, WHISPER). Difficulties in evaluating energy : (a) the ear is more sensitive to the middle range of hearing, and hears variations in pitch level better; (b) it is sometimes difficult to convert energy into sound; much of it is often wasted. Stress is therefore a combination of ENERGY, effort that goes into the production of speech sounds, and TIMBRE; it is difficult to state in exactly what proportions. For FUNCTIONS OF STRESS, *see* WORD STRESS (de la Garza).

stress accent   A variation in loudness in a word or single utterance, greater than the minimal degree of stress given a vowel or syllable; opposed to PITCH ACCENT, which consists of a raising or lowering of the voice pitch, and which depends on the frequency of the sound waves, not on their amplitude. *Synonyms:* DYNAMIC (*also* EXPIRATORY, INTENSITY) ACCENT. *See also* WORD STRESS.

stress functions   *See* WORD STRESS.

stress group   In a sentence or longer utterance, a group of syllables one of which bears stronger stress than the others; a unit of speech sound constituted by a single primary stress, usually marked by open juncture or pause before and after; a single syllable with primary stress, or a series of syllables, united by the fact that there is among them only one that has primary stress (Webster III). *See also* WORD STRESS.

stress phonemes   Variations in stress which are segmental, phonemic, or distinctive; they are described for American English as PRIMARY (first syllable of *mother*); SECONDARY (second syllable of *blackbird*); TERTIARY (third syllable of *elevator*); and ZERO (last syllable of *mother*). *See also* WORD STRESS.

string (structured)   A sequence of elements characterized by a constituent structure (Gleason).

stroneme   Daniel Jones' term for STRESS (*q.v.*).

strong   1. As applied to verbs, nouns or adjectives, undergoing internal modification (*sing, sang, sung; goose, geese*). *Opposite:* WEAK. *See also* REPLACIVE.

2. Phonemically, an opposition where it is hard to determine which of two possible relevant features is really operative (the mid-vowels of *met* and *mate* differ because the first is lax and lower, the second tense and higher; is tension or height the functional element that makes the first a weak phoneme, the second a strong one?) (Dorfman).

3. *See* STRONG FORM.

strong form   *See* LENTO FORM.

structural   Pertaining to STRUCTURE (*q.v.*).

structural allophonic change   *See* ALLOPHONIC CHANGE.

structural gap   A hypothetical sequence of phonemes not represented in the language because it is not in accord with the language's distributional pattern (initial *zdr-* in English). Do not confuse with HOLES IN THE PATTERN.

structuralism   *See* FUNCTIONALISM.

structural linguistics   Linguistic study in which each language is viewed as a coherent, homogeneous entity, with inter-relation of pattern and changes. *Partial synonyms:* DESCRIPTIVE (*also* INTERNAL, STATIC, SYNCHRONIC) LINGUISTICS.

structural marker   1. A free morpheme marking a syntactic structure. *See* FUNCTION WORD.

2. A bound morpheme marking a morphemic structure (*-ed* in *founded*).

structural meaning   *See* FUNCTIONAL MEANING.

structural set   1. A group of all the phonemes occurring in a given phonetic environment and hence, in that position, directly contrasting with one another (Bloch and Trager).

2. Morphological classes having the same characteristics (English strong or weak verbs, Latin first-conjugation verbs). *See also* SET.

structural similarity   *See* AFFINITY.

structural word   *See* EMPTY WORD.

structure   The regularities and patterns of a language viewed as a system in which the elements are defined in terms of relationship to other elements (Walsh). *See also* GRAMMATICAL STRUCTURE, PATTERN.

structured string   *See* STRING.

structure word   Roberts' term for FUNCTION WORD ("*There* are books here"; "*It* is clear that he isn't coming"). *Synonyms:* EXPLETIVE, FLOATING ELEMENT.

stump word   1. Jespersen's term for CLIPPED WORD (*q.v.*) (*Trix* for *Beatrix; skeet* for *mosquito; gym* for *gymnasium; cute* from *acute*).

2. A sporadic phenomenon which could also be called CREATIVITY BY SHORTENING. *See* SPORADIC CHANGE.

stylistics 1. The study of one author's style as contrasted with the style of others, or the prevailing language practices of his community and his time (Walsh).
2. The study and art of selection among linguistic forms; the study of optional variants in sounds, forms, and vocabulary of language as characteristic of different users, situations, or literary types (Webster III).
3. Non-linguistic, non-distinctive, non-functional, paralinguistic variations in speech, which may be phonetic (some languages have free interchange between [a] and [æ] : [baθ] ~ [bæθ]; also [tomejto] ~ [tomato], [ɛkonomiks] ~ [ikonomiks]); or they may be physionomic (the use of different alternating forms in a given language, depending upon one's age, sex, size, weight, etc.); or social (the use of flapped or trilled [r] in a language, pertaining to social class; or occasional (the use of apical [r] in French comedy, and of uvular [ʀ] in Paris); or emotional (which affects especially rhythm, as happens in Hungarian). All these variations may also be called EMPHATICS, EXPRESSIVE FEATURES, INTELLECTUAL VARIATIONS. *See also* CHARACTEROLOGY OF SPEECH, IDIOLECT, PARALINGUISTICS, RANDOM VARIATIONS (de la Garza).

subjunct The modifier of an ADJUNCT (or SECONDARY WORD, *q.v.*) (Jespersen).

sub-minimal pairs Items that differ in only two, or at the most three, respects (*treasure-pressure,* where the oppositions are /t/ − /p/ and [ʒ] − [ʃ]) (Gleason). *See also* MINIMAL PAIR.

subordinating language A language where determinative particles or elements, expressing grammatical or semantic relationships, are grouped about elements expressing main ideas, as though subordinated to them (Marouzeau). *See also* AGGLUTINATIVE (*also* INFLECTIONAL, POLYSYNTHETIC, SYNTHETIC) LANGUAGE.

subordinative construction An endocentric construction (*q.v.*) having only one head ("fresh milk," where *fresh,* the attribute, modifies *milk,* the head) (Hockett). *Synonym:* ATTRIBUTIVE CONSTRUCTION. *See also* CO-ORDINATIVE CONSTRUCTION.

subordinator A generic term for subordinating conjunctions (*if, because*), relative pronouns or adverbs ("the man *whom* I saw") and other forms by means of which subordination is achieved (Hall).

subphonemic *See* ALLOPHONIC.

subrelationship The different ways in which two or more languages may be related to one another (the non-immediate connection between Oscan and French, the latter being a descendant of Latin, a sister language of Oscan (Hoenigswald).

subset A JARGON or CLASS LANGUAGE (*q.v.*) (Lehmann). *See also* CLASS CLEAVAGE, SOCIAL STRATIFICATION.

substandard Using speech sounds or forms differing markedly from the so-called STANDARD LANGUAGE, and often labeled vulgar or incorrect; conforming to the pattern of linguistic usage of the community, but not of the prestige group. *Partial synonyms:* COLLOQUIAL, SLANG, VULGARISM. *Opposite:* STANDARD LANGUAGE.

substantival adjunct A noun used as an adjective without a suffix or other change ("*class* distinctions"). *See also* FUNCTIONAL CHANGE, TAXEME (OF ORDER).

substantive A noun; any word or group of words used as a noun or instead of a noun, as opposed to an ADJECTIVE. *See also* EPITHETOLOGUE.

substitute A word standing for another word; a pronoun (*I, all, any, who, this*) (Hockett).

substitute language A language that can be used in a given area in the place of the indigenous or national tongue (French in Algeria; English in India). *Partial synonyms:* AUXILIARY (*also* SECONDARY, TERTIARY) LANGUAGE.

substitution 1. *See* PHONEMIC (*also* PHONE) SUBSTITUTION.

2. Harris' term for Hjelmslev's COMMUTATION TEST (*q.v.*).

3. The replacement, for practical purposes of communication, of the indigenous or national tongue by another language that is in widespread use in the area. *See also* SUBSTITUTE LANGUAGE.

substitution class Elements that can be substituted for one another in a given syntactic position ("He" may replace "the man" in "the man is here") (Hall).

substitution frame *See* MULTIPLE SUBSTITUTION FRAME.

substratum A language displaced as the dominant tongue in its area by another language of conquerors, colonizers, etc., but possibly responsible for certain linguistic changes in the language that suppresses or replaces it. *See also* ADSTRATUM, SUPERSTRATUM.

substratum theory The belief that the linguistic substratum is the cause of linguistic or phonological changes in the replacing or superimposed language, and that as the speakers of socially, politically, economically or otherwise subordinate languages adopt the language of the conquerors or colonizers, or of a culturally or economically more advanced nation, differences in pronunciation cause words, forms and constructions to be affected by under-surface speech habits.

suction stop A stop attended by a downward or backward movement of the speech organ at the point of inner closure, so that when the outer closure is broken there is a small inrush of air into the mouth (Bloch and Trager). *Opposite:* PRESSURE STOP. *See also* INGRESSIVE.

suffix A formative consisting of a single phoneme, syllable or syllables added to the end of a word to modify its meaning or to form a new derivative (*dog-s, working,* Latin *vid-entur*). *See also* AFFIX, PREFIX, INFIX, PRODUCTIVE (*also* UNPRODUCTIVE) PREFIX (or SUFFIX).

superfix 1. A distinctive stress-and-juncture feature that accompanies a phoneme or succession of phonemes (*light housekeeper* vs. *lighthouse keeper*) (Whitehall).

2. A recurrent, predictable pattern of stress characterizing small stretches of speech where the constituents are parallel in relationship (*flattop, redhead*).

3. A change in stress or pitch from base form to compound (*fórmulàte* vs. *fòrmulátion*) (Hall).

superimposed language The language, usually of a colonizing power, which imposes itself as official in a country to which it is not indigenous (English in India, Dutch in the former Dutch East Indies). *Synonyms:* COLONIAL LANGUAGE, LANGUAGE OF COLONIZATION. *Partial synonym:* AREA LANGUAGE.

superstratum The language of a culturally, economically or politically superior nation or conquering group introduced into a foreign national or geographical territory, and affecting the language of the latter, while itself eventually disappearing (Germanic in the western Roman Empire; Norman French in England). *See also* ADSTRATUM, SUBSTRATUM.

superstratum theory The belief that the language of the SUPERSTRATUM (*q.v.*) influences the language of the original inhabitants of an invaded area. *See also* ADSTRATUM, SUBSTRATUM (THEORY).

suppletion 1. The morphological process whereby there is a replacement of a missing verb-form by another verb (*went,* serving as the past tense of *go*) (Gray).

2. A complete change in the form of a stem (*good, better*) (Gleason).

3. The occurrence of phonemically unrelated allomorphs of the same morpheme, whether with change of base (*good, better*) or of affix (*ox, oxen,* vs. *box, boxes*) (Hockett).

4. The most irregular type of alternation, where only one case of a kind exists (de la Garza).

suppletive A morphological form used to replace a missing form in a defective conjugation or declension, and derived from a word other than the existing forms in the paradigm (*went* for *go; was* for *be; worse* for *bad; tuli* for Latin *fero*). Do not confuse with the REPLACIVE in the process of INTERNAL MODIFICATION.

support vowel In traditional grammars, defined as a parasitic vowel developing at the end of a word to facilitate the pronunciation of a troublesome consonant cluster (final [ə] of French *peuple*). *Synonym:* VOYELLE D'APPUI.

suprasegmental morpheme Ives' term for INTONATION (*q.v.*).

suprasegmental phoneme 1. Pitch, stress, juncture, occasionally nasalization, voice or voicelessness in clusters occurring simultaneously with a succession of segmental phonemes (minimal suprasegmental contrasts are illustrated by "He bought it" vs. "He bought it?"; "black bird" vs. "blackbird"; "What are we having for dinner, mother?" vs. "What are we having for dinner, steak?"). *Synonyms:* NON-LINEAR PHONEME, PROSODEME, MARGINAL PHONEME. *See also* PROSODIC, PROSODY, SEGMENTAL PHONEME.
2. Phones belong to the suprasegmental set if, whatever their phonetic character, they behave grammatically like a separate system. Those features which clearly extend over a series of several segmental groupings are suprasegmental; a sound may be sometimes segmental, sometimes suprasegmental; what is phonetically segmental may be phonemically suprasegmental. This classification for phones depends on function as well as on phonetic character. *Synonym:* NON-LINEAR PHONEME. Do not confuse with PROSODIC FEATURES (de la Garza).

surd *See* HARD CONSONANT, UNVOICED, VOICELESS SOUNDS. *Opposites:* SOFT CONSONANT, SONANT, VOICED SOUNDS.

suspension pitch *See* PAUSE PITCH.

suspicious pairs In phonemic analysis, pairs of sounds

which are phonetically similar and could therefore be allophones of one phoneme until they are proved to be separate phonemes (Gleason).

switching A bilingual's alternate use of two languages in the same speech situation. *See also* CODE SWITCHING.

syllabary A collection of the written syllabic signs of a language arranged in a conventional order (Japanese HIRAGANA, KATAKANA).

syllabic The sound that has the maximum degree of sonority in a given syllable, constituting a PEAK OF SONORITY; the segment during which the speed of the initiator is greatest in the syllable (nest); all other segments in the syllable are NON-SYLLABIC. *Synonyms:* CREST, PEAK.

syllabication *See* SYLLABIFICATION.

syllabic contoid *See* CONTOID.

syllabic dissimilation *See* DISSIMILATION, HAPLOLOGY.

syllabic pattern The favored arrangement of consonants and vowels constituting a syllable in any given language (English favors the pattern CVC; Japanese favors CV). *See also* CANONICAL FORM.

syllabic peak The vowel or continuant within a syllable (nest; Czech krst). *Synonyms:* CREST, PEAK, SYLLABIC.

syllabic sign *See* SYLLABLE SIGN.

syllabic stress The stress within a syllable.

syllabic writing *See* SYLLABLE WRITING.

syllabification Dividing words into syllables according to the syllabic pattern of the language. *See also* CANONICAL FORM, SYLLABIC PATTERN.

syllable 1. A group of phonemes consisting of a vowel or continuant, alone or combined with a consonant or consonants, representing a complete articulation or complex of articulations, and constituting the unit of word formation; the syllable is OPEN if it ends in a vowel, CLOSED if it ends in a consonant.

2. In view of the fact that TIMBRE distinctions seem to

take care of it, the syllable could be called an ARCHE-TYPE OF THE TIMBRE DISTINCTION (de la Garza).

3. The syllable is marked by a PROSODEME (*q.v.*), whereas the pseudo-syllable is unmarked by any prosodeme (Hjelmslev).

4. The PHONETIC syllable is identifiable with the CHEST PULSE; the PHONEMIC syllable is definable as a unit of stress or tone placement, and also of timing of vowel length, or of morpheme formation (Pike).

5. The syllable is defined in terms of CREST OF SONORITY (Bloomfield, Gleason).

syllable sign A written sign representing an entire syllable or single vowel capable of forming a syllable. *Synonym:* SYLLABIC SIGN.

syllable writing The use of syllabic characters representing spoken syllables or vowels that can constitute syllables. *Synonym:* SYLLABIC WRITING.

syllabogram *See* SYLLABLE SIGN.

symbiosis The peaceful coexistence of two or more languages in the same area (Latin and Greek in the Roman Empire).

symbolic system A communications system based on unanalyzable signs, with identity between the form of the content and the form of the expression (traffic lights, gestures, ideographic writing) (Hjelmslev). *See also* FIGURAE SYSTEM.

symbolism 1. In nineteenth-century typological morphology, the term used to describe the FUSION that took place when root changes occurred; i.e., the morphemic process of INTERNAL MODIFICATION with REPLACIVE MORPHEMES (especially in Indo-European), and discontinuous morphemes consisting of root plus infix (especially in Semitic). At that time, this was considered as the greatest point of development or sophistication a language could attain.

2. Sapir's term for the fusion which takes place where there is internal modification or alteration of the mor-

pheme, and replacives are used to express grammatical relationships.

3. The fusion which takes place in a PORTMANTEAU MORPHEME; i.e., a simultaneous morph component (de la Garza).

symmetry (in **linguistic development**)   The theory of the Prague school that language change proceeds in a harmonious fashion, so that the phonemic pattern of the language at all times tends to present regular, symmetrical features. *See also* CASES VIDES, HOLES IN THE PATTERN, NEATNESS OF PATTERN, PATTERN CONGRUITY.

symmetry of pattern   *See* NEATNESS OF PATTERN, PATTERN CONGRUITY.

synchronic   Viewing linguistic phenomena as occurring at one point of time, without reference to historical changes. *Opposite:* DIACHRONIC.

synchronic grammar   Grammar that is limited to recording and studying a given stage of a language. *Opposites:* DIACHRONIC (*also* HISTORICAL) GRAMMAR. *See also* DESCRIPTIVE GRAMMAR.

synchronic linguistics   A study of language that is limited to recording and analyzing a given linguistic state or stage. *Partial synonyms:* DESCRIPTIVE (*also* INTERNAL, STATIC, STRUCTURAL) LINGUISTICS. *Partial opposites:* DIACHRONIC (*also* DYNAMIC, EVOLUTIONARY, HISTORICAL) LINGUISTICS.

synchronic phonemics and phonetics   The recording of phonemes and combinations of phonemes in general, or in a given language at a given date or stage of linguistic development.

syncope (or **syncopation**)   The loss of a medial vowel, due generally to stress accent elsewhere in the word (Latin *domina* > Vulgar Latin *dom'na* > Italian *donna*). *See also* JAMMING. Do not confuse with HAPLOLOGY.

syncretic form   A grammatical form that has absorbed the meaning and function of another form now obsolete, and is now used not only in its original function, but also in constructions where the other is required.

syncretism 1. In historical linguistics, the merging of inflectional categories once distinct, due to sound change (Anglo-Saxon *stāne* and *stāna* merge into Modern English *stone,* by reason of the weakening of final vowels; Latin *mūrus, mūrō, mūrum* merge into Italian *muro*) (Bloomfield). *Synonyms:* DEFLECTION, LOSS OF INFLECTION. *See also* MERGED FORM, OBLIQUE CASE. 2. Descriptively, said to occur where a form is lacking in a paradigm, and the latter is therefore not symmetrical (for adults, we have the gender distinction appearing in *man, men; woman, women;* at an earlier age, we have only *child, children,* with the gender distinction missing). *Opposites:* BIFURCATION, DOUBLING (de la Garza).

syneresis Drawing together into one syllable two like vowels usually pronounced separately (*seest*) (Webster III).

synonym A word having the same meaning as another (*shun–avoid*). *Opposite:* ANTONYM. *See also* RADIATION OF SYNONYMS.

synonymic attraction The tendency for subjects widespread in the interests or activities of the speaking community to attract a large number of synonyms (the many slang terms for "money," "drunk," "to die," etc.) (Ullmann).

syntactic category The classification of a word according to its grammatical function and distribution.

syntactic compound A compound whose members show the same grammatical relationship to each other as individual words in a phrase. *See also* COMPOSITION.

syntactic construction A grammatical construction having only free forms as its immediate constituents ("He went to school"). *Opposite:* MORPHOLOGICAL CONSTRUCTION. *See also* CONSTRUCTION.

syntactic doublets Two allomorphs, alternating in accordance with the environment (the English indefinite articles *a* and *an;* French *bel* arbre vs. *beau* livre) (Marouzeau). *See also* COMPLEMENTARY DISTRIBUTION, MORPHOPHONEMIC, PHONEMICALLY CONDITIONED ALTERNANTS.

syntactic molecule   The combination of a semanteme and one or more grammatical signs, form words, or link words, required for the semanteme's being able to function in a phrase (Bally).

syntactic order   The use of the taxeme of word order in sentences to indicate grammatical or syntactical relations and functions of words. *See also* TAXEME.

syntactic phonology   *See* LENITION, LIAISON, LINKING, MUTATION, SANDHI.

syntagm   1. The fusion of two or more linguistic signs or elements in a word, phrase, or idiomatic construction; a combination based upon the linear sequence of linguistic terms as they occur in the speech act, having its origin and value solely in articulated speech (Saussure).

2. An AUTONOMOUS SYNTAGM is a combination of two or more monemes whose function does not depend on its position in the speech chain ("last year"), and which is often marked by a functional moneme (*with* in "with my parents," where *with* marks the relation of *my parents* to the context); a PREDICATIVE SYNTAGM is one which is independent rather than autonomous (in "Yesterday there was a feast in the village," "there was a feast" is independent and predicative; "yesterday" is an autonomous moneme; "in the village" is an autonomous syntagm) (Martinet). *Partial synonym:* SYNTAGMA.

syntagma   1. An arrangement of units in a syntactic construction (Whatmough).

2. A group of primary and subordinate symbols bound together by sense and action, and entering into relations with other similar groups of symbols to form sentences

("I shall go") (Entwistle). *Partial synonyms:* SYN-
TAGM, TAXEME (Hall).

syntagmatic Pertaining to a SYNTAGM (*q.v.*); characterizing the ordered arrangement of phonemes and morphemes in the flow of speech (Martinet).

syntagmatic economy The use of a smaller rather than a
larger number of monemes to render a new idea (the
French use of *Bendix* instead of *machine à laver* to render the newly imported concept of "washing machine";
machine à laver consists of three monemes with which
French speakers are already familiar; *Bendix* consists
of a single moneme, but it is one which French speakers
have to learn) (Martinet). *Opposite:* PARADIGMATIC
ECONOMY.

syntagmatic sound change *See* SPONTANEOUS SOUND
CHANGE.

syntax The study and rules of the relation of words to
one another as the expressions of ideas and parts of
structures of sentences; the study and science of sentence
construction; the combination and arrangement of
words in phrases, clauses and sentences; the study of
word order. *Opposite:* MORPHOLOGY. *See also* GRAM-
MAR, WORD ORDER.

syntax language Language by means of which the syntactic structure of another language (the OBJECT LAN-
GUAGE, *q.v.*) is described; it need not be a separate language or METALANGUAGE, but may be part of the object
language (Dorfman).

synthesis The process of combining two or more elements to form a new unit or complex; the combination
of several concepts into a single word by the use of
suffixes (Latin *am-a-b-o,* "I shall love"). *Opposite:*
ANALYSIS.

synthetic compound A compound in which one member
is a bound form that could not occur alone (French
orfèvre, where *or* represents the Latin genitive *auri* of
auri faber).

synthetic index   The classification of languages by morphological criteria, which consists of : (a) the ratio of morphs per word; (b) the amount of agglutination; (c) the morpheme classes per word; (d) the affixes per word; (e) the indication of relationship by word order, pure inflection, or concord (Greenberg). *See also* LINGUISTIC TYPOLOGY, TYPOLOGICAL CLASSIFICATION.

synthetic language   A language in which the grammatical relationships of words are expressed chiefly through inflections that unite long strings of bound forms into single words, and several concepts are put together into one word (Latin *am-a-b-o-r,* "I shall be loved"). *Opposite :* ANALYTICAL LANGUAGE.

system   1. The process of transformation whereby one word is turned into another by the substitution of phonemes having an "either . . . or" function (LOGICAL DISJUNCTION); (the word *set* is turned into the word *bid* by replacing *s, e* and *t,* respectively, with *b, i* and *d;* between each of the pairs, *s-b, e-i, t-d,* there is DISJUNCTION or ALTERNATION, since we can have only one of the two possibilities; these couples form PARADIGMS (Hjelmslev).

2. *See* PATTERN.

T

taboo   The avoidance of the use of certain words, and their replacement by euphemistic expressions, for superstitious, moral, or social reasons (English four-letter words). *See also* NOA WORD.

tabulation In phonemic analysis, the recording of the distribution of allophones.

tactic form A combination of taxemes, or a single taxeme, occurring as a conventional grammatical arrangement (Bloomfield).

tactile sensation *See* FEEDBACK.

tagmeme 1. The smallest meaningful unit of grammatical form (Bloomfield); a constituent of a meaningful grammatical relation that cannot be analyzed into smaller meaningful features; it may be marked by features of word order, selection of allomorphs, agreement with finite verb forms, elaboration by preceding adjectival modifiers (Webster III).

2. A class of grammatical forms that function in a particular grammatical relation (Webster III). *See also* EPISEMEME, GLOSSEME, SLOT (Hall).

tainting (of suffixes) When a suffix acquires a given connotation, it may be extended to other words (the contemptuous connotation attached to the *-eer* suffix of *privateer, pamphleteer,* etc., goes on to *profiteer, patrioteer, bonuseer,* etc.) (Jespersen). *See also* PRODUCTIVITY.

tap A short, single FLAP (*q.v.*) of the tongue (Spanish pe*r*o, British ve*r*y). *See also* TRILL.

target language A foreign language that is being learned. *Opposite:* SOURCE LANGUAGE.

ta-ta theory The belief that language arose out of an attempt of the speech organs to imitate the shape of bodily movements.

taxeme 1. A simple feature of grammatical arrangement; the smallest unit of form in grammar (Bloomfield).

2. A minimum grammatical feature of SELECTION (selecting the bound form *-ess* to follow *actor,* in forming the feminine; of ORDER (the fact that *actr-* precedes *-ess*); of MODULATION (the occurrence of one main stress on the first syllable of *actress;* the interrogative final pitch in "She is an actress?"); of PHONETIC MODI-

FICATION (the change in form of *actor* to *actr-* before *-ess*).

3. A significant unit of syntactic combination (the word order in *nous vous en donnons,* where the subject pronoun *nous* precedes the object pronouns, the indirect object pronoun *vous* precedes *en,* and all the pronouns precede the verb) (Hall). *See also* ALLOTAX, TACTIC FORM.

taxeme of expression *See* CENEME (Hjelmslev).

teknonymy The practice of naming a parent after a child ("Christ's Mother" for "Mary"). *Opposites:* MATRONYMIC, PATRONYMIC.

telescoped word A word formed by combining parts of two or more words (*smog, motel*). *Synonyms:* BLEND, CROSSING, PORTMANTEAU WORD (Lewis Carroll), WORD-CROSSING.

tempo Duration of utterance; ALLEGRO or LENTO; may be increased or decreased from a norm (Trager).

tense 1. As applied to a vowel, pronounced with greater tension on the muscles of the articulator ([e], as opposed to [ɛ]). *Synonym:* NARROW VOWEL. *Opposites:* LAX, WIDE VOWEL.

2. Articulated with glottal opening and air pressures relatively close and taut (de la Garza).

3. Genetically, a sound produced with greater deformation of the vocal tract (away from its rest position); acoustically, there is a higher total amount of energy in conjunction with a greater spread of energy in the spectrum and in time (Jakobson and Halle). *Opposite:* LAX. *See also* SECONDARY FEATURES.

tenuis A devoiced plosive; an unaspirated voiceless stop. *See also* FORTIS, LENIS, MEDIAL (*also* MIDDLE) CONSONANT.

terminal *See* CLAUSE TERMINAL.

terminal contour INTONATIONAL PATTERNS (*q.v.*) that characterize the end of an utterance (rising, falling,

or level; often transcribed with arrows : ↑, ↓, →, or with
slant lines connecting the pitch-level indicators : ╲ ,
╱) (Walsh).

terminal stress Stress on the final syllable. *See also* OXY-
TONE.

tertiary language A language that can be used in a country to which it is not indigenous, but not to the same
degree as a SECONDARY LANGUAGE (*q.v.*) (Latin in
Italy, where French is a secondary language).

tertiary stress *See* STRESS PHONEMES.

thematic Relating to, attached to, or constituting a stem;
relating or attached to the stem before another bound
form, inflectional or derivational, is added. *Opposite:*
ATHEMATIC. *See also* THEMATIC MORPHEME.

thematic flection Inflection where the thematic morpheme appears between the root and the inflectional
affix (*hipp-o-potamus*).

thematic morpheme Usually a morpheme consisting of
a single vowel (THEMATIC VOWEL, *q.v.*) attached to the
root of a noun or verb to form the stem (-*o*, thematic
vowel for the Latin second declension; -*a* for the first
declension; -*o*- in *therm-o-meter*). Gleason calls this
the STEM FORMATIVE MORPHEME.

thematic vowel *See* THEMATIC MORPHEME.

theme *See* BASE, RADICAL, ROOT, STEM.

theoretical base form A most conveniently recognized
base form, which never actually occurs (Latin /niks/,
nix, /ni:wis/, *nīvis*, having the theoretical base form
/nigw-/) (de la Garza).

til(de) 1. A diacritic used over letters in writing to indicate a modified pronunciation (Spanish *ñ*, Portuguese
ã, *õ*).
2. The curve (~) used to indicate alternation among
morphs.
3. The symbol (~) used to designate phonologically
defined alternation (de la Garza).

timbre 1. A cluster of tones, one of which, the fundamental, is dominant, while the others (harmonics) are in harmony with it; since the resonator reinforces some of the harmonics more than others, the tone receives a character which permits the listener to distinguish between one voice and another, or one instrument and another, though both produce the same bass note (Hughes).

2. That which reflects the action in the glottis and above it; i.e., the buccal cavity, where the resonant cavities modify (dampen and filter) the sound waves coming from the glottis, thus giving each class of sounds a characteristic quality (different number of harmonics). Timbres are segmental sounds, and represent the absolute qualities of sound. *Synonym:* VOWEL QUALITY. *Opposites:* PROSODIC FEATURES (relative qualities), VOWEL QUANTITY. *See also* AFFRICATE, FRICATIVE, LIQUID, NASAL, SEGMENTAL, SEMI-VOWEL, STOP, VOWEL (de la Garza).

3. *See* PITCH.

time-depth   The time of separation between two kindred languages, said to equal the logarithm of the percentage of cognates (*c*) divided by twice the logarithm of the percentage of cognates retained after a millennium, in accordance with the formula $t = \dfrac{\log c}{2 \log r}$ (Lees); the period of time a language has undergone independent development (a language with a time-depth of two thousand years). *See also* GLOTTOCHRONOLOGY, LEXICOSTATISTICS.

tone   The musical pitch of the voice; a rising, falling, level, or falling-rising inflection of the voice in pronouncing certain words which serves a phonemic purpose (as in Chinese). *See also* TONE LANGUAGE.

tone language   A language which uses PITCH (*q.v.*) as a distinguishing mark of morphemes; the pitch levels must be distinctive and phonemic; i.e., the language must maintain a relative difference between one level and the next; these may also be called TONE REGISTERS (Chinese, Thai, Vietnamese) (de la Garza). *Synonym:* POLYTONIC LANGUAGE.

toneme 1. The stress or tonal element distinguishing two otherwise identical words or forms (Dorfman); a phoneme consisting of a specific tone in a tone language; tonal qualities of considerable duration, with abrupt and describable changes in loudness and pitch (American English is said to have four levels of loudness, four of pitch, and four types of juncture); the toneme is a signaling entity similar to but different from the phoneme (Pike).

2. A phonemic unit of intonation made up of pitches (Chinese *hǎo*) (Hall).

3. Daniel Jones' term for PITCH (*q.v.*).

tone registers *See* TONE LANGUAGE.

tongue advancement The position of the tongue from the back to the center to the front of the mouth; one of the three factors important in the articulatory description of the vowels. *See also* LIP POSITION, TONGUE HEIGHT.

tongue height The position of the tongue from high to low (Hall). *See also* LIP POSITION, TONGUE ADVANCEMENT.

tonic accent 1. Relative phonetic prominence, as from greater stress or higher pitch, of a spoken syllable or word.

2. Pitch stress as distinguished from dynamic stress (Webster III). *Synonyms:* CHROMATIC (*also* MUSICAL, PITCH) ACCENT.

tonic syllable The syllable that receives the main accent. *Synonyms:* ACCENTED (*also* STRESSED) SYLLABLE. *Opposites:* ATONIC (*also* UNSTRESSED) SYLLABLE. *See also* POST-TONIC, PRETONIC.

topic Roughly, for most languages, what traditional grammar defines as the SUBJECT (Hockett). *See also* COMMENT, PREDICATIVE CONSTRUCTION.

toponomasiology The study and analysis of place names

in a geographical area or a given language. *Synonyms:*
TOPONOMASTICS, TOPONOMATOLOGY.

toponomastics   *See* TOPONOMASIOLOGY.

toponomatology   *See* TOPONOMASIOLOGY.

toponymic   1. A place name (*New York*).

   2. A word denoting a geographical feature (*bayou, butte, crevasse*) (Marckwardt).

trade language   A language used as a medium of communication among speakers of various languages. *See also* CONTACT VERNACULAR, CREOLE, LINGUA FRANCA, PIDGIN, VEHICULAR LANGUAGE.

transcendental linguistics   A linguistic science that has its presuppositions in something outside of language (Hjelmslev).

transcription   1. The rendering of a speech unit into IPA characters (PHONETIC TRANSCRIPTION), or into phonemic symbols (PHONEMIC TRANSCRIPTION). *See also* TRANSLITERATION.

2. Rendering speech by the graphic method, with speech as the input and writing as the output. The mode of transcription may be (a) ANALYTIC or COMPONENTIAL, where the goal is to give an immediate picture of the relationship between sound and symbol, to show internal changes in producing sounds, and to render speech production (ARTICULATION) in a more satisfactory way (componential analyses have been done by Bell, Jespersen, Techmer and Jakobson, among others); or it may be (b) LITERAL; literal transcriptions may be MONOTYPE (using only graphic symbols), or DIACRITIC (using symbols plus diacritics to indicate new types of sounds). The FRAME OF REFERENCE of transcriptions may be on different levels: (a) PHONETIC ([ ]); (b) PHONEMIC (/ /); (c) MORPHEMIC ({ }). A phonetic alphabet usually has sixty to eighty symbols; there are many possibilities of adjusting one to the needs of particular languages (using Greek letters, such as [θ], conversion symbols, such as [ə], using diacritics [č],

etc. Transcription should not be confused with TRANS-
LITERATION (*q.v.*) (de la Garza).

transfer grammar Gleason's term for CONTRASTIVE
GRAMMAR (*q.v.*).

transferred meaning The metaphorical use of a word
("fox" or "wolf" as applied to a man, "angel" or
"peach" as applied to a girl). *Synonym:* METAPHOR.

transformation A statement of the structural relations of
a pair of constructions, treating the relation as a process (Gleason).

transformational analysis A process which decomposes
each sentence into transformed, and ultimately elementary, sentences and operators, without residue (Harris).
See also EQUIVALENT SENTENCES.

transformation(al) grammar 1. Grammar based on
TRANSFORMATIONAL ANALYSIS (*q.v.*).
2. A theory treating most sentences as derivations of
more basic sentences, with rules for deriving them
("This house was built by my grandfather" is a transform of "My grandfather built this house") (Walsh).
See also BIDIRECTIONAL.

transform grammar *See* TRANSFORMATIONAL GRAMMAR.

transition *See* ACOUSTIC PHONETICS, JUNCTURE, CLOSED
(*also* OPEN) JUNCTURE.

transitional sound *See* GLIDE.

transitional writing A system of using pictographs and
ideographs with written letters ("I shall pay you $10").

transition area A region between two FOCAL AREAS
(*q.v.*), participating in some of the characteristics of
each (southwestern Connecticut, sharing some features
with the New York area, others with New England).
Synonym: GRADED AREA. *See also* PRESTIGE LANGUAGE,
RELIC AREA.

translation loan word A word modeled more or less
closely after a foreign word, but consisting of speech
material of the language in which it is created (German
Fernsprecher, Wasserleitung, for "telephone," "aque-

duct") (Jespersen). *Synonyms:* CALQUE, HETERONYM 2, LOAN TRANSLATION. *See also* LOAN BLEND, LOAN-SHIFT.

transliteration 1. The representation of a sound, phoneme, word, or utterance from one language in the conventional symbols of another language or writing system (Khrushchev for Russian Хрущев). *See also* TRANSCRIPTION.

2. Rendering one type of graphic convention into another; here the input is writing and the output is writing. This is not a PHONETIC TRANSCRIPTION. Romanization and Cyrillization are two transliteration types, where Roman or Cyrillic letters are introduced into other systems which do not normally use them (de la Garza).

transmission One of the two aspects of sound which involves the intention and nervous system of the individual. INTENTION lies in the brain (repository of symbols), which contains pictures of the whole body except of itself; being the main part of the nervous system, it sends extremely rapid messages to all parts of the body through nerve cells distributed in all the muscle fibers. The nervous system involves the nerves, which end in muscles that are active in articulation. *See also* ARTICULATORY PHONETICS, ASPECTS OF SOUND, FEEDBACK, MOTOR (active) ARTICULATION, VOCAL TRACT (passive) ARTICULATION (de la Garza).

transmutation The use of a word, without change in form, in different syntactic functions; the use of the same word as a noun, adjective, verb, etc. ("I'll *up* you ten dollars"; "the *ups* and downs of life"). *Synonyms:* CONVERSION, FUNCTIONAL CHANGE (or SHIFT).

transposition 1. In historical phonetics, the act, process or result of exchanging the relative position of two elements, substituting one for the other (French *moustique* from Spanish *mosquito*). *Partial synonym:* METATHESIS.

2. The CROSSING OF BRANCHES in transformation grammar; one of a variety of transformation rules.

tree stem theory *See* FAMILY TREE THEORY, PEDIGREE THEORY, STAMMBAUMTHEORIE.

trial A grammatical number designating three, as distinct from the singular, dual and plural.

triconsonantal root *See* TRILITERAL ROOT.

trigraph The combination of three written letters to represent a single sound (Sa*pph*o, Ma*tth*ew, French b*eau*). *See also* COMPOUND GRAPHEME.

trilingualism The ability to speak and understand (possibly also read and write) three languages.

triliteral root A verbal root of the Semitic languages, consisting of three invariable consonants, with modifications of meaning shown by the interplay of vowels of the infix (Arabic QTL, "to kill"; KTB, "to write"). *Synonym:* TRICONSONANTAL ROOT. *See also* DISCONTINUOUS MORPHEME.

triliteral theory A theory to the effect that the original Indo-European roots all consisted of consonant-vowel-consonant (Benveniste, Entwistle); the first consonant is sometimes identified, on the basis of evidence discovered in Hittite, to be a laryngeal, which disappeared in the other Indo-European branches (Kuriłowicz). *Synonym:* LARYNGEAL THEORY.

trill A vibration (or several flaps or taps) of the tongue, lips, or uvula against another organ, such as the alveoli or the back of the tongue, produced by an expulsion of breath; a rapid alternation of two homorganic sounds, one more open than the other, produced by the vibration of a movable articulator, but too slow to have a perceptible pitch (Gleason). *See also* TAP.

tripartite A language system in which some stems are inflected for case (nouns), with the additional possibility of inflection for gender (adjectives); while other stems are inflected for person and number (verbs); and still others are uninflected (particles) (Hockett). *See also* BIPARTITE, INFLECTIONAL, MULTIPARTITE.

triphthong A combination of three vowel sounds functioning as a single unit (s*way*, *wow;* Italian m*iei*, b*uoi*).

triplets Three words of the same language any one of which represents a doublet with either of the other two (Italian *fiaba, fola, favola,* all from Latin *fabula*).

trough That part of the utterance which has the least sonority; the segment during which the speed of the initiator is at its lowest; sometimes described as a BORDER between syllables. *Opposites:* CREST, PEAK, SYLLABIC.

turn *See* VOICE 1.

typological classification The comparative study and classification of languages on the basis of similarities and differences in structure rather than on historical relations. *See also* GENETIC (*also* GEOGRAPHICAL) CLASSIFICATION, LINGUISTIC TYPOLOGY, SYNTHETIC INDEX.

typology *See* LINGUISTIC TYPOLOGY.

U

ultimate constituents Each of the separate morphemes that enter into a construction, and are incapable of further division or analysis ("The base ball play er s are leav ing the field"). *See also* CONSTITUENT, IMMEDIATE CONSTITUENT.

Umgangssprache The vernacular, colloquial language customarily used by the individual and the community as a means of everyday communication. *Synonyms:* COLLOQUIAL, VERNACULAR.

umgekehrte Schreibung   *See* INVERSE SPELLING.

umlaut   1. An internal vowel change caused by the partial retrogressive assimilatory influence of a vowel, semi-
vowel, or even consonant in the following syllable; the
fronting or raising of a back or low vowel (*a, o, u*)
caused by an *i* or *y* in the following syllable, now usually lost or altered; a phenomenon of ANTICIPATION.
Partial synonyms: ANTICIPATION, COMBINATIVE
CHANGE, FRONTING, METAPHONY, MUTATION, VOWEL
MUTATION. *See also* RÜCK-UMLAUT.
2. An internal vowel change caused or conditioned by
the influence of a vowel, semi-vowel, or consonant in
the syllable which immediately precedes or follows; a
phenomenon of ANTICIPATION or RETROGRESSIVE AS-
SIMILATION, LAG or PROGRESSIVE ASSIMILATION. *See
also* CONDITIONED SOUND CHANGE, METAPHONY, RÜCK-
UMLAUT. Do not confuse with ABLAUT (de la Garza).
3. A diacritic mark to indicate the occurrence of UM-
LAUT or METAPHONY, as described above (*Sätze*).

unbounded noun   A noun that requires a determiner for
the definite category only ("the milk," but only excep-
tionally "a milk"); the class meaning is "species of object occurring in more than one specimen, such that
the specimens can be subdivided or merged" (Bloomfield). *Synonym:* MASS NOUN. *Opposites:* BOUNDED
(*also* COUNT) NOUN.

unconditioned   *See* CONDITIONED.

under-differentiation   The natural tendency of a linguistic analyst to disregard significant phonemic differences
in the language he is analyzing because they do not
appear in his own (the phonemic distinction in Arabic
between *k* and *q,* to an English-speaking analyst)
(Gleason). *Opposite:* OVER-DIFFERENTIATION.

underlying form   1. A free morpheme in a complex form
(*man* in *manliness*) (Dorfman).
2. The included free form in a derived secondary word
(de la Garza).

unique constituent Bloomfield's term for a remnant in morpheme analysis; i.e., a remainder in a complex form which occurs nowhere else except in this complex form, whose common part does occur elsewhere; it is thus a unique constituent or morpheme of this complex form. *Synonym:* UNIQUE MORPHEME (de la Garza).

unique morpheme A morpheme occurring only in specific combinations (*fro* in "to and fro"; *kith* in "kith and kin"; *fangle* in *newfangled; cran* in *cranberry*) (Hockett). It may be a free or a bound form. *Synonym:* UNIQUE CONSTITUENT.

universal combination A word group where the same coordinator precedes each item in the construction (Latin *"aut vivere aut mori"*) (Hall). *See also* DISCONTINUOUS CONSTITUENT, DISCONTINUOUS MORPHEME.

universal grammar The study of language in general, and of the general principles basic to grammatical phenomena of all languages, without being confined to one specific language. *Synonyms:* GENERAL (*also* PANCHRONIC, PHILOSOPHICAL) GRAMMAR.

universal language *See* AUXILIARY LANGUAGE, INTERLANGUAGE, INTERNATIONAL LANGUAGE.

unmarked member *See* MARKED MEMBER.

unproductive Obsolescent; no longer used to produce new forms through derivation in a given language. *Opposite:* PRODUCTIVE. *See also* EXPANSION, PRODUCTIVITY.

unproductive suffix A suffix no longer used to form derivatives (*-en* of *oxen, children*) (Jespersen).

unrounding Historically, the change from a sound produced with rounding of the lips to one produced without such rounding. *Synonym:* DELABIALIZATION. *Opposites:* LABIALIZATION, ROUNDING.

unstable Prone to change or variation, especially of phonemes.

unstressed *See* ATONIC, LIGHT (VOWEL or SYLLABLE).

unvoiced A sound produced without vibration of the

vocal cords. *Synonyms:* VOICELESS SOUNDS; (for consonants) HARD CONSONANT, SURD. *Opposites:* SOFT CONSONANT, SONANT, VOICED SOUNDS.

unvoicing Historically, the change from a voiced to an unvoiced consonant (Indo-European *d* of **dent-* to Germanic *t* of *tooth*). *Synonym:* DEVOICING. *Opposites:* VOICING, SONORIZATION.

ur- Prefix meaning "primitive." *Synonym:* PROTO-.

usage doctrine (or **doctrine of usage**) The belief that there is no justification for describing linguistic forms as correct or incorrect, but that the usage of the majority of the speakers determines the standard. *Opposite:* LINGUISTIC NORM.

utterance An amount of speech put forth by a single person, before and after which there is maximum silence (Fries); a meaningful unit of speech; any self-sufficient unit of spoken language; any stretch of speech by a person, preceded and followed by silence by that person (Harris). *Synonym:* EPILEGMA.

uvular A consonant sound produced by contact between the back of the tongue and the uvula (Parisian French *r-grasseyé*). *Partial synonym:* POST-VELAR.

V

variable A FUNCTIVE (*q.v.*) whose presence is not a necessary condition for the functive with which it has a function (Hjelmslev).

variants 1. Concepts which show no formal distinction ("the man" used as subject and "the man" used as object; Danish *trae* for both "tree" and "wood") (Hjelmslev). *See also* INVARIANT.

2. Related but not identical, and non-distinctive forms, either of which may be used by the speaker at his own discretion (the difference may be phonetic: *economic* pronounced with initial [ɛ] or [i]; morphological: *indices, indexes;* orthographic: *labor, labour;* or differing by reason of the presence or absence of an affix: *biologic, biological*). *See also* CHARACTEROLOGY OF SPEECH.

3. Alternative forms or allophones in free variation. *See also* BASE FORM, COMBINATORY (*also* CONDITIONAL, CONTEXTUAL, FREE, OPTIONAL, POSITIONAL) VARIANT, REPLACIVE.

variants, phonetic *See* PHONETIC VARIANTS.

vehicular language Meillet and Cohen's term for AREA or RELATIONAL LANGUAGE (*q.v.*).

velar A consonant formed by the back of the dorsum of the tongue against the soft palate or velum (*co*ol, *go*, so*ng*, Na*ch*t). *Synonyms:* DORSAL, GUTTURAL.

velarized *See* RETRACTED.

velar vowel *See* BACK VOWEL.

verbal A part of a verb (infinitive, gerund, participle) which is used as another part of speech (Laird). *See also* DEFLECTION.

verb cluster A verb with its modifiers (Walsh). *See also* CONSTITUENT.

verbid Laird's term for VERBAL (*q.v.*).

vernacular The current daily speech of a people or geographical area, as distinguished from the literary language, used primarily in schools and in literature. *Synonyms:* COLLOQUIAL, UMGANGSSPRACHE.

Verner's law An extension or modification of Grimm's Law (*q.v.*), to the effect that the Germanic medial voiceless spirants *f, th, h, hw* and *s* become *v*, voiced *th, g, gw*, and *z*, respectively, and final *s* becomes *z* when in contact with a voiced consonant, unless the original Indo-European stress falls on the preceding vowel. *See also* CONDITIONED SOUND CHANGE, NEO-GRAMMARIANS, REGULAR SOUND CHANGE.

vibrant A sound produced with a variable number of contacts between the articulator (normally the tongue) and one of the immovable speech organs (Saussure). *Synonym:* BRANLANT. *Opposite:* OBSTRUENT.

vibratory feedback *See* FEEDBACK.

vibratory phonetics *See* ACOUSTIC PHONETICS.

virtualités *See* SEMANTIC POTENTIALITIES.

vocable A combination of spoken sounds or written signs, not viewed as a semantic symbol.

vocabulary The stock of words used by a language, a group, an individual, or a work. *Partial synonym:* LEXICON.

vocabulary change *See* LEXICAL CHANGE.

vocabulary word A word that has full meaning (*table, walk, old, soon*); normally, nouns, adjectives, pronouns, verbs, adverbs. *Synonyms:* CONTENT (*also* FULL, LEXICAL) WORD, SEMANTEME. *Opposites:* EMPTY WORD, FUNCTION WORD.

vocal characterizers Trager's term for such subsidiaries of speech as laughing, crying, yelling, whispering, etc.

vocalic Pertaining to or functioning as a vowel.

vocalic consonant A consonant (liquid or nasal, [l], [r], [m], [n], etc.) which may occasionally function as a vowel. *Partial synonyms:* SONANT, SONORANT.

vocalic off-glide *See* OFF-GLIDE, SEMI-VOWEL.

vocalism The study, descriptive or historical, of the vowel system of a language or dialect. *Opposite:* CONSONANTISM.

vocalization Historically, the change of a consonant to a semi-vowel or vowel (Latin *planum* > Italian *piano;* Latin *palma* > French *paume*).

vocal lip control The range from a heavy rasp to various degrees of openness (Trager).

vocal qualifier   An elaboration of speech that contributes to its total meaning (social relationship, emotional content, etc.), but is not part of a larger metalinguistic structure (overloudness, oversoftness, the Japanese giggle that is a token of embarrassment, drawling, clipping, rasp, openness, hollowness, breaking, whining, singing, whispering, etc.) (Lloyd). According to Trager, it is part of METALINGUISTICS, but is not part of the MICROLINGUISTIC structures in language; its intensity ranges from oversoft to overloud; its pitch height from overlow to overhigh; its extent from clipping to drawling. *Synonym:* VOICE QUALIFIER. *See also* CHARACTEROLOGY OF SPEECH, PARALINGUISTICS, PHONETIC VARIANTS.

vocal segregates   Trager's term for such metalinguistic expressions as *uh-huh, uh-uh.*

vocal tract articulation   *See* ARTICULATORY PHONETICS (PASSIVE ARTICULATION).

vocoid   A sound during which the air leaves the mouth over the center of the tongue and without friction in the mouth (therefore a non-lateral; but friction may appear elsewhere); the vocoid is a vowel when functioning as a syllable crest, but may also be non-syllabic. *Opposite:* CONTOID.

voice   1. The distinction of form or inflection of a verb to indicate the relationship of the subject to the action denoted by the verb (ACTIVE, MIDDLE, PASSIVE, etc.) (Jespersen).

2. Vibration of the vocal cords accompanying the emission of a sound. *See also* MURMURED VOWEL, WHISPER.

voiced sounds   Sounds produced with simultaneous vibration of the vocal cords (normally, these include all vowels, semi-vowels, and voiced consonants, such as [b], [d], [g], [v], [z]). *Partial synonyms:* SONANT, RESONANT.

voiceless sounds   Sounds produced without vibration of the vocal cords (such as [p], [t], [k], [f], [s]. *Synonyms:* HARD CONSONANT, SURD, UNVOICED.

voice qualifier *See* VOCAL QUALIFIER.

voicing Historically, the change of a consonant from voiceless to voiced (Latin *latus* > Spanish *lado*). *Synonym:* SONORIZATION. *Opposites:* DEVOICING, UNVOICING.

Volgare Dante's term for the Italian language that had issued from Latin; *sermo* (or *lingua*) *vulgaris* appears in much earlier writings to designate the Italian vernacular.

vowel 1. A sound produced with vibration of the vocal cords, by unobstructed passage of air through the oral cavity, and not constricted enough to cause audible friction.

2. A sound produced with air flow moving centrally and orally, forward through the mouth, and into the open air, thus exciting the unobstructed buccal cavity, which forms a filtering cavity; the filtering effect is affected by three factors : tongue height, tongue advancement, and lip position (*q.v.*). It is immaterial how the buccal cavity is excited; the air may be ingressive or egressive (*q.v.*). The sound is usually voiced; if voiceless (i.e., where the vocal cords are not excited), all that results is a "blowing," or an [h] sound. If the oral exit is closed, a nasal sound results (de la Garza).

vowel cluster Bronstein's term for DIPHTHONG (*q.v.*).

vowel fracture Historically, diphthongization of a simple vowel under the influence of neighboring sounds (Latin *manum* to French *main,* where the change from [a], *a* to [aj], [ɛ], *ai* is conditioned, in a free syllable, by the following nasal). *Synonyms:* BREAKING, BRECHUNG, DIPHTHONGIZATION.

vowel gradation 1. Historically, the change in internal vowels of words to show distinctions in meaning, such as difference of tense in a verb; the gradation may be QUALITATIVE, consisting of change to a different vowel (Latin *facio,* perfect *feci*), or QUANTITATIVE, consisting of lengthening, shortening or suppression of the vowel

(Latin *venio,* perfect *vēni*). *See also* ABLAUT, ABSTU-FUNG, ABTÖNUNG.

2. Descriptively, *see* (for QUALITATIVE VOWEL GRADA-TION) INTERNAL MODIFICATION, REPLACIVE; (for QUAN-TITATIVE VOWEL GRADATION) REDUPLICATION, REDU-PLICATING MORPHEME.

3. The change in length and quality of a vowel in accordance with the stress placed upon the word that contains it ("This is *the* place!") (Bronstein).

vowel harmony 1. A form of DISTANT PROGRESSIVE AS-SIMILATION or LAG (*q.v.*) prevailing in the Uralic and Altaic languages whereby the vowels are divided into two or three classes (front, middle or neutral, and back), and the vowels of all suffixes must be modified to harmonize with the vowel of the root (Finnish *muuttumattomuudestansa,* "from his unchangingness," vs. *tytymättömyydestänsä,* "from his discontentedness"; Turkish *ev-de,* "in the house," vs. *oda-da,* "in the room") (Sweet).

2. Process whereby affixes have allomorphs conditioned by the vowel of the preceding syllable. *See also* AUTO-MATIC ALTERNATION, ECHOISM, MORPHOPHONEMIC AL-TERNATION, NON-CONTIGUOUS ASSIMILATION (de la Garza).

vowel mutation Process whereby a vowel change is caused by the presence of a front vowel, semi-vowel, or consonant in the following syllable; this may be a highly productive process in a given language. *Synonyms:* MUTATION VOCALIQUE, UMLAUT. *See also* AN-TICIPATION, FRONTING, RETROGRESSIVE ASSIMILATION (de la Garza).

vowel quality The characteristic property in the acoustic effect of a particular vowel, which distinguishes it from any other vowel. *Synonym:* TIMBRE. *Opposite:* VOWEL QUANTITY. *See also* PROSODIC FEATURES (RELATIVE QUALITIES) (de la Garza).

vowel quantity Relative length or duration of a vowel

sound. *Opposites:* TIMBRE, VOWEL QUALITY. *See also* PROSODIC FEATURES, QUANTITY.

vowel shift In the development of modern English, the change whereby nearly all the long vowels of Chaucer's period rearranged themselves according to a new pattern, many of them diphthongizing (*bite,* from /biːte/ to /bajt/), while others were raised (*spon,* /spoːn/ to *spoon,* /spuːn/) (Lehmann). *Synonym:* (GREAT) ENGLISH VOWEL SHIFT. *See also* PATTERN, PHONETIC LAW, UNCONDITIONED CHANGE.

vox nihili *See* GHOST WORD, PHANTOM WORD.

voyelle d'appui *See* SUPPORT VOWEL.

vulgar A form of language used by the masses, as opposed to the literary form.

vulgarism A word or expression violating purity of diction; a debased form of colloquialism. *See also* COLLOQUIAL, SLANG, SUBSTANDARD.

Vulgar Latin The vernacular of Rome and the Roman Empire, as opposed to the Classical literary Latin; the successor or contemporary of SERMO FAMILIARIS (*q.v.*), it survived in the west; it is scantily recorded in literary works, but attested in inscriptions, documents of a specialized nature, and it may in part be reconstructed from the later Romance languages and dialects. *Synonyms:* LOW LATIN, PRIMITIVE ROMANCE.

vulgate English A substandard cultural level of the language (Perrin, Kenyon).

W

wave theory   The belief that related languages, originating from a common parent language, spread from the center in all directions, like the waves in a pool when a stone is thrown into the water, and that linguistic innovations spread in the same fashion (Schmidt). *Synonym:* WELLENTHEORIE. *See also* FAMILY TREE THEORY, STAMMBAUMTHEORIE.

weak   1. As applied to Germanic verbs, those which form the past and past participle by the addition of the regular inflectional ending, without internal vowel change (*work, worked, worked*). *Synonym:* REGULAR. *Opposites:* IRREGULAR, STRONG.

2. As applied to nouns and adjectives, those having a less full declension (Germanic noun stems in -*n*, such as Anglo-Saxon *oxa, oxan,* German *Ochs, Ochsen;* Germanic adjectives preceded by the definite article and similar words, as illustrated by *der gute Mann* vs. *ein guter Mann*).

3. Phonetically, bearing a minimal degree of stress, often with obscuration of the vowel sound (French *me* as opposed to *moi*). *Synonym:* ALLEGRO FORM. *Opposites:* LENTO (or STRONG) FORM.

weakening   1. Historically, the change from a complex to a simple sound, or from a diphthong to a monophthong (Latin *caelum* to Vulgar Latin *celum*).

2. Historically, the change from an open to a close vowel, usually as the result of loss or change of stress (Latin *perficio* from *facio;* Italian *prǫviamo* vs. *prǫvo*).

3. Historically, the process whereby a form, when unstressed, is cut down to a shorter form (*Miss* from *Mistress, m'sieu* from *monsieur, don* from *domine*). *See* ALLEGRO FORM, WEAK.

weak grade Descriptive of a member of an ABLAUT (*q.v.*) series (such as a low or neutral vowel) occurring in a syllable having reduced stress.

weak stress *See* STRESS PHONEMES.

Wellentheorie *See* WAVE THEORY.

whisper Speech in which the vibration of the vocal cords is replaced by a fricative sound made by the breath in the whisper glottis while the cord glottis is closed (Webster III); the sound produced by narrowing the glottis almost to the position for voice, and then stiffening the vocal cords to prevent vibration; in whispered speech, voiced sounds are replaced by whispered sounds, while voiceless sounds are unchanged (Bloch and Trager). *See also* MURMURED VOWEL, (FULL) VOICE.

widened meaning The use of a word that has a specific meaning in an extended and more general sense (*cat* for *lion* or *tiger*). *Opposite :* NARROWED MEANING.

wide vowel *See* LAX, LOOSE VOWEL, OPEN VOWEL.

word A speech sound or a series of speech sounds symbolizing and communicating meaning without being divisible into smaller units capable of independent use; a linguistic form that is a minimum free form (Webster III); a phonetic group which, owing to its permanence of form, clearness of significance, and phonetic independence, is readily separated from the whole sentence (Boas); the spoken or written symbol of an idea, regarded as the smallest independent sense unit; the smallest significant unit of speech and language (Ullmann); a minimum free form (Bloomfield); the smallest speech unit capable of functioning as a complete utterance (Palmer); an autonomous syntagm formed of non-separable monemes (Martinet).

word class A linguistic form class whose members are words (Webster III). Such forms are not defined according to function. *Synonyms:* MAJOR FORM CLASS, PART OF SPEECH.

word-crossing *See* BLENDING. *Synonyms:* CONTAMINATION, CROSSING, TELESCOPED WORD. *See also* PORTMANTEAU WORD.

word formation The formation of new words in a language by the processes of INFLECTION and DERIVATION (including COMPOSITION, *q.v.*). *See also* BACK FORMATION, COINAGE, CONTAMINATION, STUMP WORD.

word order The order in which words may occur in a phrase, clause or sentence. *See also* SYNTAX, TAXEME (of ORDER).

word sign A visual symbol or group of symbols representing a word; a single character used to represent a word in a regular system of writing (Webster III). *Synonym:* LOGOGRAM.

word stress The stress within the word (i.e., marking morphemic constructions), as distinguished from SENTENCE STRESS (*q.v.*); word stress may be FIXED (or BOUND), and predictable, i.e., always marking a particular part of a morphemic construction in a given language (initial stress in Icelandic, Czech, Hungarian, etc.), in this function stress is permanent or CULMINATIVE, and DEMARCATIVE; in other languages (English, Russian) stress may be the only feature to differentiate two words otherwise consisting of the same succession of phonemes (*billow*, /bílou/ vs. *below*, /bilóu/); here stress acts as another (segmental) phoneme in the sequence, is free, and has a DIFFERENTIATIVE function; in still other languages (Spanish, Italian), there is a RESTRICTED stress, neither bound to one particular position in the word nor free to occur in any position; lastly, stress may indicate emotive contrast, but without changing the quality of the sound. Assumptions about degrees of stress vary among linguists (de la Garza).

See also BOUND (*also* FREE) STRESS, CONTRASTIVE (*also* EXPRESSIVE, OPPOSITIONAL) FUNCTION.

wrenched accent 1. In poetry, a stress which for the sake of the meter is forced from the normally stressed sylla- ble of a word to a syllable normally unstressed (*England* stressed on the last syllable to make it rhyme with *hand*) (Webster III).

2. An incorrectly placed vocal stress, due to ignorance, error, deliberate intent, or other causes (a Frenchman's rendering of *potatoes* as POT-a-toes). *See also* SHIFT OF ACCENT.

writing The representation of thoughts, ideas, and speech by conventional material signs or symbols. *See also* LINEAR (*also* LOGOGRAPHIC, PICTOGRAPHIC) WRIT- ING, ORTHOGRAPHY.

Y

yield *See* FUNCTIONAL YIELD.

yod The glide or transition sound heard in *yes*; the name comes from a letter of the Semitic alphabet which in- variably has that value. *See also* SEMI-VOWEL.

yodization A palatalization which acoustically equals the sound of *y* added to the consonant (Marouzeau); historically, the changing of a pure vowel, usually *e* or *i*, in hiatus, into a semi-vowel (Latin *vi-ne-a* to Vulgar Latin *vi-nya* to Italian *vi-gna*). *See also* SEMI-VOWEL.

yo-he-ho theory The belief that human speech origi- nated in sounds produced by the strong expulsion of breath by primitive man performing work involving strong muscular effort; more generally, that the origin of speech lies in sounds produced spontaneously, without conscious effort to imitate natural sounds (Noiré).

Young Grammarians *See* JUNGGRAMMATIKER, NEO-GRAMMARIANS.

Z

zero   The lack or absence of a feature, considered as a positive feature in the paradigm, for the sake of paradigmatic regularity (*zero* tonality, *zero* ending); in morphemic analysis, it indicates that no change has taken place (the plural of *sheep;* the plurals of most nouns in spoken French; the feminine of French and Spanish adjectives ending in *-e;* the past tense of *cut* or *hit*) (Walsh). *See also* ZERO CHANGE.

zero allomorph   An allomorph which represents or is characterized by ZERO CHANGE (*q.v.*) (the plural form *deer* (*deer* + 0), which has the same spoken form as the singular), but is called ZERO for the sake of paradigmatic regularity.

zero anaphora   *See* ANAPHORA.

zero change   The absence of an overt linguistic feature, when this absence is itself significant because of the presence of such a feature at a corresponding point in the language (Webster III).

zero connector   A connector which is understood or omitted ("I consider him [to be] my best friend"; "The man [whom] you saw yesterday") (Hockett).

zero ending   The bare root of the word, used as such in discourse (Latin nominative singular *puer;* the nominative singular ending of *puer* is represented by a ZERO

ALLOMORPH, which represents ZERO CHANGE in the root). *Synonym :* ZERO ALLOMORPH.

zero grade The most reduced form of weak ABLAUT grade, where the vowel disappears entirely. *See also* ABLAUT, ABSTUFUNG, WEAK GRADE.